MW01284535

BUDDHISM AND
POLITICAL THEORY

BUDDHISM AND POLITICAL THEORY

Matthew J. Moore

OXFORD

UNIVERSITY PRESS

OXFORD
UNIVERSITY PRESS

Oxford University Press is a department of the University of Oxford. It furthers
the University's objective of excellence in research, scholarship, and education
by publishing worldwide. Oxford is a registered trade mark of Oxford University
Press in the UK and certain other countries.

Published in the United States of America by Oxford University Press
198 Madison Avenue, New York, NY 10016, United States of America.

Library of Congress Cataloging-in-Publication Data
Names: Moore, Matthew J.
Title: Buddhism and political theory / Matthew J. Moore.
Description: New York : Oxford University Press, 2016. | Includes
bibliographical references and index.
Identifiers: LCCN 2015038588 | ISBN 9780190465513 (hardcover : alk. paper)
Subjects: LCSH: Buddhism and politics.
Classification: LCC BQ4570.S7 M66 2016 | DDC 294.3/372—dc23
LC record available at http://lccn.loc.gov/2015038588

1 3 5 7 9 8 6 4 2
Printed by Sheridan, USA

CONTENTS

ACKNOWLEDGMENTS

ALMOST ALL OF THIS BOOK was presented at various academic and professional conferences. I thank my fellow panelists, discussants, and other attendees for their helpful comments and questions on those occasions.

An earlier version of chapter 1 appeared as "Political Theory in Canonical Buddhism" in *Philosophy East and West* 65, no. 1 (2015): 36–64. Some material from that article also appears in chapter 7. An even earlier version of this chapter was presented at the Western Political Science Association Annual Meeting, San Francisco, California, April 2010.

Earlier versions of chapter 4 were presented at the Association for Political Theory Annual Meeting, University of Notre Dame, South Bend, Indiana, October, 2011, and at the Western Political Science Association Annual Meeting, Portland, Oregon, March 2012.

An earlier version of chapter 6 was presented at the Association for Political Theory Annual Meeting, Nashville, Tennessee, October 2013. A portion of this chapter also appeared as part of "Immanence, Pluralism, and Politics," *Theory in Action* 4, no. 3 (July 2011): 25–56, and appears here courtesy of the Transformative Studies Institute.

Earlier versions of chapters 2 and 3 were presented at the Western Political Science Association Annual Meeting, Hollywood, California, March 2013.

An earlier version of chapter 7 was presented at the American Political Science Association Annual Meeting, Washington, DC, August 2014.

The research and writing of this book were generously supported by the California Polytechnic State University, San Luis Obispo, in part through a sabbatical in the 2011–2012 academic year, a State Faculty Support Grant in the 2010–2011 academic year, the ongoing support of the College of Liberal Arts for faculty research, and finally the support of the Department of Political Science (and its generous alumni).

Finally, special thanks to Ron Den Otter for his invaluable help at every stage, to Michaele Ferguson for some inspired advice about reorganizing the argument, and to my wife Jolie, and children Eli and Sasha, for their patience and generosity along the way.

BUDDHISM AND POLITICAL THEORY

INTRODUCTION

Buddhism and Political Thought

OVER ROUGHLY THE PAST FIFTEEN years there has been an explosion of scholarship in comparative political thought. There have been numerous articles and monographs published on Islamic political thought, Confucianism, African political thought, and other traditions.[1] Curiously, virtually none of this work has focused on Buddhism and political theory, despite that Buddhism is the fourth- or fifth-largest religion in the world, that its teachings guide hundreds of millions of people, and that several Asian nations (such as Cambodia, Bhutan, Thailand, and the government in exile of Tibet) identify their governments as being guided by Buddhist principles. Indeed, over the past thirty to forty years, there has been only a trickle of political theory scholarship published in English that seriously discusses Buddhism in any way.[2]

This neglect of Buddhism by Western political theorists is not only puzzling but unfortunate, because Buddhist political theory not only addresses many of the same issues of interest to Western theorists (such as identity, agency, the duties of citizenship, metaethics, the role of politics in life, and so on), but it takes positions on many of those issues that are profoundly different from those taken by Western thinkers, and in many cases the Buddhist positions are better thought out, better argued, more willing to take arguments to their logical conclusions, and

I

more consistent with actual political practice and experience. In short, Western theorists not only have a lot to learn *about* Buddhism, they have a lot to learn *from* it.

In particular, my interpretation is that Buddhist political theory rests on three underlying ideas that simultaneously are familiar to Western thinkers and represent positions than almost no Western thinkers have been willing to embrace. First, Buddhist political thought is based on a denial of the existence of a self—not merely that there is no immortal soul, but that there is nothing at all that remains continuous over time to be the basis of personality or selfhood. This position allows Buddhism to diagnose a belief in the existence of a self as being the main source of interpersonal and social conflict, while also allowing it to avoid argumentative dead ends like the West's interminable debate about how agency can be possible given the reality of subjectification and socialization by external forces. Second, Buddhism is radically deflationary about the importance of politics to human life, coming about as close as possible to being overtly antipolitical without actually embracing anarchism. On the Buddhist view, politics is inevitable and is probably even necessary and helpful, but it is also a tremendous waste of time and effort, as well as being a prime temptation to allow ego to run rampant. Buddhist political theory denies that people have a moral duty to engage in politics except to a very minimal degree (pay the taxes, obey the laws, maybe vote in the elections), and it actively portrays engagement in politics and the pursuit of enlightenment as being conflicting paths in life. Third and finally, Buddhist political theory rests on a theory of ethics that sees moral claims as being both naturalistic, in the sense that they arise from natural facts about the universe and not from any supernatural source such as a deity, and also irrealist, in the sense that moral claims do not reflect obligatory normative truths but rather optional (though wise) advice about how to achieve certain goals. If you want to achieve enlightenment, act in the following manner. If you prefer to pursue some other goal, you are free (if foolish) to do so, and no normative judgment attaches to your decision.

These issues should be familiar to Western-trained political theorists, and yet Buddhism's conclusions are quite different from the positions taken in the mainstream of Western thought, and in some places different even from anything on the fringes. Thus many Western thinkers, notably Hume and Nietzsche, have questioned or even denied the reality of the self, but no major Western thinker has argued that we not only could get rid of the idea of the self but that we would also be much better off if we did. Similarly, Western political thought is profoundly committed to the importance of politics to human life. Even the anarchists, in vehemently denying the *value* of politics, inadvertently admit its tremendous *importance*. Buddhism's claim that politics, while necessary, is distinctly less important than other concerns has a parallel in a minor Western tradition stretching from Epicurus to Stanley Hauwerwas. Buddhist political theory suggests that that minor tradition deserves a much broader hearing and that most Western theorists need to reexamine their priorities. Finally, Buddhism's naturalistic, irrealist ethical theory also echoes a minor tradition in the West, but one that has primarily been speculative. Buddhist political theory offers the tremendous advantage of describing a living tradition of organizing social (and to some extent political) life on this philosophy, and thus allows Western thinkers to take immanent ethics out of the seminar room and into the real life of society. For all of these reasons, Buddhist political theory represents not just an inviting *terra incognita* for those interested in non-Western traditions but also a rich tradition and sharp challenge for all Western political theorists.

Overview

The aim of this book is to introduce Western political theorists to the Buddhist political theory tradition and to argue that there are some especially important connections and disconnections between the two traditions. Given the lack of political theory scholarship on these issues, the book is also intended to be a roadmap for other scholars interested in engaging with Buddhism. Thus I have discussed all the major primary texts (and provided citations to good quality English translations) and the existing secondary literature (mostly coming from academic disciplines other than political science and philosophy).

The book is divided into two parts, with the first looking at the *theory of government* found in Buddhist texts (that is, the particular regime type that the Buddhist texts recommend), and the second looking at the *political theory* that I argue we can find in those texts (that is, the underlying normative commitments that drive the Buddhist view of government and which may not be tied to any particular regime type). While part I is largely descriptive, part II is analytical and synthetic, presenting my own reading of Buddhist political theory.

Within part I, chapter 1 looks at the political ideas expressed in early Buddhism (on periodization, see Collins and Bechert[3]), the era that extends from the lifetime of the historical Buddha (c. sixth-fifth centuries BCE) until the first century BCE, when the first Buddhist texts were written down (having been preserved orally for several hundred years up to that point).[4] The texts of early Buddhism are especially important, not only because they are the oldest texts in the tradition, but also because all Buddhists, regardless of other sectarian disagreements, recognize the early texts as being authentically the teachings of the historical Buddha (though they may also believe that later texts clarify or modify the early teachings in important ways). Thus, all branches of Buddhism are rooted in these early texts. Chapter 1 examines what the early texts themselves say about government and political theory and suggests some inferences that we can draw from them.

Chapter 2 examines key texts of traditional Buddhism (c. first century BCE to about 1850 CE) that touch on political theory and government. This chapter argues that despite the otherwise substantial doctrinal differences among the various branches of Buddhism, all of them carried forward the early Buddhist theory of government—more-or-less-absolute monarchy with an enlightened monarch ruling in the collective interest—though with some interesting and telling modifications.

Chapter 3 focuses on the puzzle of the complete transformation of Buddhist political thinking as the traditional period ended and the modern period began, starting roughly in 1850 CE. Over the course of 100 years, between 1850 and 1950, every Buddhist-majority country went from openly embracing monarchy to openly embracing republican government (with the exception of Tibet, which currently lacks political autonomy), though in many cases their commitment to republicanism is more a matter of rhetoric than reality. For 2,000 years, everyone agreed that Buddhist politics meant monarchy, and over the course of 100 years, everyone changed their minds, at least officially. Chapter 3 examines how and why that happened and also looks briefly at Buddhist political thinking today.

In part II, I turn to the question of whether we can draw a useful and interesting political theory from the political texts of Buddhism. Chapters 4, 5, and 6 collectively argue that contemporary political theorists have much to gain from engaging with Buddhism. Thus chapter 4 compares the Buddha's teachings on the (nonexistence of) the self with Nietzsche's similar but crucially different theory of identity and agency. Chapter 5 argues that the early texts' vision of politics amounts to a theory of "limited citizenship," which has Western parallels in the writings of Epicurus, Henry David Thoreau, and John Howard Yoder. Finally, chapter 6 argues that the early Buddhist theory of ethics is best understood as being both naturalistic (it grounds ethics in natural facts, not in anything supernatural) and nonrealist (it treats ethics as a kind of practical advice, rather than as absolute moral commandments). That approach to ethics also has a Western counterpart, frequently called "immanence" theory, and examining the two traditions together sheds helpful light on both.

Finally, by way of a conclusion, chapter 7 argues that Buddhist political thought is not only alive and well in the twenty-first century, but that it promises to be of ongoing interest and importance for Western political thinkers. Indeed, Western thinkers have a great deal to learn about their own ideas by studying how similar ideas have played out in Buddhism.

What Political Theory Is

For this book to make sense and be helpful, we need a common understanding about what political theory is and what Buddhism is. Very generally, political theory is concerned with the philosophy of government, politics, and related issues. It asks how government should work, what politics should concern itself with, and how we should understand normative concepts like justice, equality, freedom, property, individual autonomy, the relationship between individuals and collectives, and so on. Inevitably, there are many differences of approach and disagreements among political theorists about what political theory is and should be,[5] with some scholars focusing on understanding texts in their historical context, others treating texts as an opportunity to engage in various kinds of critical analysis, yet others seeking to offer novel answers to age-old philosophical questions, and some seeking to use political theory to affect practical politics.[6] For my purposes in this book, political theory is normative ideas about government—that is, advice about how government should be, along with arguments about why it should be that way. This is purposefully a very narrow, conservative definition of politics and political theory. In this book I am interested in what Buddhism has to say about government (i.e., the formal, institutional processes of collective rule) and how it should be conducted. Buddhism may also have things to say about politics conceived more broadly, as any collective social activity or institution, and in passing I mention a few authors who discuss that issue, but it is not my present focus.

What Buddhism Is

On the most basic level, Buddhism is the religious/philosophical system taught by Siddhattha Gotama (Sanskrit: Siddhārtha Gautama) (c. sixth-fifth centuries BCE[7]), subsequently elaborated by many other teachers, and today practiced in many different forms by several hundred million people, primarily in Asia. The name Buddhism comes from the title adopted by Gotama, Buddha, which means "awakened one." Waking up is a central metaphor in Buddhism, which teaches that humans (and other sentient beings) live in a realm called *saṃsāra*, characterized by birth, death, and rebirth, in an endless cycle. Like the Vedic religion from which it arises (and which itself later evolved into modern Hinduism), Buddhism teaches that intentional action (*kamma*; Sanskrit: *karma*) cultivates certain dispositions of character, which ultimately determine one's next birth (and may shape one's character for many incarnations). The central goal of Buddhism is to escape *saṃsāra* and attain *nibbāna* (Sanskrit: *nirvāṇa*), which is an ineffable state beyond suffering, life, and death.

In his first sermon after achieving enlightenment,[8] the Buddha taught five of his former companions the basics of the religion, which remained at the center of his teachings for the rest of the Buddha's life. This basic message is summarized in the Four Noble Truths: (1) that life is *dukkhā* (suffering, or characterized by persistent unsatisfactoriness); (2) that *dukkhā* is caused by clinging (*taṇhā*; literally "thirst"), that is, clinging to the way one would like life to be, and thus resisting contrary conditions; (3) that if one could overcome clinging, the experience of *dukkhā* would cease (*nirodha*, "cessation"); (4) that clinging can be overcome by living according to the Noble Eightfold Path, which entails right understanding, intention, speech, action, livelihood, effort, mindfulness, and concentration. The best-known Buddhist practice, meditation, is a concentrated effort to train oneself to see the world aright and live according to the path.

In later sermons, the Buddha taught that human beings are characteristically motivated by three particular drives, often called the three poisons: greed, hatred, and delusion. In other words, we act to get what we want and to avoid what we don't want, all the while laboring under false impressions that harm our real interests. The most important delusion is our failure to recognize what the Buddha called the three characteristics or marks of existence:[9] *dukkhā* (that life is/contains suffering), *anattā* (that there is no self), and *anicca* (that everything is impermanent). Wrongly believing that things are permanent, we seek happiness in things that will inevitably die or be destroyed, thus ensuring our ultimate sorrow. Wrongly believing that we are or have a self or soul, we act to ensure what we perceive to be our self-interest, often harming others and even ourselves in the process.

In essence, the rest of the Buddha's early teachings are elaborations of these basic points, often in an effort to help his audience see the insubstantiality of the self, the inevitability of suffering in the realm of *saṃsāra*, and the impermanence of all things. Three such teachings are especially important for our purposes. The first is the elaboration of the idea of *anattā* or no-self. The Buddha teaches not only that there is no immortal soul (in sharp contrast to the Vedic religion) but further that there is no self of any kind—no inner essence, no psychological unity over time. Instead, there are only phenomena bound together by causality and hypostatized into a self by a persistent mistaken belief. (I examine this teaching in greater depth in chapter 4.)

The second teaching that will be helpful to bear in mind combines the no-self message with the idea of *anicca* or impermanence. Thus the Buddha teaches that all objects of our experience, including ourselves, are made up of five aggregates (*khandhas*; Sanskrit: *skandhas*): form or matter (*rūpa*); sensation or feeling (*vedanā*); perception or cognition (*saññā*); mental formations or volition (*saṅkhāra*); and consciousness or discernment (*viññāṇa*).[10] Crucially, there is no self to be found among the *khandhas* (literally "heaps" or "bundles"), and all of them are impermanent, in the sense that they will inevitably eventually die or decay.

The third and final teaching that is especially important for my purposes is the Buddha's theory of dependent origination or arising (*paticcasamuppāda*; Sanskrit: *pratītyasamutpāda*).[11] This theory plays several roles in Buddhism, including explaining the process of reincarnation. For my purposes, I want to focus on its role of explaining the interdependence of all of existence. The teaching argues that every thing that exists is the effect of prior causes, that nothing could be what it is without those prior causes, and that given those prior causes everything must be what it is. (This theory raises some difficult questions about freewill and determinism, which are thankfully beyond the scope of this book.[12]) Ultimately, the whole of existence arises interdependently, with the various parts mutually conditioning one another. Everything is related to everything, even if often only by infinitesimal degrees. This teaching reinforces the idea that there is no self, since we generally think of the self as being to some degree independent of external causality, and also the idea that everything is impermanent, since today's effects are merely tomorrow's causes.

This short description of the basic teachings of Buddhism is similar to many other such brief summaries,[13] and would not likely arouse much controversy among Buddhists. But scholars rightly have different concerns and considerations, and some may object to the idea that there is a single entity called Buddhism to be found either in the early texts or today. After all, those early texts amount to some 12,000 pages in translation, and there is good reason to think that (despite what the texts themselves purport), they are not simply transcriptions of what the Buddha and some early disciples taught, but are instead the result of several hundred years of selection, editing, and misremembering on the part of hundreds or, more likely, thousands of people, who may have had very different ideas of what Buddhism was. On one level, that criticism is obviously true. As we've seen with biblical scholarship over the past 100 years, any large corpus that has been influenced by large numbers of people over long periods of time will inevitably be internally fragmented, contested, and the result of complex struggles for power and influence. But, on another level, too much can be made of that point. For the several hundred million people alive today who think of themselves as Buddhists, there most certainly is a single, coherent entity called Buddhism (even if they don't all agree on what it is or what it says), and it is both appropriate and perhaps helpful to ask what it has to say about a variety of subjects, including politics. In the end, even among scholars there is room for both ways of approaching the texts, early, traditional, and modern. Some scholars will prefer to emphasize the internal complexity and disunity of texts, while others will prefer to ask what overall messages or lessons we can draw from the texts if we take them as a more-or-less unified whole. This book takes the latter approach.

Why These Three Elements?

Apart from the issue of the connections that I assert exist between the Buddhist and Western political theory traditions, you might wonder why I am focusing on the three aspects of Buddhism I identified as central to Buddhist political theory: the theory of no-self (*anattā*), the view that politics is necessary but relatively unimportant, and the claim that Buddhist ethics is both naturalist and irrealist. After all, Buddhism is a rich and complex tradition, with lists and categories aplenty. Why these three elements and not others?

In his first sermon, the Buddha teaches the Four Noble Truths and the Noble Eightfold Path. The core message of the sermon is that sentient beings experience suffering, that their suffering arises from them clinging to certain beliefs and desires/aversions, and that they could train themselves to no longer suffer by learning not to cling. In his second sermon, the Buddha expands that teaching to include the point that one of the most destructive false beliefs is the belief that one is a self (both that one has an immortal soul, and that one is a more-or-less coherent psychological entity that endures over time).

At first glance, these two sermons appear to be fatally mutually contradictory—if there is no self, what is it that suffers, and what is it that could be trained not to suffer? But by the principle of charity, we have to attribute to the Buddha a coherent theory that unifies these two teachings without self-contradiction. To do that, we have to assume that at any given moment there are sentient beings who are capable of sensation, cognition, and intention, that those beings habitually hold false beliefs and engage in false habits that lead them to suffer, and that those beings are capable of pursuing an intentional course of conduct that could lead them to escape suffering.

We can posit those things without assuming that there is a self that animates or unifies such beings—they do not need an immortal soul to have these qualities (just as most Westerners do not attribute a soul to animals, which are nonetheless capable of some degree of sensation, cognition, and intention), and they do not even need a continuous psychological entity, provided that we assume that they have some capacity for memory. We don't need to reify such beings—they may merely be momentary (or short-lived) phenomena that emerge from the interaction of energy and matter, like waves on the sea (to pick a common Buddhist metaphor). But we have to treat them as having at least a phenomenal identity—they appear to themselves to be real things that persist over time—because otherwise there is no possible actor/thinker/percipient for the Buddha to refer to and address.

If one of these beings is persuaded of the truth of the Buddha's teachings, it has to follow a subtle and paradoxical path. To continue to exist as a sentient being, so that it can pursue its intention to escape from suffering, it must continue to act as if it is a persistent self—it must eat, drink, seek shelter, and so on. To make progress toward overcoming suffering, it must act as if its memories reflect real experiences in the life course of a single being, and as if its intentions have some real effect on its future behavior. But if it reifies any of the aspects of its experience—if it treats anything as having a fixed, natural essence—it will remain trapped in suffering, since it will believe something false that it will cling to despite contradictory evidence and inevitable change. Thus it must simultaneously act in some ways as if it were a persistent self and in other ways as if it had no real existence at all.

As we will see in chapter 1, one aspect of the experience of such beings is that they are unable to meet their needs without the cooperation of other such beings. A related aspect is that such beings typically prefer to fulfill their own needs and desires before helping fulfill the needs of others, in some cases without helping others at all, and in extreme cases actively harming others to fulfill their own perceived needs and desires. These facts lead to the necessity of creating some system of social cooperation that is capable of coordinating most of the behavior of most of the beings most of the time, such that everyone's needs are met and harm to beings is minimized. Given these beings' selfishness, such a system will have to employ coercion and force, though those tactics will inevitably themselves cause other social conflicts.

If such a system is to succeed, it too must perform the balancing act of fulfilling the apparent, phenomenal needs of such beings, while simultaneously avoiding reifying (a) the existence of those beings, (b) the principles by which their social interactions are guided, and (c) its own existence and importance. For example, government must avoid making claims about the nature of human beings, about the possession of souls, about what happens to them after death, and so on, so as not to encourage people to believe false things that contradict the truth of *anattā*. Similarly, it must avoid making claims about the principles that guide social life, since the *anicca* doctrine teaches that all things are impermanent—there are no principles that are always and everywhere true or right or helpful; rather, there are only the principles that are helpful for particular people at particular times and places in the pursuit of particular goals. Finally, the government must not exaggerate its own importance or status. Like persons and principles, government is impermanent, something that can be helpful in some circumstances but that has no claim to an absolute nature or value.

All of those component parts of government are phenomenal rather than substantial or essential, and government must play its part without ruining the whole enterprise by either intentionally or unintentionally leading beings to believe that any part of the enterprise is real in some ultimate sense, which would leave them trapped in *saṃsāra*. In other words, Buddhists seeking liberation need government, but government can only work if it acknowledges that the people are not selves; that the principles of social interaction (i.e., ethical rules) do not reflect ultimate, real, absolute, unchangeable truths (which would be the only things not subject to decay and destruction); and that government itself is of merely relative importance, given the nature of the phenomena of which it is composed. Those three elements are essential to any system of government consistent with the overall beliefs and commitments of Buddhism.

A Note about Pāli and Sanskrit

The early texts were memorized and written down in a language called Pāli, which is roughly to Sanskrit what Italian is to Latin. Many words used in the texts come from the Vedic religion, whose sacred texts were written in Sanskrit. Many Buddhist terms are familiar in the West in their (Westernized) Sanskrit forms, such as dharma, karma, nirvana, and so on. Because the early texts are in Pāli, and since therefore most of the translations quoted in the text below use the Pāli versions of Buddhist terms, I have decided to keep the language consistent throughout the book by using the Pāli terms, except when quoting texts that use the Sanskrit.

PART I

BUDDHISM'S THEORY
OF GOVERNMENT

I

Theory of Government and Political Theory in Early Buddhism

ASKING WHAT "BUDDHISM" SAYS ABOUT politics is roughly like asking what "Christianity" says about politics—it's an impossibly large and vague task. The existing literature on "Buddhism and politics" breaks down into a number of main types: descriptive literature about how Buddhists have actually engaged in politics and/or are doing so today;[1] normative literature about what Buddhism (or Buddhists) say about whether (and how) Buddhists *should* engage in politics;[2] historical/ sociological literature on the social and political context within which Buddhism first arose;[3] literature on Buddhist ethics, some of which touches on politics;[4] and political advocacy from a Buddhist point of view.[5]

Part I of this book focuses on what the texts of Buddhism say about politics. This chapter focuses on "Early Buddhism," [6] that is, the contents of the Pāli Canon, which is the scripture of one tradition of Buddhism (Theravada), and is recognized by the other traditions (Mahāyāna and Vajrayāna) as being authentically the teachings of the Buddha. Thus whatever conclusions we can draw about political theory from the early texts are relevant to all Buddhists, though some Buddhists may believe that there are other valid teachings on these topics as well.

Although political theorists have largely ignored Buddhism, there is an existing literature from other disciplines on the early texts and normative political theory. Within that literature, there are three debates that are interesting for political theorists. The first debate is whether Early Buddhism contains a theory of government at all or whether the various comments about politics in the texts are better understood as parables, illustrations, or comments on important contemporary events. Max Weber influentially argued that Buddhism is entirely unconcerned with politics, while contemporary scholars like Stanley Tambiah, Steven Collins, Richard Gard, and Balkrishna Gokhale have argued that politics plays at least some role in the early teachings.[7] As I argue below, the evidence of the primary texts makes clear that there is indeed a normative political theory in the early texts, one that has been underappreciated.

The second debate is over whether any theory of government ostensibly put forward in the early texts supports monarchy or some form of republicanism, which in this context means broader popular participation in decision-making (though typically nothing approaching the level of semidemocratic participation of contemporaneous Athens). Here, the clearly dominant view is that the early political theory of Buddhism supports monarchy,[8] although a handful of scholars argue that reading is mistaken and that there is a subtle but detectable preference for republicanism.[9] This issue will also be addressed below, though I will ultimately argue that the issue of the particular political system embraced by the early texts is less important than the question of the underlying political theory. We find that same divergence in the Western tradition—no one reads Hobbes because they want to create a monarchy on his model; they read him to uncover and assess his underlying theoretical insights and commitments.

The third and final debate is over the role or significance of politics within Buddhism overall. On the one hand, some scholars argue that any politics in the early texts is relatively peripheral to the main concerns of Buddhism, which are primarily about individual transformation,[10] while other scholars argue that politics and salvation cannot be separated in the Buddhist theory, and thus that politics should be understood as central to Buddhism.[11] This question is central to my discussion below, where I argue that politics is distinctly secondary to individual enlightenment and to some degree actually irrelevant.

The Relevant Early Texts

The early texts that are relevant to normative political theory are the *Aggañña-Sutta*, the *Cakkavatti-Sīhanāda Sutta*, the *Mahāsudassana Sutta*, the beginning of the *Mahāparinibbāna Sutta*, and various discussions in the *Jātaka Tales* about the ten duties of the righteous king (the *Rajādhamma*), such as in *Jātaka* 385.[12] (A few other tangentially relevant texts will be mentioned below and in later chapters.) I briefly summarize these key texts here.

Aggañña-Sutta

The *Aggañña-Sutta* purports to be an explanation of the origin of the four main castes: *brāhmaṇa* (clergy and teachers), *khattiya* (warriors), *vessa* (farmers and merchants), and *sudda* (servants and peasants). It is widely accepted among scholars that it is intended to be a satire of Vedic origin myths, in that it undermines Vedic claims for the intrinsic superiority of the Brahmans.[13] The story begins as a creation myth about the origin of the cosmos (though apparently the cosmos has no true beginning, only periods of expansion and contraction):

> There comes a time . . . when, sooner or later after a long period, this world contracts . . . But sooner or later, after a very long period, this world begins to expand again. At a time of expansion . . . beings . . . are mostly reborn in this world. Here they dwell, mind-made, feeding on delight, self-luminous, moving through the air, glorious—and they stay like that for a very long time.[14]

As the world continues to become more material and less ethereal, "savoury earth" spreads itself out on the surface of the ocean. One of the beings tastes it, and craving arises in that being. Seeing the first being enjoying the savory earth, other beings taste it, and craving arises in them. As these beings continue to eat, they lose their luminosity and slowly transform from being mind-made to being matter-made. This same process occurs several times, with several different kinds of foods, and each time the beings become more bodily and also more disposed to misconduct of various kinds, such as arrogance, spite, lust, and so on.

With each successive coarsening of the bodies and characters of the beings, the foods available to them become less tasty and harder to obtain. Eventually they reach a stage where the main food is rice, which needs to be cultivated with a familiar degree of steady effort. This leads the beings to divide the fields into individual plots, so that each person could be assured of reaping the benefits of his or her own labor. But ownership inevitably leads to theft.[15]

To solve the ongoing problem of theft, the beings decide to appoint one among them to serve as enforcer of the rules. This appears to be a simple social contract (though see below):

> Then those beings came together and lamented the arising of these evil things among them: taking what was not given, censuring, lying and punishment. And they thought: "Suppose we were to appoint a certain being who would show anger where anger was due, censure those who deserved it, and banish those who deserved banishment! And in return, we would grant him a share of the rice." So they went to the one among them who was the handsomest, the best-looking, the most pleasant and capable, and asked him to do this for them in return for a share of the rice, and he agreed.[16]

This king, whose title was Mahā-Sammata, which the text argues means "People's Choice," was the first *khattiya*, which the text argues means "Lord of the Fields."[17] Some of the people in this society began to reflect on the evils that had arisen and committed themselves to refraining from evil: "'They Put Aside Evil and Unwholesome Things' is the meaning of Brahmin, which is the first regular title to be introduced for such people."[18] Finally, the names for the *vessa* and *sudda* castes are simply occupational titles—merchants and hunters.[19] Hence the Vedic division of castes is purely historical and occupational, and the castes reflect nothing about the origins or natural qualities of their members. Further, the Buddha's own *khattiya* caste were originally the political and social leaders, as opposed to the *brahmanas* valorized by the Vedic literature.

Cakkavatti-Sīhanāda Sutta

Right next to the *Aggañña-Sutta* in the collection called the *Dīgha Nikāya* is the *Cakkavatti-Sīhanāda Sutta*. This *sutta* (Sanskrit: *sūtra*) concerns a *cakkavatti* or "wheel-turning monarch." The Buddha's first sermon after achieving enlightenment was called the *Dhammacakkappavattana Sutta*, or the *Sutta on the Turning of the Wheel of Dhamma*.[20] *Dhamma* (Sanskrit: *dharma*) in this context means truth or teaching, and in that first sermon the Buddha's teaching set the truth rolling through the world.[21] Similarly, the *cakkavatti*, or wheel-turning monarch, is a king who advances the *dhamma* through his governance. A basic description of how a king becomes a wheel-turner, and of the seven treasures that he obtains by doing so, is given in the *Mahāsudassana Sutta*.[22] Very briefly, a king can only become a *cakkavatti* through achieving personal moral purity, and then can only maintain that status through ruling in a way that encourages the people to also achieve moral purity. The symbol of a king's status as a *cakkavatti* is the wheel treasure, which is a visible but magical wheel that allows the king to peacefully conquer and rule neighboring states (and, by implication, the whole human world). The *Cakkavatti-Sīhanāda Sutta* recounts what happens when a *cakkavatti* rules in the wrong way.

The story begins with Daḷhanemi, a wheel-turning monarch who realizes that he is reaching the end of his life and decides to spend his last days seeking spiritual wisdom as a wandering ascetic. After the king leaves the kingdom, the wheel treasure disappears. The newly crowned king consults the royal sage, who explains that the wheel treasure cannot be passed from one king to another but must be earned by each king individually fulfilling the duties of a wheel-turning monarch, which are as follows: "you should establish guard, ward, and protection according to Dhamma for your own household, your troops, your nobles and vassals, for Brahmins and householders, town and country folk, ascetics and Brahmins, for beasts and birds. Let no crime prevail in your kingdom, and to those who are in need, give property."[23]

That king and the next seven of his successors follow this advice and become wheel-turners. But the eighth makes the fatal mistake: "[H]e ruled the people according to his own ideas, and, being so ruled, the people did not prosper as they had done under the previous kings who had performed the duties of a wheel-turning monarch."[24] He tries to mend his ways but doesn't follow the sages' advice carefully; in particular, he does not give property to the needy. This leads the poor to steal; interestingly, the king's initial response is to give the thieves enough property that they don't need to steal anymore, but eventually the king realizes that this will have the perverse effect of encouraging theft. The king decides to execute the next thief, which has the unintended consequence of legitimating the use of force, thus making theft both more common and more dangerous.

This starts a cycle of moral degradation, parallel to the one in the *Aggañña-Sutta* in which physical craving for food leads to moral degradation:

> Thus, from the not giving of property to the needy, poverty became rife, from the growth of poverty, the taking of what was not given increased, from the increase of theft, the use of weapons increased, from the increased use of weapons, the taking of life increased—and from the increase in the taking of life, people's life-span decreased, their beauty decreased, and a result of this decrease of life-span and beauty, the children of those whose life-span had been eighty-thousand years lived for only forty thousand.[25]

This same cycle continues, with novel crimes being committed (always caused by the previous crime), until the life span is only 100 years—that is, until today. The Buddha predicts that in the future there will be further degradation, until the life span is only ten years. Then the cycle reverses:

> And for those of a ten-year life-span, there will come to be a "sword interval" of seven days, during which they will mistake one another for wild beasts. Sharp swords will appear in their hands and, thinking: "There is a wild beast!" they will take each other's lives with those swords. But there will be some beings who will think: "Let us not kill or be killed by anyone! Let us make for some grassy thickets or jungle-recesses or clumps of trees, for rivers hard to ford or inaccessible mountains, and live on roots and fruits of the forest." And this they will do for seven days. Then, at the end of the seven days,

they will emerge from their hiding-places and rejoice together of one accord, saying: "Good beings, I see that you are alive!" And then the thought will occur to those beings: "It is only because we became addicted to evil ways that we suffered this loss of our kindred, so let us now do good! What good things can we do? Let us abstain from the taking of life—that will be a good practice." And so they will abstain from the taking of life, and, having undertaken this good thing, will practise it. And through having undertaken such wholesome things, they will increase in life-span and beauty. And the children of those whose life-span was ten years will live for twenty years.[26]

In the future, when the life span has again reached 80,000 years, a new Buddha will appear, named Metteya. At the same time, a new *cakkavatti* will arise, named Sankha. The two will rule the two spheres—spiritual and temporal—side by side, by implication creating the best possible human society. Ultimately, Sankha will become a disciple of Metteya and achieve enlightenment, thus demonstrating the superiority of the spiritual to the temporal.

There appears to be widespread agreement among scholars that this story represents a novel theory in the history of Indian political thought, sometimes referred to as the Two Wheels of Dhamma[27]—the identification of both religious life and political/social life as being governed by the same underlying moral laws, and the assertion that ultimately the temporal powers were subordinate to the spiritual powers.[28] This theory is frequently contrasted with the realist theory of politics put forward by Kautilya in the later *Arthasastra*. Later Buddhist thinkers identified King Aśoka (died c. 238 BCE) as having been a wheel-turning monarch.[29]

Mahāparinibbāna Sutta

The *Mahāparinibbāna Sutta* is the last of the major texts that offers normative political guidance (more on the *Jātaka* tales below). In this passage, the Buddha learns that King Ajātasattu intends to attack a people called the Vajjians. The king sends a minister to the Buddha to inform him of this plan and to report back to the king whatever the Buddha says in response. The Buddha tells the minister that he had previously advised the Vajjians to follow seven principles and that as long as they followed those principles they would prosper and not decline. Those seven principles were (1) "hold regular and frequent assemblies"; (2) "meet in harmony, break up in harmony, and carry on their business in harmony"; (3) "do not authorise what has not been authorised already, and do not abolish what has been authorised, but proceed according to what has been authorised by their ancient tradition"; (4) "honour, respect, revere and salute the elders among them, and consider them worth listening to"; (5) "do not forcibly abduct others' wives and daughters and compel them to live with them"; (6) "honour, respect, revere and salute the Vajjian shrines at home and abroad, not withdrawing the proper support made and given before"; and (7) "that proper provision is made for the safety of Arahants [enlightened beings], so that such Arahants may come in future to live there, and those already there may dwell in comfort."[30]

The subtext of all this is that the Vajjians had a quasi-republican form of government. Some scholars have read this passage to say that the Buddha had told the Vajjians to uphold their republican traditions and was thus implicitly criticizing monarchy. On this reading, it's significant that the aggressive king is Ajātasattu, who had murdered his spiritually advanced father, Bimbisāra, to obtain the throne. (Elsewhere the Buddha reveals that, after his death and due to his spiritual virtue, Bimbisāra was reborn in one of the heaven realms and that he would achieve enlightenment after only one more human birth, thus demonstrating that political leaders can make spiritual progress.[31]) Bolstering this reading, the Buddha then gives parallel advice to his monks about how they should govern the *sangha* (the community of monks) after his death. The structure of the *sangha*, which the Buddha himself had set up, was republican. For example, there was no leader of the *sangha*, and all decisions were made in open meetings, where all monks had equal rights to make proposals and vote. Indeed, given that the *sangha* was the only community that the Buddha ever created, some have argued that we should see it as representing his preferred model of social organization.[32] Further, the Buddha had grown up in a society governed by semirepublican principles, though during his lifetime that form of government was rapidly disappearing.[33]

Jātaka Texts

Finally, there are passing comments about normative political theory in the *Jātaka* texts, parables about the previous incarnations of the Buddha. In a number of places, they list a series of duties to be observed by kings who would be righteous. These *Rajādhamma* duties are as follows: "Alms, morals, charity, justice and penitence, Peace, mildness, mercy, meekness, patience."[34]

The Theory of Government of Early Buddhism

It will be helpful for us to distinguish between the *theory of government* or political regime that the early texts endorse and the *political theory* that underlies that endorsement. Although this reading will require some elaboration, in brief the political system that the early texts endorse is enlightened monarchy based on a primal social contract. The king's authority originally arose from the consent of the governed but is maintained by the spiritual righteousness of the king himself. The king's legitimate power extends to preserving order and preventing extreme poverty, though the people apparently have no right to resist even an incompetent or evil king,[35] and there appears to be no possibility of reopening the terms of the social contract. Social and political inequalities are inescapable facts of life, though they are based on human conventions rather than on any natural or spiritual differences among the people. *Cakkavattis* will not need to use violence, but inferior kings will inevitably rely on it, though such semilegitimate violence also is ultimately socially destructive.

This brief summary of the political system that is laid out by the early texts touches on three controversies in the existing literature that need to be addressed before we move on. First, Andrew Huxley has objected to reading the *Aggañña-Sutta* as depicting a social contract on the grounds that the Buddha's society had no tradition of legal contracts to draw upon—the ideas of mutually independent parties voluntarily accepting certain duties and obligations and of a breach either dissolving the relationship or justifying coercion simply weren't available. Huxley suggests that instead we should read the *Aggañña-Sutta* as depicting merely the necessity that those governed accept or acquiesce in being ruled.[36] However, as Steven Collins argues in response to Huxley, we can read a bit more into the *Aggañña-Sutta*, even if we accept the point that we cannot treat it as simply another instance of social contract theory.[37] First, as I noted above, we can read the *Aggañña-Sutta* as a statement of the moral equality of persons and also of their original social equality. Second, we can read the *Aggañña-Sutta* as a claim that the only way that original social equality could have justifiably been broken was through the choice of the people themselves. Third, we can find in the *Aggañña-Sutta* some rudimentary criteria for judging the performance of kings, though not the later idea found in the social contract tradition that failure on their part could give rise to justifiable rebellion. For these reasons, it is reasonable to discuss the *Aggañña-Sutta* as depicting something closely analogous to a social contract, even if that exact model was not available at the time of its composition.

Second, in my summary above I suggest a reading that synthesizes what are ostensibly different and possibly conflicting theories of the origin of legitimate authority. Both the *Aggañña-Sutta* and the *Cakkavatti-Sīhanāda Sutta* offer theories about the nature of political legitimacy. The *Aggañña-Sutta* suggests that a king's authority rests on the initial consent of the people and implies that subsequent kings inherit authority as a birthright. The *Cakkavatti-Sīhanāda Sutta* appears to offer a very different theory of legitimacy, which is based on the king's personal spiritual purity (though rule still appears to be passed to a male heir). An explanation of the relationship between the two texts that is widely cited by other scholars is the one given by Balkrishna Gokhale: "In the second phase of theorizing [the *Cakkavatti-Sīhanāda Sutta*] the early Buddhists endeavored to use the state to further the ends of *dhamma* by asserting the supremacy of the *dhamma* over *āṇā* [the power of the state]."[38] On that reading, the change from *Aggañña-Sutta* to *Cakkavatti-Sīhanāda Sutta* represents a strategic attempt on the part of the Buddha or *sangha* to benefit from state patronage or protection by depicting kings in a flattering light as possessing unusual spiritual grace. In that way, Gokhale suggests, the *sangha* hoped to become the arbiter of political legitimacy by evaluating the spiritual fitness of kings. However, in other places Gokhale suggests that the change was due to the rapidly increasing power of monarchical states during the Buddha's lifetime and a desire on the Buddha's part to try to restrain state power.[39] The *Rajādhamma* texts seem to support this latter reading, indicating an effort on the part of the Buddha to restrain kings. I'm not convinced that there is really a problem here. The *Aggañña-Sutta* and *Cakkavatti-Sīhanāda Sutta* depict very different stages of government— the *Aggañña-Sutta* its origins, and the *Cakkavatti-Sīhanāda Sutta* its perfection (and inevitable cyclical decline). In the era depicted in the *Aggañña-Sutta*, there had never been kings. In the era depicted in the *Cakkavatti-Sīhanāda Sutta*, kingship was an accepted background fact about society, and the interesting question was how kings could be better or worse. There doesn't seem to be any insuperable problem to reading them synthetically, as I have proposed above.

Before we move to the third and final controversy in the literature, we should address one additional issue about the nature of legitimate authority in the early texts. One of the main purposes of the social contract tradition in Western thought is to tell a story of the origins of coercive authority that appropriately respects the moral autonomy and agency of the citizens. That is, one of the background assumptions of Western thought (especially since the seventeenth century) is that society is composed of more-or-less independent, rational individuals whose autonomy and subjectivity must be respected by the political system for that system to be legitimate. We see this illustrated very clearly, for example, in Locke's *Second Treatise of Government*, where he argues that since human beings have all been created by God, and since we can therefore infer that God must want us to exist, it is a violation of God's will to harm any human being (including oneself) or hinder anyone from peacefully pursuing their goals.[40] This raises an additional problem for reading the *Aggañña-Sutta* as (resembling) a social contract argument, because Buddhism rejects the idea that human beings are at base atomistic, rational beings endowed with natural rights. As will become clear in chapter 4, this traditional Western conception of human subjectivity conflicts directly with the *anattā*, or no-self doctrine, that the Buddha taught. If human beings are not rational essences endowed with natural rights, the idea that legitimacy arises from consent seems arbitrary rather than logically necessary. In other words, if human beings are ultimately just more-or-less contingent phenomena, what does it matter whether they are ruled by someone they choose or by someone who seizes power against their wills?

What exactly would be the normative problem with that? It might be tempting here to say that the concept of legitimacy doesn't have a place in Buddhist political theory, because it assumes that citizens have some kind of natural essence (expressed as natural rights) that could either be respected or violated. But draining the bathwater of legitimacy would also entail tossing out the baby of normative political theory. At the end of the day, political theory just *is* the idea that some forms of government are normatively good and others normatively bad, in other words that some forms are legitimate and others are not. Thus if Buddhism is to have a normative political theory, there must be some criterion of legitimacy other than one based on the natural rights of rational individuals. I believe we get the clue to that alternative criterion in the *Cakkavatti-Sīhanāda Sutta's* implicit lesson that some forms of government elicit lower levels of social conflict and individual spiritual regress than others, in particular that rule by a spiritually advanced king minimizes social conflict while maximally encouraging individual spiritual progress. By implication, any other type of rule would be less beneficial to the ultimate goal of achieving enlightenment. Thus legitimacy is not about adequately respecting the autonomy of rational selves but rather about creating conditions to allow human beings to make spiritual progress (though, as I argue below, the political system can do no more than create a conducive atmosphere—the individual must make the choice to pursue enlightenment).

Returning to the third and final controversy in the existing literature, there is the question (mentioned above) about whether the early texts really endorse monarchy or whether there is a subtle but detectable preference for republicanism present in them, as briefly sketched in the summary of the *Mahāparinibbāna Sutta* above. I believe that the evidence is overwhelming that the texts endorse monarchy rather than republicanism for several reasons. First, the *Mahāparinibbāna Sutta* is the only place in the early texts where the Buddha even appears to recommend republican government for lay society (as opposed to the community of monks, or *sangha*). In every other place where the Buddha discusses lay government, either descriptively or prescriptively, he is talking about monarchy. Second, when the Buddha offers a utopian vision of a much better political future, at the stage of the *Cakkavatti-Sīhanāda Sutta* when humanity once again lives for

80,000 years, the form of lay government is still monarchy. Indeed, the implication of the sine-wave view of time that underlies the *Cakkavatti-Sīhanāda Sutta* is that this would be the best possible form of lay society: monarchy led by a spiritually advanced king, in an era during which a fully enlightened Buddha is also teaching. Especially given the semifantastic nature of the *Cakkavatti-Sīhanāda Sutta's* predictions of the future, this is precisely where we would expect the Buddha to endorse republicanism as a distant-but-obtainable ideal; the fact that he did not do so suggests that the Buddha did not see republicanism as the ideal for lay society. Finally, it's worth taking seriously the differences between the *sangha* and lay society. While it is true that the only society the Buddha ever set up, the *sangha*, was republican, there are at least two good reasons to think that the *sangha* may not have been intended as a model for the larger society. First, the *sangha* was an intentional community, with a long list of rules and precepts whose violation could mean expulsion. Many of the typical social problems of the larger society could be eliminated without the use of force in the more restrictive setting of the *sangha*. For example, the *sangha* required celibacy, a practice that the Buddha never proposed for society at large. Second, the *sangha* could count on the guidance of (relatively) enlightened members to help resolve disputes through peaceful discussion, again avoiding the use of force or coercion that typifies government. Thus, the *sangha* could employ republican methods in part because it didn't face the same problems as a lay political society. For both of these reasons, I believe that we should treat the *Mahāparinibbāna Sutta* as primarily emphasizing the value of tradition and continuity, rather than seeing it as a subtle endorsement of republicanism. This conclusion suggests that when it comes to the form of government, the Buddha either supported or acquiesced in monarchy as the only practical form.

An Early Buddhist Political Theory

Seen solely as an endorsement of a political system, the theory of government of the early texts isn't of much interest—it's just another iteration of the very familiar defense of enlightened monarchy based on a primeval and unrecoverable social contract. We find much the same theory in the *Republic*, *Leviathan*, and *Reflections on the Revolution in France*, among many other texts. If this were all Buddhist political thought had to offer us, it wouldn't be worth the trouble for anyone but Buddhologists and antiquarians. Happily, Buddhism has a great deal more to offer, because the political theory that underlies the political system is radically different from comparable theories in the Western tradition. In particular, the political theory of the early texts rests on three ideas: a deflationary account of the role of politics in human life; a naturalistic and nonrealist theory of morality; and the claim that individual identity is both illusory and harmful. It is these three underlying arguments that are really of value—indeed, although the vast majority of Buddhists living today have abandoned monarchy in favor of some form of republican government, they have preserved these underlying rationales of Buddhist political theory.

These three elements add up to a distinctive political theory, which is explained and elaborated further in chapters 4, 5, and 6. Here I present a brief summary: The most basic human desire is happiness. Unfortunately, life is characterized not by happiness but by suffering. Even our happiest moments are marred by the knowledge that they must end, that everyone involved must eventually sicken and die, and that even as we are enjoying them we are wasting precious time worrying about the future and fretting about the past. Every human being has a natural and powerful incentive to try to escape from the suffering of life. That escape is possible but only through individual effort. The incentive to seek enlightenment is entirely pragmatic. There is no moral duty to seek enlightenment, and one is perfectly free to continue in the cycle of *saṃsāra* forever. Since the universe is without beginning or end, there isn't even a threat of running out of time before making spiritual progress—when the universe collapses and reexpands, one will simply be reborn and start right back into the cycle of birth and rebirth.

It is helpful on the path to enlightenment to have support from like-minded friends and to live in a relatively peaceful and stable society, but neither of those conditions is necessary—it is possible to achieve enlightenment without them. The primary goal of politics is to ensure social stability and peace by promulgating laws and rules, punishing violations, and preventing extreme poverty (which typically leads to crime). Politics is a useful and inescapable human activity since some human beings will inevitably seek to benefit at other people's expense through theft, violence, and fraud, and the victims of those actions will seek to create laws and institutions to protect themselves. However, individuals have no moral duty to participate in politics, and one should participate only to the extent that doing so helps one make spiritual progress. Typically, active participation beyond merely obeying the laws and paying taxes will be a distraction from the more important goal of individual salvation. Government actions and policies will inevitably have an effect on the spiritual progress of the citizens, but that effect is not dispositive—good policies will not ensure that individuals make progress, and bad policies cannot prevent them from making progress. Obviously, helpful policies are to be preferred to obstructive policies, but generally one should not take an active role in politics for the purpose of making better policies and should instead focus on one's spiritual life. Indeed, the Buddha himself gave up his claim to rule a kingdom precisely so that he could seek enlightenment, despite a prophecy that he would have become a *cakkavatti* if he had become a political ruler.

Finally, one of the key steps toward enlightenment is realizing the illusory nature of the self. Overcoming the illusion of the self has both soteriological and political consequences. On the one hand, as discussed above, it is a necessary step in letting go of clinging, and thus learning to suffer less from life. On the other hand, since the basic problem of believing that one is or has a self is that it leads one to act egocentrically, always seeking to fulfill one's needs before or at the expense of the needs and desires of others, letting go of the idea of the self should make one extremely unlikely to commit any crimes. Although the Buddha never discusses this possibility, it seems that a society made up entirely of enlightened individuals would operate according to some form of pacifist anarchism. Further, as the *Cakkavatti-Sīhanāda Sutta* clearly implies, a society of people who have each weakened their sense of self, though not yet totally eradicated it, would apparently be more harmonious and less conflicted than the societies with which we are familiar (and the citizens would all live to be 80,000 years old!).

Thus, government is both necessary and inevitable in any plausible human society, but it doesn't matter very much what form it takes. In any event, one should not play an active role in government if one can avoid it. Real social and political change and improvement will come from the transformation of individuals, which is only modestly affected by politics and is largely the responsibility of each person.

2

The Traditional Buddhist Theory of Government

IN THIS CHAPTER I TURN TO investigate Buddhist normative political theorizing after the early period. At first glance this task is impossibly large, as even by the end of the early period Buddhism had already divided into several sects and had begun to develop substantial regional differences.[1] Over the next 2,000 years, Buddhism divided into three main sects: Theravada, Mahāyāna, and Vajrayāna. It also developed into numerous local variants as it mixed with various national cultures and evolved under different historical circumstances. To give just one example, the Sri Lankan national epic the *Mahāvaṃsa* is central to Sinhalese Buddhists' understanding of what Buddhism says about politics, and is very influential for other Southeast Asian versions of Buddhism, but has no obvious relevance to Buddhists in Tibet or Japan, who in turn have their own texts and traditions. Off the cuff, it seems as if one would have to investigate the development of Buddhist political theory separately in each national context.

Although there is obviously great value in such nation-specific studies (many of which have been done), I argue that there is such a high degree of commonality among the various national traditions that we can identify and meaningfully examine what I will call (again following Collins and Bechert[2]) a *traditional* Buddhist political theory. As chapter 1 argues, the early texts endorse a political system of enlightened monarchy based on a primal social contract. The king's authority originally arose from the consent of the governed but is maintained by the spiritual righteousness of the king himself. The king's legitimate power extends to preserving order and preventing extreme poverty, though the people apparently have no right to resist even an incompetent or evil king, and there appears to be no possibility of reopening the terms of the social contract.[3] Social and political inequality are an inescapable fact of life, though they are based on human conventions rather than on any natural or spiritual differences among the people, and the monarch has a moral duty to support the poor and unfortunate. *Cakkavattis* will not need to use violence, but inferior kings will inevitably rely on it, though even such semilegitimate violence is ultimately socially destructive.

In the early traditional period, the most important and durable sectarian division within Buddhism, that between Theravada and Mahāyāna, emerged. Theravada Buddhism has been the dominant strain in Sri Lanka and Southeast Asia, while Mahāyāna Buddhism has been the dominant strain in the East Asian countries of China, Korea, and Japan. The Vajrayāna tradition is itself an offshoot of Mahāyāna and has been most influential in Tibet, Bhutan, and Mongolia. Although the several traditions disagree about doctrine, history, and the authority of various texts and teachers, they maintained remarkably similar ideas about political theory, largely preserving the theory of the enlightened monarch (*cakkavatti*) developed in early Buddhism, while modifying it in similar ways. In particular, we see three kinds of changes in the traditional-period political texts of all three traditions: (1) identifying the Buddha with the mythical first king, either by claiming that the Buddha was in fact Mahāsammata himself in a previous incarnation or that the Buddha is a direct descendant of Mahāsammata, thus uniting spiritual and temporal power; (2) identifying kingship with the status of being a Bodhisattva or future Buddha, thus rendering kings semidivine; (3) identifying contemporary and historical kings as being descendants of Mahāsammata and/or the Buddha, thus further sacralizing the king and blurring the distinction between sacred and secular power.[4]

I turn now to examining the major traditional-era texts that appear to offer normative advice about politics. One preliminary note: Although it is easiest to group these texts in a way that lines up with the three main traditions of Buddhism, the guiding principle for sorting them has been the tradition in which their influence has been greatest, not necessarily the tradition with which their authors have explicitly identified.

For example, the work of Nāgārjuna was written before the emergence of the Mahāyāna, but over time it has been more influential in that tradition than in the Theravāda, and thus it is included in the Mahāyāna section.

The *Mahāvastu*

A noncanonical text apparently written between the second century BCE and fourth century CE and important as an early influence on what would later become the Mahāyāna tradition, the *Mahāvastu* provides a genealogy of the Buddha that is repeated in many later traditional-era texts, thus giving this text an unusually central and important role. In particular, this genealogy includes the noncanonical claim that the Buddha was a descendant of Mahāsammata,[5] tracing his lineage as follows: Mahā-sammata, Kalyāna, Rava, Uposadha, Māndhātar, Iksvāku (also called Sujāta), Opura, Nipura, Karandaka, Ulkāmukha, Hastikaśīrsa, Simhahanu, Śuddhodana, Śākyamuni (the Buddha).[6]

In addition, the *Mahāvastu* also recounts a tale similar to *Jātaka* 521, in which three talking birds give advice to King Brahmadatta about how to govern well: avoid anger, judge fairly, restrain the senses, act justly, give generously to those in need, prevent violence, reward righteousness, act ethically (no adultery, gambling, abuse of power for personal gain), cultivate friendship with neighboring kings, keep one's ideas and the advice of one's counsel secret, act decisively, acquire and preserve wealth (within the bounds of ethical behavior), be lenient, appoint wise and scrupulous ministers, employ spies to bring you information that would otherwise be difficult to obtain, and finally be confident that righteousness is rewarded in this life and in the next.[7]

The text also frequently references the idea of the *cakkavatti*, for example in stories of the lives of previous Buddhas. In many of these stories, the wheel-turning kings who rule during the era of a Buddha are Bodhisattvas destined to eventually become Buddhas, and they use their period of earthly rule to help their subjects make spiritual progress.[8] There are also various scenes depicting wheel-turning kings showing generous support and due deference to the Buddha and *sangha* in case any contemporary kings should be confused about their duties in that regard.

Traditional-Era Theravāda Texts

Visuddhimagga

This text, written by Buddhaghosa and dated to the fifth century CE, adds to the canonical *Aggañña Sutta* story the important traditional-era claim that the Buddha himself had been Mahāsammata in a previous incarnation.[9] The text says:

> When beings had come to an agreement in this way in this aeon, firstly this Blessed One himself, who was then the Bodhisatta (Being due to be Enlightened), was the handsomest, the most comely, the most honourable, and was clever and capable of exercising the effort of restraint. They approached him, asked him, and elected him. Since he was recognized (*sammata*) by the majority (*mahā-jana*) he was called Mahā Sammata. Since he was lord of the fields (*khetta*) he was called khattiya (warrior noble). Since he promoted others' good (*rañjeti*) righteously and equitably he was a king (*rājā*). This is how he came to be known by these names. For the Bodhisatta himself is the first man concerned in any wonderful innovation in the world. So after the khattiya circle had been established by making the Bodhisatta the first in this way, the brahmans and the other castes were founded in due succession.[10]

Dīpavaṃsa/Mahāvaṃsa

These two texts, the former from the third to fourth century CE, and the latter from around the sixth century, are both the national chronicles of Sri Lanka and tremendously important sources for Theravada Buddhism elsewhere in Southeast Asia. Both identify the Buddha as being a descendant of Mahāsammata.[11] Hence, chapter II of the *Mahāvaṃsa*, "The Race of Mahāsammata" begins thus: "Sprung of the race of Mahāsammata was the Great Sage [i.e., the Buddha]."[12] The text goes on to give a genealogy similar but not identical to that in the *Mahāvastu*.[13] These texts also provide a genealogy of early Sri Lankan kings that makes them descendants of the Buddha's Sākya clan and thus of Mahāsammata.[14]

Traiphum Phra Ruang

This Thai text, traditionally dated to the fourteenth century CE (though recent scholarship has raised the possibility that it was really an eighteenth century compilation[15]), identifies Mahāsammata as a previous incarnation of the Buddha.[16] The text also elaborates on the theory of the *cakkavatti*, depicting the wheel-turning king as a kind of substitute Buddha in eras when there is no Buddha teaching: "The great Cakkavatti king knows merit and Dhamma, and teaches the people to know the Dhamma; it is just as if a Lord Buddha had been born and was teaching the people to live according to the Dhamma."[17]

One duty of the *cakkavatti* is to preach to lesser rulers about how to rule. One central piece of advice is for kings to obey the *rajādhamma* rules: "Let the rulers and king observe the ten Dhammic rules for kings, and do so without ever ceasing."[18] Another set of injunctions reminds kings that they are subject to the five precepts, which apply to all laypersons:

> Now I will speak to you about the five kinds of evil deeds that you rulers should avoid. One kind of evil deed concerns various animals or insects that have life, consciousness, mental processes, or move about, right down to every single ant or termite—you must not kill any of these![19]

> Another kind of evil deed concerns the wealth and property of others that is not given by its owner—such things rulers must never take![20]

> As for the kind of evil deed that concerns the wives of others, that is, committing adultery with the wives of others—you who are rulers must never do it! You must never do it, even the least bit![21]

> Another kind of evil deed concerns lying—that is saying things for which there is no basis; such things you who are rulers must never say![22]

> Another kind of evil deed concerns intoxicating liquor—when you who are rulers associate with one another, you must not drink it![23]

There is much additional advice, aimed at keeping taxes reasonable, enabling the ordinary people to earn a living, treating social inferiors respectfully, judging fairly, taking care of monks and the *sangha*, and rewarding virtue and punishing vice. The text also contains a version of the *Aggañña-Sutta* origin story. It differs from the canonical version of that story by identifying Mahāsammata as a previous incarnation of the Buddha:

> After they meet and speak to one another like this, they go to pay their respects to the Lord Bodhisatta asking *him* to be their *lord* and their leader and to have them as his servants. They then consecrate the Lord Bodhisatta to be their king by endowing him with three names; one name is Great Elect [Mahāsammata], another name is Khattiya, and another name is King.[24]

Jinakālamālī

This text, composed in the fifteenth or sixteenth century CE in the Thai kingdom of Lān Nā, unites the central innovations of the traditional-era texts in that it both claims the Buddha as a descendant of Mahāsammata and says that the Buddha was himself Mahāsammata in a previous incarnation.[25] Hence: "And at the very beginning of this aeon, on account of the fact that our Aspirant to Enlightenment had first of all been selected by the common people, he became the king called Mahāsammata (Popular Choice)."[26] The text goes on to give genealogy similar to that given in the *Mahāvaṃsa*, making the Buddha a descendant of Mahāsammata.

Southeast Asian Legal Codes

Tambiah and Huxley separately note that the historical legal codes of several Southeast Asian countries, particularly Burma and Thailand, explicitly identified Mahāsammata as the person who first developed the codes themselves, and that these references to Mahāsammata continued to be present in the codes until the end of the traditional period in the nineteenth century.[27]

Traditional-Era Mahāyāna Texts

Ārya-satyaka-parivarta or *Ārya-bodhisattva-gocara*
(*The Range of the Buddha*)

This text, composed between the third century BCE and first century CE, covers a wide range of issues.[28] A central part of the narrative is the visit of King Caṇḍapradyota to the *nigranthaputra* (lay teacher[29]) Satyavādin, who gives the king various pieces of advice, all of them consistent with the early teachings. For example, he tells the king: "Your majesty, you should also not inappropriately dominate the kingdom. You should not generate harmful thoughts towards two-legged, four-legged, many-legged, or legless species."[30] The advice goes on to discourage the king from killing, lying, stealing, and using harsh words.

Interestingly, this text says explicitly something that many texts imply without making overt: enlightened beings don't need government. Thus: "Some sentient beings during their lifetime are endowed with the meritorious power of their previous karma.... They had no need for a ruler's domination."[31] The text also addresses head-on the difficult issue of whether it is legitimate for kings to use violence to secure social peace:

> The ruler should chastise wicked people [with the purpose of] convincing them to assume, not to neglect, their obligations. . . . If a ruler realizes that he can accomplish [the purpose of] his punishment just by [mere] criticism, then a ruler should castigate strongly those wicked people, but he should not [really] hurt them by binding or killing, etc. . . . When a ruler believes that punishment [of the wicked] will not be effected by means of mere obloquy, then, concentrating on love and compassion and without resort to killing, damaging of sense organs, or cutting off of limbs, he should try warning, scolding, rebuking, or beating them, or confiscating their property, exiling them from the state, tying them up, or imprisoning them. A ruler should be tough, but not in any heavier ways than these. . . . He is tough, but he has no wish to abandon or harm them.[32]

Otherwise, the text follows the general patterns of traditional-era texts by explaining the theory of the *cakkavatti* and arguing that the Buddha was descended from previous *cakkavattis* and would have become a universal ruler if he had not pursued enlightenment.

Suhṛllekha (*Letter to a Friend*) and Ratnāvalī (*Precious Garland*)

Both of these texts were written by Nāgārjuna (c. 150–250 CE), widely considered to be the most important Buddhist thinker after the Buddha. Although both texts are explicitly framed as advice to kings, they contain mostly general advice about the *dhamma* that would be applicable to anyone. The *Suhṛllekha* does offer some advice specific to kings, such as how to choose a good queen, but the overall point is that kings should rule in accordance with *dhamma*.[33] Similarly, the *Ratnāvalī* encourages kings to rule in accordance with the *rajādhamma* principles and promises them worldly success if they do.[34]

Buddhacarita and Saundarananda-kavya

These two texts were written by Aśvaghoṣa (c. second century CE). The *Buddhacarita* argues that the Buddha's father, Suddhodana, was himself a *cakkavatti*,[35] and that the Buddha's birth brought great good fortune to Suddhodana's kingdom.[36] Thus it continues themes from the early texts without modifying them. The *Saundarananda-kavya* repeats a portion of the genealogy of the Buddha as deriving from the sons of Iksvaku,[37] whom other sources such as the *Mahāvastu* and *Mahāvaṃsa* identify as being descendants of Mahāsammata, thus continuing the traditional-era identification of Buddha with the first king.[38]

Catuḥṣataka (Four Hundred Verses)

This text, written by Āryadeva (c. third century CE), a student of Nāgārjuna, contains advice directed to kings about how to rule in accordance with the *dhamma* and how to avoid letting their position lead them to a false view of self and of their own merit.[39] The main focus of the (brief) political portion text is avoiding arrogance and bad behavior inspired by it:

> 77. Society's servant, paid with a sixth part,
> Why are you so arrogant?
> Your becoming the agent of actions
> Depends on being placed in control.[40]

> 82. Those who act at others' insistence
> Are called fools on this earth.

> There is no one else at all
> So dependent on others as you.[41]

> 86. If giving proper protection is
> A ruler's religious practice,
> Why would the toil of artisans too
> Not be religious practice?[42]

> 88. The sensible do not acquire kingship.
> Since fools have no compassion,
> These merciless rulers of men,
> Although protectors, are irreligious.[43]

> 90. Virtuous rulers of the past
> Protected the people like their children.
> Through the practices of this time of strife
> It is now like a waste without wildlife.[44]

But, despite this generally humbling tone, the text does repeat the idea that *cakkavattis* are usually Bodhisattvas:

> 123. Why should anyone who takes birth
> Through constant control of the mind
> Not become a ruler
> Of the entire world?[45]

Kāruṇīkarāja-Prajñāparamitā-sūtra (*The Prajñāparamitā Sūtra For Humane Kings Who Wish to Protect Their States*)

This text, of unknown authorship and dating to the third or fourth century CE,[46] is directed to kings and advises them to rule in accordance with the *dhamma*, especially in times of civil disorder. This *sutta* played a major role in forming East Asian societies' view of the relationship between Buddhism and monarchy, particularly the idea that kings were similar to (or perhaps identical with) Bodhisattvas.[47] This *sutta* differs from the others we've discussed so far in that instead of giving advice about how to behave, it primarily gives advice about the preservation and ritual recitation of the *sutta* itself as a more-or-less thaumaturgical means of preventing and healing political and social strife. Hence:

> The Buddha said to the great kings: "Listen attentively, listen attentively! Now I shall explain on your behalf the Law of Protecting the Country. In all countries, when riots are imminent, calamities are descending, or robbers are coming in order to destroy (the houses and possessions of the inhabitants), you, the Kings, ought to receive and keep and read this *Prajñā-pāramitā*, solemnly to adorn the place of worship (the altar), to place (there) a hundred Buddha images, a hundred images of Bodhisattvas, a hundred lion-seats, to invite a hundred Dharma-masters (priests) that they may explain this *sūtra*. And before the seats you must light all kinds of lamps, burn all kinds of incense, spread all kinds of flowers. You must liberally offer clothes, and bedding, food and medicine, houses, beds and seats, all offerings, and every day you must read this *sūtra* for two hours. If kings, great ministers, monks and nuns, male and female lay-members of the community, listen to it, receive and read it, and act according to the Law, the calamities shall be extinguished. Great Kings, in the countries there are innumerable demons and spirits, each of whom has innumerable relatives (followers); if they hear this *sūtra*, they shall protect your countries."[48]

Suvarnaprabhāsauttamarāja-sūtra (*Suvarṇaprabhāsa-sūtra*; Golden Light Sūtra)

This *sutta*, dating to some time before the fifth century CE, is one of the most important Mahāyāna *suttas*. Several of its sections discuss kingship and argue that the Buddha and other celestial beings will protect kings who rule according to *dhamma* and punish kings who do not. Further, the text suggests that kings rise to their social position due to merit earned in previous lives and with the blessing of various gods.[49] Hence:

> Venerable Transcendent Victor, should a king of humans listen to the King of Glorious Sutras, the Sublime Golden Light, and having

listened, should he then give protection, give refuge, care for and save those monks from all their enemies, then Venerable Transcendent Victor, we the four great kings [Vaishravana, Dhrtarashtra, Virudhaka, Virupaksha] will protect, give refuge, care for, save and give peace and well-being to the beings living in the entire country of that king of humans.[50]

Further, the text reinforces the idea that universal kings have some kind of special spiritual merit that leads to their attainment of the monarchy:

> Blessed by divine kings
> They enter into their mother's womb;
> Being first blessed by gods,
> Afterwards, they enter her womb.
>
> Once born in the human world,
> They become kings of humans.
> From gods they are born;
> Thus they are called "divine son."
>
> Granting them a share of royalty
> And saying, "You are the son of gods,"
> The divine rulers of Thirty-Three
> Create such human kings in this way
> In order to bring misconduct to an end,
> Thwart what is against the Dharma
> And set beings in virtuous deeds.[51]
>
> When a king does not perform the function
> For which kingship had been bestowed,
> He demolishes his own realm
> As the elephant lord destroys a lotus pond.[52]

Other Mahāyāna Texts

Finally, some later Mahāyāna texts, such as Saicho's *Shugo-kokkai-sho* (818 CE) and Nichiren's *Rissho-ankoku-ron (On Establishing the Correct*

Teaching for the Peace of the Land[53]) argue that government can only be successful if it adheres to the *dhamma*, in these two cases specifically to the versions of the *dhamma* favored by these two authors. However, they don't reflect any substantive changes from the mainstream of the traditional-era texts.[54]

Traditional-Era Vajrayāna Texts

Many of the texts already discussed are important in the Vajrayāna tradition, though they are not unique to it. Among texts unique to Vajrayāna Buddhism, the only one that I am aware of that explicitly comments on government and the conduct of kings is the *Dulva*, the Tibetan version of the canonical *Vinaya*, which lays out the rules for monks and nuns, as well as recounting a number of the Buddha's teachings. The *Dulva*, but not the early/Pāli version of the *Vinaya*, identifies the Buddha as a descendant of Mahāsammata.[55]

Conclusion

Thus, despite the important differences among the various Buddhist sects, it seems clear that throughout the traditional period the only form of government that Buddhists of all kinds considered a serious possibility for lay society was monarchy, and that all the schools adopted the early ideas that monarchy was the first form of government, that Mahāsammata was the first king, and that righteous and/or enlightened kings could and should rule according to *dhamma*. In both Theravada and Mahāyāna texts we see a persistent effort to identify the Buddha with Mahāsammata, either through descent, through previous incarnation, or both. We also see persistent efforts to identify contemporary and historical kings with the lineage of the Buddha and/or Mahāsammata, and in some texts we see a further emphasis on identifying kings as Bodhisattvas.[56] As we will see in the next chapter, all that changed rapidly and dramatically in the nineteenth century.

3

Buddhist Modernism, 1850–1950

BEGINNING IN THE MID-NINETEENTH CENTURY, the traditional Buddhist theory of government changed rapidly and radically. The first changes were mostly efforts at modernization and Westernization of the various monarchies, largely in response/resistance to colonization.[1] Eventually the changes shift toward embracing either popular republicanism or constitutional monarchy (with relatively little power for the monarch). By the early twenty-first century, all Buddhist-majority countries are republican in form, and some are effectively republican in practice (to varying degrees), though a few retain kings with some degree of power (quite a lot in Bhutan, less in Thailand and Cambodia,[2] though still more than most European monarchs), and many are republican in name more than in practice.

From my perspective, the interesting question is not how or why this change happened, since it seems obvious that colonization and globalization made it clear to all concerned that the traditional monarchies were not a sustainable form of government, both because they could not (with the exceptions of Thailand and Bhutan) defend themselves against colonization, and because they could not compete with Western countries in the global arena. Rather, the interesting question is how it was possible for Buddhists to justify the change to themselves. What stories did Buddhists tell themselves about why it was acceptable to abandon 2,000 years of monarchy and embrace republicanism in lay government? How did they (re)interpret the early and traditional-era texts to justify the change? Was this seen as a crisis, or were the philosophical issues largely ignored?

To my knowledge, these questions have not been directly examined before, though a number of studies on Buddhism and politics touch on the issue in passing. From those studies, we can extrapolate several possible explanations, which boil down to two basic positions: (1) that the republican transformation has no justification in the early or traditional texts and is flatly a pragmatic and/or cynical invention in response to circumstances; (2) that the transformation rests on some themes in the various historical texts, and that the shift from monarchy to republicanism represents a defensible change in interpretation and emphasis, rather than wholesale invention.

The first view—that the transformation has no basis in the historical texts—is argued by Heinz Bechert in the context of Sri Lanka, Emanuel Sarkisyanz in the context of Burma, and Donald Smith as a general causal argument about political development in the Buddhist-majority countries. Both Bechert and Sarkisyanz argue that the experience of colonialism led to something that they call Buddhist modernism.[3] For Bechert, Buddhist modernism was an attempt to respond to both colonialism and modernization by referring back to, but also liberally reinterpreting, the Buddhist canon. Hence he writes: "In 'modernistic' Buddhism, Buddhists have the 'freedom to construct a Buddhist economic and social ethic suited to the age,' as Gananath Obeyesekere has termed it. Such constructions may or may not be in conformity with, or at least not in contradiction with, the teachings of the Buddha. In any case, they are not 'Buddhist' in the sense of being legitimized by the teachings of the historical Buddha himself."[4] Further: "Certain references to political questions in the scriptures are now interpreted as the Buddha's guidelines for political life, and the old structure of the *sangha* is described as a model for a democratic state."[5] (However, Bechert is slightly sympathetic to the idea that there were some democratic strains within traditional Buddhism.[6])

For Sarkisyanz, whose study of Burma raises questions for all Buddhist countries, Buddhist modernism was an inevitable syncretism of the indigenous Buddhist tradition and the culture imposed by colonialism: "Though democracy and socialism were adapted by Burma from Britain, they were accepted within the context of a Buddhist social ethos.... [I]deological syncretism was inevitable."[7]

Finally, for Donald Smith, the transformation represents an incomplete attempt to legitimate government after the colonial powers took over. He suggests that the traditional Buddhist theory of government was irreparably damaged by the colonial victories, and that the embrace of republicanism was inevitable and only partially effective:

> For those societies which came under Western-imperialist rule, the question of legitimacy was never fully resolved. According to traditional criteria, European Christians were ipso facto illegitimate rulers when governing . . . Buddhist . . . subjects[.] . . . After independence, liberal, democratic, and socialist currents of thought, merged with nationalism, produced legitimating ideological formulations which were deemed satisfactory to the political elite, despite their Western origin and their near-unintelligibility to the masses still steeped in traditionalist modes of thought.[8]

The second major line of explanation for the republican transformation is that it drew upon genuine republican and democratic elements in the Buddhist tradition, and thus that it represents a justifiable change in interpretation or emphasis rather than either the invention of a specious new tradition or the outright destruction of Buddhist political models. The strongest version of this is argued by Joanna Macy, Trevor Ling, Laksiri Jayasuriya, K. N. Jayatilleke, Nandasena Ratnapala, and Anthony Warder,[9] who separately argue, based in part on the Buddha's advice to the Vajjians in the *Mahāparinibbāna Sutta*, that Buddhism has always been philosophically republican and that the historical embrace of monarchy was pragmatic rather than principled, reflecting a practical need to maintain good relations with the governments of the time, all of which were monarchical.

A more modest claim is made by Donald Smith, who argues that Buddhism has always contained elements amendable to republican government (even if, as above, he ultimately concludes that the way in which the transformation was imposed made the transition to republicanism a rupture with the Buddhist tradition rather than a reinterpretation of it). Hence he writes: "The primary implications of the

Buddhist values of individualism and egalitarianism for political culture are obvious. Buddhist authority patterns are highly incongruent with authoritarian political systems and supportive of systems which recognize a broad area of individual freedom."[10] Also: "It is quite clear that the Buddhist tradition has within it ideational elements which can be used to legitimate change in the direction of democratic socialism or modernity in general."[11]

Richard Gard offers a similar interpretation:

> Early Indian Buddhist political thought would seem appropriate for modern constitutional monarchies and parliamentary and presidential governments in Buddhist Asia. The early social compact and governmental contract theories and the juridical conception of kingship could perhaps be adapted more meaningfully, at least for Buddhist peoples, for the new republics than borrowed Western political theories which necessarily have different historical and social contexts. The Buddhist principle that the essential purpose of political authority—whether located in kingship or in village or clan legislative assemblies—is to [e]nsure individual and collective security and wellbeing could still apply to contemporary states. Similarly, the early Buddhist theory and practice concerning the qualifications and selection of those who exercise political authority on behalf of the people, and the repudiation of those who fail, might be restated in modern terms for democratic political processes; whereas the later conceptions of the Cakravartin [*cakkavatti*], Devaputra, and Buddha-rāja, which induced and sanctioned political absolutism . . . may no longer be appropriate.[12]

Burmese political dissident and leader Aung San Suu Kyi suggests that the important issue in Buddhist political theory has always been creating a government that both reflects and nurtures Buddhist values, and that the particular form that government takes is a matter of convenience rather than principle:

> By invoking the Ten Duties of Kings the Burmese are not so much indulging in wishful thinking as drawing on time-honoured values to reinforce the validity of the political reforms they consider necessary.

It is a strong argument for democracy that governments regulated by the principles of accountability, respect for public opinion and the supremacy of just laws are more likely than an all-powerful ruler or ruling class, uninhibited by the need to honour the will of the people, to observe the traditional duties of Buddhist kingship. Traditional values serve both to justify and to decipher popular expectations of democratic government.[13]

The Fourteenth Dalai Lama comes to a similar conclusion, noting that the *sangha* was organized democratically; that democracy enables the kind of open search for the truth that the Buddha encouraged (for example, in his often-cited advice to the Kalamas to trust only their own experience of religious teachings[14]); and finally that "Buddhism is essentially a practical doctrine. In addressing the fundamental problem of human suffering, it does not insist on a single solution."[15]

In the next section, I sketch the various national experiences of the transformation to assess which of the rival explanations of the republican transformation is most accurate. I conclude that both have some explanatory power. While the Buddhist political tradition is explicitly (and virtually exclusively) monarchist, there are in fact some republican and democratic elements in Buddhism that reformers did draw upon. But those reform efforts were largely driven by Western-influenced or educated elites, and they met with varying degrees of success. Thus, while Thailand and Bhutan (and to a lesser degree the government-in-exile of Tibet) have successfully and relatively peacefully reinterpreted the Buddhist tradition to support their republican governments, Cambodia and Burma/Myanmar have had a much more turbulent experience, and the stability of their more-or-less republican institutions remains in doubt.

Whichever broad explanation is right, it's clear that today virtually all Buddhists see Buddhism as being compatible with republican government and, perhaps, as requiring it to some degree. There are no influential Buddhist thinkers calling for a return to absolute monarchy, even if many Buddhists retain a fondness for kings and their special role in traditional Buddhism (for example in Thailand, where lèse-majesté remains a regularly prosecuted crime and many citizens have pictures of King Mongkut/Rama IV in their homes or workplaces, or in Tibet and the Tibetan diaspora, in which the Fourteenth Dalai Lama has led the charge to reduce his own authority, often over the objections of the citizens he is trying to empower). Especially since the 1960s, Buddhism has even come to be associated with democratic governance and liberation movements of various types.[16]

The Various National Experiences of the Transformation

In this section, I briefly summarize some of the experiences of various countries of the transition from the traditional to the modern Buddhist conception of politics. I look only at countries that have Buddhist majorities and in which Buddhism was embraced by the political power structure at the time that government shifted from monarchy to republicanism (very broadly conceived). Thus, for example, I do not look at China, Vietnam, or Korea,[17] where Buddhism had been displaced by Confucianism as the state ideology well before those countries' republican transitions. I also omit India, since Buddhism had died out there more than 700 years earlier and was only reborn in the mid-twentieth century. Mongolia is excluded because it was incorporated into the Qing dynasty in the eighteenth century and only became an independent country in 1921, after the Chinese empire had gone through its own republican transformation. Japan is a closer case, but I have decided to omit it on the grounds that the Meiji government's disestablishment of Buddhism and embrace of state Shintō in the late nineteenth and early twentieth centuries resulted in Buddhists there not facing the same challenge that Buddhists faced in countries whose governments officially embraced Buddhism and its apparent commitment to more-or-less absolute monarchy.[18]

My discussion is also focused narrowly on the beginnings of the various national transitions to republicanism—the moments at which Buddhist thinkers and practitioners had to justify their belief that Buddhism might be separated from monarchy. There is already a great deal of excellent work on the larger histories of the role of Buddhism in the politics of these countries during the modern period,[19] but little on the question of how the people involved understood the political transformation.

Bhutan

The case of Bhutan is unique.[20] Although the country was unified in 1616, and was technically a more-or-less-absolute monarchy until the early twenty-first century, political power was not effectively centralized and made stable until 1907, when the monarchy was made hereditary by the creation of an explicit social contract that stated (in part): "Now therefore a contract has been drawn up in firm conclusion containing a unanimous agreement ... made evident to all gods and men, that Sir Ugyen Wangchuk, the leader of Bhutan and Tongsa Penlop, has been empowered as hereditary monarch ... accordingly we the above mentioned lamas and officials, subjects and followers, great and small, shall place our loyalty and render service and honor to the king ... and to the succession of his royal heirs."[21] This first hereditary king, Ugyen Wangchuk, immediately began a process of modernizing and centralizing Bhutan's system of government. Thus Bhutan was not a traditional Buddhist monarchy in the model of Thailand or Tibet, and its full embrace of hereditary monarchy was in fact the earliest stage of its process of modernization. The major push began in the 1950s, when King Jigme Dorji Wangchuk began a process of moving the country from absolute monarchy toward republican government, establishing a legislature and a cabinet. His son and successor, King Jigme Singye Wangchuk, continued and deepened these reforms, overseeing the creation of a constitution, transferring most of his powers to the cabinet, and permitting the impeachment of the king by the legislature. In 2008 Bhutan held its first general election.

Although the constitution of Bhutan asserts that the new form of government is consistent with Buddhism, there is very little discussion in the document about that issue. The most explicit reference comes in Article 9(20): "The State shall strive to create conditions that will enable the true and sustainable development of a good and compassionate society rooted in Buddhist ethos and universal human values."[22] Buddhism remains the dominant (though not the official) religion, and the king must be a Buddhist, but all citizens are guaranteed religious freedom. Similarly, in a series of speeches given by the king and various officials surrounding the process of drafting and ratifying the constitution, only very indirect reference is made to Buddhism, and the major emphasis is on national stability, security, and happiness.[23] As Mathou notes, the constitution "is inspired by traditional principles of conciliation, pragmatism, and compassion. Its support of public welfare is a modem version of the Buddhist doctrine's 'fundamental need for harmony in human relations.' While not necessarily ideological, such an approach does provide a political basis to the regime, which is rather new to Bhutan."[24]

The motivations for these changes are difficult to uncover. There is a relatively small political opposition, mostly in exile in India and Nepal and concentrated in people expelled from Bhutan as noncitizens during a tightening of citizenship laws in the 1980s, as well as some indigenous militant and ethnic dissident groups. Mathou argues that these groups have posed a real threat to Bhutan's system of government and that some of the impetus from the reforms may be a response to that threat, as well as to threats from militant groups in neighboring countries who cross the borders relatively easily.[25] Further, the changes do not appear to be driven by primarily religious motives—we don't see evidence of a transformation in the traditional version of Vajrayāna Buddhism that has long been established in Bhutan. Although the government asserts that the constitution is consistent with Buddhism, there is no claim that Buddhism requires republicanism. Mathou argues that the motivation for the change is largely explained by King Jigme Singye Wangchuk's invention of the idea that government's main task is to promote gross national happiness (GNH), which is typically explained as being a practical application of Buddhist principles.[26] Mathou suggests that GNH played the role of political ideology, allowing national unity and collective purpose while also providing a standard to evaluate both existing institutions and proposed changes. Thus, this appears to be something of a mixed case—at minimum, it seems that the Bhutanese elite sees otherwise-expedient republican reforms as not contradicting Buddhist values, and at most, perhaps, it sees republicanism as the best way to achieve those values under modern conditions.

Burma/Myanmar

Like most of the states in Southeast Asia, Burma/Myanmar has a long and complex history of shifting boundaries, degrees of power and autonomy, and ethno-cultural diversity. For our purposes, the relevant era begins with the Konbaung dynasty (1752–1886) that ruled Burma during the three Anglo-Burman Wars (1824–1885), which ultimately resulted in Burma losing its independence and becoming a British colony.[27] The British remained in complete power until 1937, when Burma was granted limited autonomy. During World War II, Burma was a major battleground; the Japanese took formal political control in 1942, but practical power was disputed until the end of the war. In 1948 Burma became an independent republic, based on the Panglong Agreement negotiated by Aung San before he was assassinated by rivals in 1947. A multiparty civilian government, led by U Nu, ruled until 1962, when the military, led by General Ne Win, seized power in a coup d'état and established a one-party socialist state. In 1988 a rival group in the military, led by General Saw Maung, seized control and declared martial law, with the professed aim of returning power to an elected civilian government. However, the junta refused to acknowledge the results of the multiparty elections in 1990, placing opposition leader Aung San Suu Kyi under house arrest. Since 2008 there have been numerous signs of reform and moves toward civilian government, including the release of Aung San Suu Kyi in 2010 and the holding of multiparty elections in 2012.

In the Burmese case, the beginnings of Buddhist republicanism are relatively clear. In 1871 U Hpo Hlaing (1829–1883), one of King Mindon's (1808–1878) principal ministers, wrote a text called *Maha-Samata Vinicchaya Kyàn* (*An Analysis of the Mahāsammata Concept*[28]), emphasizing that in the Buddhist tradition monarchical power rested on the consent of the people. When King Mindon died in 1878 there was a bloody succession battle. During that period U Hpo Hlaing exercised effective political power and attempted to impose constitutional limits on the heir, Prince Thibaw, which he outlined in his book *Raja-Dhamma-Singaha-Kyàn (Companion of Dhamma for Royalty*[29]). In that text he argued for parliamentary monarchy as being the appropriate manifestation of Buddhist principles. The effort was short-lived, and within three months Thibaw had consolidated power and dismissed U Hpo Hlaing from office. During the same period, U Kyaw Htun, a government official in a part of Burma that had already been colonized by Britain, wrote his *Essay on the Sources and Origins of Buddhist Law*

(1877), which argued that Buddhist principles supported the idea of restraining government power by subordinating it, through a constitution, to higher laws.[30]

These texts appear to be the first articulations in Burma (and perhaps anywhere) of the idea that Buddhism might be compatible with, or even require, republican government. Both were written by members of the political elite, and both offered detailed reinterpretations of the Buddhist tradition to support their claims. Emmanuel Sarkisyanz argues that the subsequent defeat of the monarchy by the British in 1886 effectively destroyed the traditional model of political legitimation, with its elaborate cosmology, and made finding a practical alternative an urgent practical, rather than philosophical, matter.[31] In the period immediately before and after independence, the nationalist movement led by Aung San was largely secular; whereas the civilian government led by U Nu was explicitly Buddhist and actively sought to integrate a republican, socialistic Buddhism into government, including making Buddhism the state religion. Given that the earliest republican texts came before the British takeover, and that they were explicitly cast as detailed readings of the early Buddhist texts, I think we can class Burma/Myanmar as an example of a transformation genuinely motivated by aspects of Buddhism (even if the immediately historical motivation was the ongoing British threat).

Cambodia

In 1863 King Norodom signed a treaty with France making Cambodia a protectorate, largely as a way of protecting Cambodia from the rival ambitions of Thailand and Vietnam, both of which had been trying to exercise control over Cambodia for centuries.[32] Although the treaty gave effective sovereignty to France, it preserved the monarchy, which lasted (despite French interference with the succession and Japanese occupation during World War II) through independence in 1953. In 1955, Norodom Sihanouk, who had been king since he was installed through French machinations in 1941, abdicated in favor of his father, Norodom Suramarit, so he could enter politics directly. He was promptly elected prime minister on a platform of creating a Buddhist, socialist state. In 1960, upon the death of his father, he resumed the throne (taking the

title prince rather than king) and in 1963 made changes to the constitution that effectively made him a hereditary monarch once again. In
1970 Prime Minister Lon Nol took advantage of the king's absence on a
trip and convinced parliament to depose Sihanouk, creating the Khmer
Republic, which claimed to be the true representation of Buddhist
political values. Sihanouk went into exile but also actively supported
the Khmer Rouge insurgency. When the Khmer Rouge defeated the
Lon Nol government in 1975, it nominally made Sihanouk head of
state but gave him no real power and forced him out again in 1976.
The Vietnamese invasion of 1978 ousted the Khmer Rouge regime and
replaced it with a socialist government controlled by Vietnam, which
Sihanouk opposed from exile. In 1991 the pro-Vietnamese government
and the Sihanouk-led opposition forces signed a settlement, allowing
Sihanouk to return to Cambodia. He became king again in 1993 and
remained on the throne until 2004, when he was succeeded by his
son, Norodom Sihamoni, though in this later period the power of the
monarchy was significantly constrained within the framework of a
parliamentary republic.

In the Cambodian case, it's hard not to see the ostensible shift from
Buddhist monarchy to Buddhist republicanism as being largely a cynical
ploy by elites, specifically Sihanouk, to preserve their power under
changed conditions. Gyallay-Pap argues that the Cambodian monarchy
had been less damaged as an institution by colonialism than the monarchies of other Southeast Asian nations and survived the colonial period
largely intact.[33] Gyallay-Pap and Suksamran separately argue that, in
the postwar period, there was growing pressure for republican reforms,
largely driven by Western-educated, elite, urban Khmers, and that this
movement was encouraged and helped by the French.[34] In the period
between 1955 and 1963, Sihanouk managed to both abandon monarchy
and create a form of republicanism that was as close to the traditional
monarchy as was practically possible under the conditions, all explicitly
in the name of Buddhism. When Lon Nol seized power in 1970, he
enlisted the help of Ven. Khieu Chum, a prominent Buddhist monk
and intellectual, to help justify the change from monarchy to republicanism as being more consistent with Buddhism than Sihanouk's
regime had been.[35] The Khmer Rouge attempted to destroy Buddhism
in Cambodia, forcing monks to disrobe, and destroying temples and

libraries. During the period of Vietnamese occupation, Buddhism slowly returned to Cambodian political life, and in 1991 the dominant Cambodian People's Party once again declared Buddhism the official state religion. As Suksamran concludes: "In the modern history of Cambodia since the 1950s, Khmer Buddhism has continuously been mobilized to achieve the political goals of the ruling élite."[36]

Laos

Modern Laos is made up of what had been three kingdoms (Luang Phrabang, Vientiane, and Champasak), united in the kingdom of Lan Xang in the fourteenth century, separated in the eighteenth century, and then reunited by the French colonial power in 1893.[37] France made King Sisavang Vong of Luang Phrabang nominal ruler of the newly reunified Laos, though the French retained control over Laos until independence in 1953, with a brief period of Japanese occupation during World War II and an abortive attempt at independence in 1945. When Laos emerged from French control, it established itself as a constitutional monarchy. Beginning in the early 1950s, the communist Pathet Lao were the main opposition force, occasionally entering into unity governments, but primarily acting as an armed insurgency. Beginning in 1968, Vietnamese forces supported the Pathet Lao, who eventually took power in 1975 and established a communist state.

Stuart-Fox and Suksamran separately argue that French colonization effectively destroyed the traditional sources of legitimacy of the Laotian monarchy by making plain to everyone the impotence of the king.[38] Both suggest that by the time independence came, Buddhism as a basis of legitimation was no longer a serious option and that Western-educated elites were primarily interested in creating a constitutional monarchy based on Western models. Buddhism remained culturally important but was no longer politically significant. We see that reflected in the Constitution of the Kingdom of Laos, adopted in 1947, which makes Buddhism the state religion (Title I, Article 7) and requires the king to be a Buddhist (Title II, Article 8), but otherwise says nothing about Buddhism and government.[39] Hence Stuart-Fox argues: "French rule effectively eliminated any political influence for Buddhism in Laos.... [S]ince evidently the king ruled not by karmic right but by benevolent permission of the French Résident Supérieur, religious ritual legitimizing his right to rule was reduced to little more than entertainment, in the eyes of some, at least, of the French-educated Lao élite. Buddhism may have retained a nostalgic cultural significance, but it almost entirely lost its political legitimizing function."[40] Suksamran agrees: "The French colonial rule over Laos was long enough (1893–1954) to orient the Lao elite to Western modes of thought on constitution and government. These modernizing elite, when they came to power after independence were ambitious to pattern the Lao government after the Western democratic form.... Legitimacy for the government now rested on popular participation in government through party politics and elections."[41]

Thus, the case of Laos seems closest to the situation described by Donald Smith above: there never was a question of justifying the transition from monarchy to republicanism, because colonialism destroyed the possibility of Buddhist monarchy altogether, and when independent, republican government became a possibility as the traditional sources of legitimation were simply no longer available to be accepted, rejected, or modified.

Sri Lanka

Buddhism came to Sri Lanka very early—by tradition in the second century BCE—though the island has long had substantial non-Buddhist ethnic minority populations.[42] Monarchy was the dominant form of government, though Sri Lanka has a complex history of internal warfare and invasion by outsiders. Starting in 1517, the Portuguese colonized Sri Lanka gradually. In 1638 the king of Kandy, the last independent monarchy on Sri Lanka, signed a treaty with the Dutch to secure their help in expelling the Portuguese, which was accomplished in the Dutch-Portuguese War in 1656, but which also resulted in Dutch colonization. Starting in the late eighteenth century, the British began to attempt to take control of Sri Lanka, and in 1815 Sri Lanka lost its independence to Britain. The British brought all of Sri Lanka under unified political control and eventually established a system of domestic representative government. In 1948 Sri Lanka became an independent member of the Commonwealth, governed by a parliament and with the queen as head of state. In 1972 the country adopted a republican constitution, with a prime minister as head of state. That constitution was replaced in 1978 by another republican constitution, which remains in place today. Sri Lanka has retained a republican system of government since independence, though its political culture has been intensely conflictual, especially concerning relations between the Buddhist Sinhalese majority and the minority, mostly Hindu, Tamils.

Sri Lanka was subject to colonial rule for a longer period than any of the other Buddhist-majority monarchies, which perhaps helps explain its unique experience. Starting in the late nineteenth century, we see the emergence of a Buddhist revival, which was closely tied to a resurgence of Sinhalese nationalism and anticolonialism. At least for the Sinhalese majority, Buddhism as a religious and cultural identity became a major focus and impetus of anti-British activism. At the same time, we do not see any serious effort to reestablish a Buddhist monarchy. By this point, several generations of Sri Lankans had received Western-style educations and participated in colonial institutions, and it seems that, at least, the Sri Lankan elite had accepted that republican government was inevitable and perhaps preferable. It is this situation that leads Bechert to conclude that the Buddhist "revival" would be better described as a Buddhist reinvention:

> Another factor which contributed to change was the reinterpretation of traditional Buddhist values by the movement of Buddhist modernism. As a consequence of the leading role played by the new elite of the colonial period which had been intensively influenced by European education, the nationalist Buddhist movement made no attempt to restore a traditional form of monarchy in Ceylon, but aimed at the establishment of a democratic republic controlled by the Buddhist majority of the population. The ideals of democracy were searched for and found by the modernists within Buddhist tradition, e.g., in the structure of the early Buddhist *Sangha*.[43]

Stanley Tambiah, though more sympathetic to the idea that early Buddhism contains strains of both monarchism and republicanism, largely agrees:[44]

The most vivid and consequential formulation of Sinhala Buddhist revivalism with nationalist overtones is to be witnessed in the anti-Christian movement begun by monks like Migettuwatte Gunananda and Hikkaduwe Sumangala in the mid-nineteenth century, then given an institutional and propagandist basis by the Theosophists, notably by Colonel Olcott as their leader in the 1880s, and taken to its ideological limits by the charismatic Anagarika Dharmapala (1864–1933) . . . the major features of [whose] Buddhist revivalism [include] a selective retrieval of norms from canonical Buddhism.[45]

Sri Lanka seems to share with Laos the experience that by the time independence became practically possible the tradition of Buddhist monarchy was completely dead, and no one was interested in reviving it. It also seems that there was no indigenous republican movement prior to the British takeover, and thus that the ultimate embrace of republicanism was largely the result of the influence of the colonial power and the lack of any plausible indigenous alternative. If Bechert and Tambiah are right, the connection of Buddhism to republicanism really only emerges as part of the Sinhalese nationalist revival. The question, then, is whether the assertion that Buddhism was compatible with, and perhaps even required, republicanism was an opportunistic ploy to make Buddhism appear relevant to the modern world or was a good-faith reinterpretation of the evidence from the early texts. Bechert clearly thinks it was the former; Tambiah, while acknowledging that the reinterpretation of the canon was selective, also argues that the early texts contain conflicting viewpoints on politics and government, and denies that it is obvious that they unambiguously endorse monarchy. Given these conflicting interpretations, we will need to treat Sri Lanka as an indeterminate case.

Thailand

In contrast, the case of Thailand is fairly clear, if complex. During the period of Western colonization in Asia, the Chakri dynasty (1782–present) was in power [46] Unlike most of the other monarchies of Asia, the Chakri successfully resisted colonization, and Thailand remained sovereign. The future king Mongkut (Rama IV, 1804–1868) entered

Buddhist monastic life in 1824. Later that same year, his father, Rama II, died. Although Mongkut was technically the rightful heir, the court preferred his half-brother Prince Jessadabodindra, who was crowned Rama III. Mongkut remained a monk and in 1833 started a monastic reform movement, which ultimately became the influential Thammayut sect that emphasized a return to the canonical teachings and disciplines of early Buddhism. When Jessadabodindra died in 1851, Mongkut was crowned as Rama IV and ruled until his death in 1868. He was succeeded by his son Chulalongkorn (Rama V).

Mongkut initiated a sweeping set of reforms to government and Thai culture, all aimed at strengthening Thailand in its struggle against Western powers. He also continued to champion the religious reforms he had initiated as a monk. On the political side, his reforms centralized and strengthened the power of the monarchy, although he did seek to either abandon or deemphasize some of the practices that elevated the king to divine status. On the religious side, his reforms simultaneously emphasized a return to "pure" tradition while also arguing that Buddhism was compatible with the findings of modern science.

Chulalongkorn (Rama V, ruled 1868–1910) continued and broadened his father's reform efforts. In 1886 a group of Western-educated Thai princes and officials submitted a petition to Chulalongkorn asking him to change Thailand's form of government to a constitutional monarchy. Chulalongkorn declined to make the suggested changes, but he responded courteously to what could have been interpreted as treason and expressed his support for a constitutional monarchy, though he thought that Thailand was not yet ready for that change.[47] In 1892 Chulalongkorn began a series of changes that moved several steps toward republican (and more fully centralized) government, without fully embracing it.[48]

Chulalongkorn's son, Vajiravudh, became Rama VI in 1910 and ruled until 1925. He continued the governmental reforms, still modernizing and moving toward further centralization of political power, but he retained an absolute monarchy. In response to a letter from his brother and closest friend Chakrabongse, Rama VI also declared his support for a constitutional monarchy, but, like his father, thought that Thailand was not yet able to sustain that system of government.[49] At the same time, other elements of the Thai elite were pressing for more rapid moves toward a constitutional monarchy with a strong parliament, such as some of the plotters of the failed 1912 Palace Revolt.[50] After the natural death of Vajiravudh in 1925, his brother Prajadhipok became Rama VII. Prajadhipok was on the throne during the successful Revolution of 1932, also led by disenfranchised, Western-educated Thai elites, that ended the absolute monarchy and replaced it with a constitutional system in which the king retained sharply limited powers.[51] Since 1932 Thai politics has been famously conflictual, though it has retained a republican structure (at times only nominally) with a relatively weak king.

It seems clear that the reform initiatives of Mongkut and Chulalongkorn (perhaps especially their encouragement of Thai elites to send their children to Europe to be educated) played a large role in the eventual change from monarchy to republicanism, and it seems that, at least from Chulalongkorn on, the kings of Thailand were open to the idea of a constitutional monarchy, though none ever thought the time was ripe. In both the political and religious arenas, their changes led to demystification and an increased respect for science and reason, all of which had the ultimate effect of making the semisacred monarchy open to rational doubt and contestation. Along those lines, Keyes argues that the reforms changed Thais' conception of karma from one that was relatively fatalistic to one that encouraged the possibility of both karmic and social mobility and agency.[52] Especially in the case of Mongkut, who was a monk for twenty-seven years before ascending the throne, and who had largely stayed out of palace politics during that period, it seems fair to conclude that his religious reforms were inspired by an earnest belief that they represented a purer form of Buddhism than what had evolved over Thai history, and that his political reforms were carried out in the earnest belief that they were at least not in conflict with Buddhist teachings. The motivations of the plotters of the 1912 Palace Revolt and the Revolution of 1932 appear to have been primarily secular and political.[53]

Tibet

Tibet was effectively a monarchy, under the rule of the Dalai Lama, with a long and complicated history of dependence on other powers, independence, and various degrees of autonomy, until the Chinese took effective power in 1951.[54] The Chinese permitted the existing government to remain in place until a failed uprising in 1959, when the Chinese government deposed the Fourteenth Dalai Lama, who fled into exile in India. Today Tibet remains an autonomous region within China, with the Chinese government exercising effective control. The Tibetan government in exile is a constitutional republic.

In the Tibetan case, the origins of the move from monarchy to republicanism are very clear: they largely affect the Tibetan diaspora in exile and are almost entirely the brainchild of the Fourteenth Dalai Lama. These efforts began in 1962–1963 with the publication of the Dalai Lama's autobiographical *My Land and My People*, and the promulgation of a draft republican constitution for the government in exile and for Tibet proper should the government in exile be permitted to return. While it's certainly possible to offer a cynical reading of that transformation—that the Dalai Lama recognized that the world would be much more sympathetic to the plight of a democratic government in exile than to a theocratic and semifeudal one—the Dalai Lama has consistently defended the new form of government as being better suited to Buddhism than the old regime, and his arguments on that topic seem to be consistent with his other interpretations of Buddhism. For example, he writes:

> I am deeply committed to the political modernization and democratization of my native Tibet and have made efforts to develop a democratic system for Tibetans living in exile. In 1963, I promulgated the democratic constitution of Tibet, and our exiled community has, under difficult circumstances, responded well to the challenge of this experiment with democracy. In 1969, I declared that whether the institution of the Dalai Lama should continue to exist depended on the wishes of the Tibetan people. And in 1991, our legislature, the Assembly of Tibetan People's Deputies, adopted the Charter of Tibetans in Exile, which expanded the Assembly's membership and transferred from me to it the power to elect the Cabinet.[55]

Elsewhere he characterized the new constitution as "based on the principles of the doctrine of Lord Buddha and the Universal Declaration of Human Rights."[56]

Thus, while it's debatable whether Tibet would have transitioned to republicanism absent the events of 1951–1959, it seems like a reasonable interpretation that the Dalai Lama's commitment to republicanism is genuinely based on a reappraisal of the Buddhist tradition and not simply the result of cynical calculation.

Conclusion

Of the various national experiences of the transition from Buddhist monarchy to republicanism, two (Burma and Tibet) seem to have been driven by Buddhist religious convictions; three (Thailand, Bhutan, and Laos) seem to have been motivated by largely nonreligious factors that the actors apparently perceived as being consistent with Buddhism; one (Cambodia) appears to be a cynical use of Buddhism to justify elite power; and one (Sri Lanka) is indeterminate. As I indicated above, this suggests that both of the broad explanatory schema—that the transition was largely cynical, and that the transition was rooted in a good-faith reinterpretation of the early texts—have some explanatory value. There are some clear cases in each category, and some cases that reflect a mixture of the two motivations. What that means for Buddhists going forward is that while there are textual and historical bases for a republican or democratic interpretation of Buddhist political theory, we cannot simply flatly assert that Buddhism is fundamentally democratic, nor forget its long embrace of monarchy, nor finally deny that some may use Buddhism cynically, as a fig leaf for power politics.

Since 1950, there has been an enormous amount of Buddhist political theory written, from many different doctrinal, national, and political points of view. On my reading, it is all or nearly all republican, with most of it endorsing some form of democratic government. While there are, of course, individuals or institutions who speak for particular versions of Buddhism, such as the Dalai Lama for Tibetan Buddhism, there is no one who speaks for "Buddhism" generally, and thus there is no single Buddhist political theory today. Rather, there are many different strains of Buddhist political thinking, united (as I argue in part II) by some common normative commitments, but diverging on the particulars of how those should play out practically. Since my ultimate concern is those underlying normative claims, I do not provide a catalog of contemporary Buddhist political writings here but rather turn to the political theory that inspires them.

PART II

A BUDDHIST
POLITICAL THEORY

4

Overcoming versus Letting Go

Nietzsche and Buddha on the Self and Politics

IN PART I WE SAW THAT one of the key teachings of early Buddhism is the doctrine of *anattā*, or no-self. In this chapter I examine what the Buddha said about the self and its implications for politics. I then compare the Buddha's theory of self with its closest Western analogue, Nietzsche's theory of under-souls. I conclude that the Buddha's theory is preferable, even when assessed using Nietzsche's own criteria. In chapter 7, I return to this issue to examine how the *anattā* theory helps create a compelling political theory.

On the surface, Nietzsche and the Buddha appear to have remarkably similar views on the status and importance of the self. Both thinkers argue that there is no immortal soul or essential self. Both claim that our belief that we are psychologically continuous over time masks the fact that our identity is the result of a dynamic and unstable relationship among many internal and external factors. The two even agree that false self-conceptions are at the root of many and perhaps most personal and social problems. Yet Nietzsche and the Buddha offer diametrically opposed advice about how one should act based on these insights. In brief, the Buddha advocates letting go of one's sense of being a self, on the grounds that this illusory experience is not needed for any useful purpose but instead poses a permanent barrier to peaceful, harmonious relations with oneself and others. In contrast, Nietzsche advocates a process of continuous self-overcoming, constantly replacing one's existing, limiting self with a newly conceived self that allows one to fulfill one's goals more fully.

These two courses of action represent a fundamental existential choice for anyone who comes to doubt whether there is any essence or substantial continuity to the self: Shall I not conceive of myself as a self at all, or shall I remake my self to suit my existing plans and values? From the Buddha's point of view, Nietzsche's decision to affirm even a contingent, more-or-less-temporary self represents a failure of courage to live in a world without guarantees or stable essences. In other words, it represents the limit of Nietzsche's commitment to becoming. From Nietzsche's point of view, the Buddha's attempt to let go of the idea of being a self represents a passive form of nihilism, a giving up on the idea of pursuing normative ideals and standards.

The two thinkers agree that one's self-view is central to one's ability to cooperate socially and politically with others, while once again disagreeing about which self-view to adopt. The Buddha argues that letting go of one's sense of being a self will lead one to become less egocentric, less likely to do harm to others, and more likely to be willing to create peaceful means of coexistence. Conversely, he argues that holding onto the conception of being a self is one of the primary causes of social conflict. Nietzsche conceives of his self-overcoming view as the mean between the destructive, reactive egoism of *ressentiment*, which is premised on the existence of an essential self, and the nihilism that he perceives in the no-self position. He views continuous self-overcoming as generating a politics of peaceful, joyful cooperation and voluntary self-control (among equals).

However, reading these two thinkers together does not merely clarify and sharpen the terms and consequences of the choices that confront us. It also reveals that the Buddha was right and Nietzsche was wrong. As I argue below, the Buddha has the better argument for two main reasons. First, Nietzsche's claim that we should maintain a contingent self creates a barrier to our ability to accept the full truth of our experience of ourselves, and thus injects resentment against existence back into his theory. Second, Nietzsche is mistaken in thinking that the Buddhist no-self view leads to an abandonment of agency and the ability to pursue normative ideals. Indeed, precisely the opposite is true: holding onto a self-theory that one knows is false is the bigger barrier to agency and normative striving. The same line of reasoning also holds good for their political views: Nietzsche is mistaken in thinking that continuous self-overcoming avoids the dangers of both *ressentiment* and nihilism, and the Buddha's argument, that abandoning the idea of the self altogether is likely to lead to peaceful cooperation, is more plausible.

The Self

In common-sense terms, what we mean by the self is that element/ quality/essence/factor/process that makes each one of us the unique individuals that we are. More concretely, when we talk about the self we have at least three things in mind: identity, continuity, and causality. By identity I mean that whatever the self might actually be, it is what makes you you. The self is unique to each individual, and it cannot be shared with someone else or taken away. By continuity I mean that the self remains relevantly the same over time. Exactly what that means is the subject of an enormous literature in philosophy,[1] but for our purposes we can bypass that debate. If there is a self, it is the thing that makes it true to say that you are same person today who you were ten years ago, and will be ten years in the future. Further, if you believe that some part of your identity survives after the death of your body, then the self might be identical with the soul.

The causality condition is a bit more complicated. On the one hand, the self would have to be a primary cause of your experiences and actions. Really, that's just a spelling out of the identity condition—if the self is what makes you yourself, then it must be primarily causally responsible for those things that are distinctive to you: your experiences and actions. However, on the other hand, the self would need to be largely immune from being permanently affected by external causes. In effect, this is just a spelling out of the continuity condition—if your self could be changed by the influence of external factors, then it's possible that you would not be the same person today who you were ten years ago, and continuity would be lost. Thus the self might be as much as an immortal soul or as little as a minimum degree of psychological continuity over time, but whatever it is, if it exists, the self must possess the relevant qualities of identity, continuity, and causality.

In the primary texts from both Nietzsche and the Buddha, and to a lesser degree in the scholarly commentary on those texts, we find three different levels or definitions of self discussed (sometimes explicitly, often implicitly). First, there is the self as an ontological or metaphysical fact, a thing-in-itself, a natural essence, a soul, and so on. For simplicity, I'll call this the *metaphysical* self.

Second, there is what I'll call the *persistent self*, which is the self understood as an ongoing psychological unity. Thus, one might accept that there is no immortal soul or natural essence that constitutes a human self and yet still experience or believe that human cognitive functioning gives rise to a distinct psychological entity that has the necessary qualities of identity, continuity, and causality (at least during the lifetime of the body).

Finally, there is the *phenomenal self*, which is the experience of human beings as single, more-or-less unified entities at any given moment. Thus, it makes sense for each of us to refer to ourselves as "I" and for us to treat others as if they were single, more-or-less unified subjects. Both the Buddha and Nietzsche refer to human beings as phenomenal selves and do not seem to think that this commits them to any untenable metaphysical claims.

Nietzsche and the Buddha both argue that there is no metaphysical self, but that human beings naturally experience themselves as being psychologically unified over time and therefore as being persistent selves. The two thinkers agree that this experience is an illusion that covers over the fact that human "selves" are made up of unstable arrangements of psychological and somatic experiences, such as instinctual drives, memories, sensory experiences, and so on. Their major disagreement is over how we should respond to realizing that the persistent self is an illusion.

The Buddhist Theory of No-Self

As discussed in the introduction to this book, in the early texts the Buddha identified three especially important issues about which we must develop right views to achieve enlightenment, the religion's main goal. Together these three issues are called the *tilakkhaṇa*, which is variously translated as the Three Marks, Characteristics, or Signs of

Existence: that life is suffering (*dukkhā*), that all things are impermanent (*anicca*), and that all things are not-self (*anātta*).[2] The overwhelming majority of Buddhists interpret *anātta* as meaning that the Buddha taught that what I have called the metaphysical and persistent selves do not exist, and that our apparent experiences of them are illusions.[3] A small minority of Buddhists and scholars believe that the Buddha's teachings do not amount to a total denial of the existence of the self.[4] Given that the vast majority of Buddhists reject this view, I will not assess it here—for our purposes, we can assume that the Buddha did in fact teach that there is no self.

The *locus classicus* of the *anattā* doctrine is the Buddha's second sermon (the *Anattalakkhana Sutta*).[5] To understand the arguments made there, we need a little background on the theory of the *khandhas*, discussed briefly in the introduction. That theory is laid out repeatedly in the early texts, and many scholars identify *Samyutta Nikāya* 22:56 (the *Parivatta Sutta*) as being an especially clear exposition.[6] There the Buddha teaches that all the objects of experience (also called conditioned objects) are made up of five *khandhas* (the Pāli word literally means heaps or bundles): form or matter (*rūpa*); sensation or feeling (*vedanā*); perception or cognition (*saññā*); mental formations or volition (*sankhāra*); and consciousness or discernment (*viññāna*). In the *Anattalakkhana Sutta* the Buddha teaches that no self can be found in the five *khandhas*. He makes two distinct arguments along these lines.[7] First, he argues that if the *khandhas* were identical with or amounted to a self, then that self would have volitional control over the *khandhas*. Since human beings don't have volitional control over the *khandhas* that suggests that the interaction of the *khandhas* does not either flow from or give rise to a self. The text says: "Bhikkhus [Monks], form is nonself. For if, bhikkhus, form were self, this form would not lead to affliction, and it would be possible to have it of form: 'Let my form be thus; let my form not be thus.'" (The same comments are repeated for the other *khandhas*.)[8] The second argument rests on the assumption that a self would be permanent, either in the sense of being eternal and immutable (i.e., a metaphysical self) or in the sense of being consistent and stable over a long period of time (i.e., a persistent self). The Buddha points out that our actual experience shows us that the *khandhas* are impermanent, and therefore could not either be a self or give rise to a self: " 'What do you think, bhikkhus, is form permanent or impermanent?'—'Impermanent, venerable sir.'—'Is what is impermanent suffering or happiness?'—'Suffering, venerable sir.'—'Is what is impermanent, suffering, and subject to change fit to be regarded thus: "This is mine, this I am, this is my self?" '—'No, venerable sir.' " (The same comments are repeated for the other *khandhas*.)[9]

The Buddha concludes: "Therefore, bhikkhus, any kind of form whatsoever, whether past, future, or present, internal or external, gross or subtle, inferior or superior, far or near, all form should be seen as it really is with correct wisdom thus: 'This is not mine, this I am not, this is not my self.' " (The same comments are repeated for the other *khandhas*.)[10]

Remember that above I argued that whatever the self might be, it has to have the three qualities of identity, continuity, and causality. In essence, the Buddha's two arguments in the *Anattalakkhaṇa Sutta* concern the causality quality (which will in turn implicate the other two). On the one hand, he argues, if there really is a self, it ought to be the primary cause of our experiences. Since the *khandhas* constitute all the possible objects of experience, it seems that if we had a self it ought to be able to exert some degree of volitional control over our experience of the *khandhas*. Yet we do not have volitional control over (our experience of) the *khandhas*, which suggests that there is no self to be found in them. On the other hand, the Buddha argues, if there is a self, it must be identical with one or more of the *khandhas*, since by hypothesis the *khandhas* exhaust the category of possible objects of experience. By definition, the self has to be largely immune from external causality, or else it would not be adequately continuous over time. But none of the *khandhas* (or combinations of *khandhas*) is immune from causality— every aspect of our experience, of both the outer and inner worlds, is subject to constant flux and change due to the influences of external causes. In essence, the self would have to be a cause of change in the *khandhas* while not suffering changes due to them. But nothing in our actual experience has those qualities. Therefore nothing in our experience could be a self, and we are justified in concluding that there is no self (it is this last step that a minority of interpreters argue the Buddha himself does not take, arguing that the most that we can conclude is that we have no evidence of there being a self, but not the positive or dogmatic conclusion that there therefore is not one).

According to the Buddha, accepting that there is no self is central to liberation and enlightenment. We can infer this from the fact that the no-self view is one of the three marks or characteristics of existence (*tilakkhaṇa*)—believing in a self is necessarily always believing something false about the fundamental nature of existence. There are also a number of places in the early texts where the Buddha explicitly makes this point. For example, the following formula appears repeatedly and suggests that abandoning self-view is central to enlightenment:

> [Buddha:] "Is what is impermanent, suffering, and subject to change, fit to be regarded thus: 'This is mine, this I am, this is my self?'" [Bhikkhus:] "No, venerable sir.". . . [Buddha:] "Seeing thus, bhikkhus, a well-taught noble disciple becomes disenchanted with material form, disenchanted with feeling, disenchanted with perception, disenchanted with formations, disenchanted with consciousness. Being disenchanted, he becomes dispassionate. Through dispassion [his mind] is liberated. When it is liberated there comes the knowledge: 'It is liberated.' He understands: 'Birth is destroyed, the holy life has been lived, what had to be done has been done, there is no more coming to any state of being.'"[11]

There is also an often-cited *sutta* about the self-view of the monk Khemaka. A group of other monks question Khemaka about whether he finds a self in any of the *khandhas*. When he says that he does not, the monks reply (perhaps mockingly): "If the Venerable Khemaka does not regard anything among [the *khandhas*] as self or as belonging to self, then he is an arahant, one whose taints are destroyed [i.e., an enlightened being]."[12] Khemaka responds that although he intellectually knows and believes that there is no self, he cannot quite get rid of the sense that he is or has a self. In the terms I have proposed, he does not believe that he is a persistent self, but he cannot avoid the experience of feeling like a persistent self. Khemaka says: "Friends, even though a noble disciple has abandoned the five lower fetters, still, in relation to the [*khandhas*] there lingers in him a residual conceit 'I am,' a desire 'I am,' an underlying tendency 'I am' that has not yet been uprooted."[13] But, Khemaka explains: "As he dwells thus [dispassionately] contemplating the rise and fall in the [*khandhas*] the residual conceit ... comes to be uprooted."[14] As a consequence of having this conversation, Khemaka and sixty of the other monks achieve enlightenment.

Finally, in a number of places the Buddha argues that every possible self-view will lead to continued suffering. For example, in the *Sammādiṭṭhi Sutta*, the Buddha teaches that there are four kinds of clinging (the root cause of suffering): "clinging to sensual pleasures, clinging to views, clinging to rules and observances, and clinging to a doctrine of self."[15] Elsewhere the Buddha says: " 'Bhikkhus, you may well cling to that doctrine of self that would not arouse sorrow, lamentation, pain, grief, and despair in one who takes it as a support. But do you see any such doctrine of self, bhikkhus?'—'No, venerable sir.'—'Good, bhikkhus. I too do not see any doctrine of self that would not arouse sorrow, lamentation, pain, grief, and despair in one who clings to it.' "[16]

The correct view about the self, according to the Buddha, is to see every experience as merely the causal consequence of impersonal factors, whether they be external or internal. Roughly, the goal is to avoid reifying either the object or the subject of experience, and to avoid clinging to (or actively avoiding) one's experience. The Buddha did not deny the existence or relevance of mental phenomena like thoughts, emotions, memories, moods, and so on. Rather, he refused to give them special importance—they are merely some among many sources of present experience whose arising and cessation we should attend to dispassionately, and they are impersonal in the sense of arising and ceasing without the need for any subject (just as we believe that animals experience sensation, emotion, and memory and yet do not impute to animals a self).

The Buddha never gives a direct explanation of what it would be like to live without a concept of self, but there are many clues in the texts. From abundant examples, it's clear that the Buddha believed that it is possible to continue living a recognizably human life without the concept of self. Thus people who have achieved this insight still have the normal range of internal and external experiences—sensations, emotions, memories, thoughts, subconscious activity, and so on. Further, they still conceive of themselves as physically separate entities with distinct needs, desires, and intentions. The main differences are that, on the one hand, such people are able to accept all the various constituent parts that make them up without feeling the need to reject or deny some of those parts as inconsistent with their self-image, and, on the other hand, such people are able to interact with the outside world in a dispassionate way, not suppressing or denying their feelings, but also not allowing their feelings and reactions to determine their behavior. Rather, precisely because they do not have a self-image to project or defend, they can deliberate on all of their experiences—both inner and outer—and act based on reflection and choice. The Buddha argues that this will lead to the greatest possible personal happiness and also suggests that it will lead to social peace and harmony (discussed below).

Nietzsche's Theory of the Self

Although there are many passages in Nietzsche's work that are indirectly relevant to the question of the nature and status of the self, there are only a handful of passages in which Nietzsche directly discusses the issue.[17] There is also a small but surprisingly diverse secondary literature on this question.[18] Pinning down exactly what Nietzsche says about the self is challenging, both because of Nietzsche's famously elusive style of writing and because he talks about both the metaphysical and persistent selves without always clearly distinguishing between them (a problem that causes confusion in the secondary literature as well). However, a majority of interpreters agree that Nietzsche makes two main claims about the self. First, Nietzsche denies that any metaphysical self exists. Second, Nietzsche argues that our experience of being persistent selves is based on a contingent hierarchy established among a multiplicity of what he calls under-souls (drives, affects, instincts, thoughts, intentions, and so on).

In several places in both his published and unpublished writings, Nietzsche flatly denies that any metaphysical self exists. For example, he writes in the *Genealogy of Morality*: "But there is no such substratum; there is no 'being' behind the deed, its effect, and what becomes of it; 'the doer' is invented as an afterthought,—the doing is everything."[19] Similarly, In *Beyond Good and Evil*, he writes: "one must also first of all finish off that other and more fateful atomism which Christianity has taught best and longest, the *soul atomism*. Let this expression be allowed to designate that belief which regards the soul as being something indestructible, eternal, indivisible, as a monad, as an *atomon: this* belief ought to be ejected from science!"[20]

Nietzsche's comments on the persistent self are more numerous and more complicated. His main claim is that our experience of being selves arises from a contingent and unstable hierarchy established among our various "under-souls." We find this view in a number of places in both the published and unpublished work. Thus, Nietzsche writes in *Thus Spoke Zarathustra*: "The body is a great intelligence, a multiplicity with one sense, a war and a peace, a herd and a herdsman."[21] Similarly, in *Beyond Good and Evil* he writes: "But the road to new forms and refinements of the soul-hypothesis stands open: and such conceptions as 'mortal soul' and 'soul as multiplicity of the subject' and 'soul as social structure of the drives and emotions' want henceforth to possess civic rights in science."[22] Later in the same book, Nietzsche writes: "He who wills adds in this way the sensations of pleasure of the successful executive agents, the serviceable 'under-wills' or under-souls—for our body is only a social structure composed of many souls—to his sensations of pleasure as commander. L'effet, c'est moi: what happens here is what happens in every well-constructed and happy commonwealth: the ruling class identifies itself with the successes of the commonwealth. In all willing it is absolutely a question of commanding and obeying, on the basis, as I have said already, of a social structure composed of many 'souls.' "[23] In the *Nachlass* materials ultimately published as *The Will to Power*, we find: "a single individual contains within him a vast confusion of contradictory valuations and consequently of contradictory drives."[24] Later in the same text: "The assumption of one single subject is perhaps unnecessary; perhaps it is just as permissible to assume a multiplicity of subjects, whose interaction and struggle is the basis of our thought and our consciousness in general? A kind of aristocracy of 'cells' in which dominion resides? To be sure, an aristocracy of equals, used to ruling jointly and understanding how to command? My hypothesis: The subject as multiplicity."[25] Finally, again from *The Will to Power*: "The body and physiology as the starting point: why?—We gain the correct idea of the nature of our subject-unity, namely as regents at the head of a communality (not as 'souls' or 'life forces'), also of the dependence of these regents upon the ruled and of an order of rank and division of labor as the conditions that make possible the whole and its parts. In the same way, how living unities continually arise and die and how the 'subject' is not eternal."[26]

A number of commentators have argued that this theory, at least on its face, is not coherent. The basic concern is that a being made up only of a multiplicity of drives, without some additional ability for reflection and choice, simply isn't capable of the kind of subjectivity and agency that we attribute to human selves. This argument is made separately by Fennell, Janaway, Booth, and Staten.[27] Interestingly, this general argument—that without a more substantial self no reflection or choice is possible—is parallel to Nietzsche's own criticism of Buddhism, which I address below.

Some of these criticisms are based on a failure to distinguish between the metaphysical and persistent selves. If it's true that there is a persistent self of some kind in Nietzsche's theory, and if it's true that such a persistent self, made up of a variety of under-souls, is capable of reflection and choice, then the alleged incoherence of Nietzsche's theory is resolved. Hales and Welshon argue both that such a "bundle" self (in their terminology) is capable of consciousness, and that it is capable of creating a hierarchy among the various under-souls, such that the self has some criteria for making choices and pursuing intentions over time.[28] They write: "The answer is that disciplining the drives does not entail a subject distinct from the drives because the task the subject is supposed to perform is shouldered by each and every drive or set of drives that go into composing the self. Each individual drive and set of drives are instances of forces that attempt to domineer all the others, so there is no need for a subject distinct from them that engages in the domineering."[29]

Most commentators have agreed with this line of thinking, that the self-as-multiplicity could be capable of agency. Thus the major disputes in the secondary literature are over a different issue (though not always explicitly). The real debate, and the difference between the Nietzschean and Buddhist theories of the self, emerges not when we consider Nietzsche's *descriptive* claims about the self-as-multiplicity, but rather when we consider his claims about what *attitude* we should take toward our experience of being persistent selves. On this issue we find three very different interpretations. The first school of thought argues that, on Nietzsche's view, we only ever achieve a very limited unity among the various drives and that it does not or need not harden into a diachronically continuous identity or self. The second interpretation argues that for Nietzsche we do need to form and maintain a diachronically continuous personality based on a relatively stable hierarchy of drives. While this self may be capable of self-overcoming under some circumstances, and while it may (and should) acknowledge itself as contingent and potentially fluid, we nonetheless need a relatively stable self over time. The third and final school argues that while Nietzsche does indeed believe that we need relatively stable persistent selves, this is only a transitional phase and that in the future we would be able to rely on the instincts having been adequately trained and harmonized, so that we could learn to let go of our conscious, intentional sense of self, and instead allow our (tamed, harmonized) natures to guide us.

The first view, that Nietzsche's persistent self never crystallizes into a stable hierarchy of drives, is argued explicitly by Miller and implicitly by Strong.[30] For example, Miller argues: "Nietzsche's interrogation of the idea of selfhood has reached, by a complex series of dissolutions, a definition of the self as a projected, constantly changing virtuality, like the center of gravity of a moving mass. This phantasmal center, moreover, has been doubled, fragmented, multiplied, dispersed into who knows how many separate momentary centers. Each is inhabited by a will to power over the whole, a desire to dominate and be itself the center."[31] Here Fennell, Janaway, Booth and Staten have it right: it's hard to see how this is a coherent account of a self at all. To the extent that Nietzsche's persistent self is merely a temporary resolution of the conflicts among forces, and that the balance of power changes from moment to moment, without the creation of a relatively stable hierarchy, no agency appears possible.

Before considering the second school of interpretation, which I think is largely correct, I'd like to leap ahead to the third, which I believe is mistaken. Graham Parkes and André van der Braak separately argue that Nietzsche's view of the persistent self is that it is a transitional stage that can eventually be abandoned.[32] Because Parkes's version of this argument is more fully developed, I examine his argument as representative of both. Parkes agrees with the view that Nietzsche rejects the meta-physical self and that he articulates a theory of the persistent self as being composed of a multiplicity of under-souls. Parkes then argues as follows:

> The final stage of self-overcoming, then, consists of daring, after prolonged practice of self-mastery, to relax the discipline and trust to natural spontaneity. . . . The eventual relaxation takes daring because the ego, which would otherwise control the process, has been overcome—dissolved into a plurality of drives—in the course of the protracted self-discipline. What is responsible for the disciplining are various (groups of) drives, and there comes a point where the discipline is no longer necessary because these various groups have learned to live in harmony with each other.[33]

Parkes himself explicitly argues that, on this interpretation, Nietzsche's view of the persistent self is the same as the Buddha's. Although there is some dispute about this reading,[34] for the moment I think we should accept Parkes's claim. If this really is Nietzsche's view, then Nietzsche and the Buddha do take the same attitude toward the experience of being a persistent self. However, I believe that this interpretation is not the best reading of Nietzsche. There are several arguments against this reading developed in the secondary literature (though only the first is directly specifically against Parkes's work). First, Morrison argues that this reading seems to imply that there is an implicit or inchoate natural harmony among the drives that one merely has to bring to fruition. Morrison argues that this implies a greater degree of essentialism about the self than Nietzsche appeared to intend or accept, especially given Nietzsche's rejection of the metaphysical self.[35] Second, Gemes argues that this kind of reading implies that the subject has a greater degree of volitional control over the management of the under-souls than Nietzsche envisioned. Rather, Nietzsche envisioned the drives as being partially autonomous, so that they could be partially harmonized, but never fully tamed.[36] Third, Thiele and Nehamas separately argue that Nietzsche appears to have viewed the possibility of a final, stable unity of the under-souls as being a regulative ideal rather than an achievable goal.[37] Finally, Bret Davis argues that Nietzsche's texts are indeterminate on this question, that Nietzsche could not make up his mind whether completely harmonizing the self would mean dissolving the self or reifying it.[38] Parkes and van der Braak's reading of Nietzsche presents an attractive view of the attitude we should take toward our experience of being persistent selves—indeed, in the long run I will argue that it is the correct view. But I agree with Morrison, Gemes, Thiele, Nehemas, and Davis that it is not Nietzsche's view.

Thus we come to the second school of thought: that for Nietzsche we do need to form and maintain a unified personality based on a relatively stable hierarchy of drives. This is clearly the majority position among interpreters,[39] though there is some disagreement about why we need to maintain a stable hierarchy. One camp argues that we need a relatively stable self for cognitive reasons. Thus Davey argues: "Nietzsche holds that the very condition of our existence as an organisation of multiple drives will be jeopardised for without an effective cohesion between the drives that make us up, the cohesion of the whole would fall apart. For this reason Nietzsche maintains that we cannot renounce the fiction, an argument which is clearly reminiscent of Hume's case concerning mental dispositions which cannot be opposed."[40] Hales and Welshon agree: "Nietzsche thinks that it is imperative that there be a ruling drive in the service of which the other drives organize."[41] Further: "A flourishing life is thus one in which there is an overarching second-order drive or set of them that coordinates 'the inner systems and their operation' so that a person may create him- or herself."[42]

On my reading, this first camp among those who see Nietzsche as wanting us to hold onto the experience of being a persistent self has a defensible, even persuasive, reading of the primary texts. But I believe that this reading plays down Nietzsche's fundamentally normative motivations. Over and over again, Nietzsche reminds us that his major concern is the question of the value or meaning of human life. As with Kant, Nietzsche's concern with cognitive or epistemological questions is ultimately always in the service of his normative concerns. For that reason, I believe that the second camp, those who see as Nietzsche encouraging us to create and maintain a persistent self for normative reasons, has the better reading.

A number of interpreters take this general position,[43] though they do not all identify the same normative motivations behind Nietzsche's encouragement of the persistent self. Thus Davey (elsewhere) argues that

Nietzsche believes that maintaining a stable persistent self is a necessary condition for maximizing our will to power.[44] Gemes and Zuckert separately read Nietzsche as calling upon us to create a unified subjectivity to overcome nihilism.[45] Hanson argues that Nietzsche's emphasis on maintaining a stable hierarchy and will actually solves a problem in Buddhism of being unable to explain how willing is consistent with the lack of a metaphysical self.[46] Loy argues that Nietzsche can't let go of a relatively stable persistent self because his basic project is overcoming an existential sense of lack through the creation of a heroic ego.[47] Unique among interpreters, Davis argues that Nietzsche cannot make up his mind whether we can (or should) give up our experience of ourselves as persistent selves.[48]

As I have already suggested, I believe that this is the best reading of Nietzsche's thoughts on the attitude we should take toward the experience of being a persistent self. We see this point in a number of passages from Nietzsche, including: "One thing is needful.—To 'give style' to one's character—a great and rare art! It is practiced by those who survey all the strengths and weaknesses of their nature and then fit them into an artistic plan until every one of them appears as art and reason and even weaknesses delight the eye.... It will be the strong and domineering natures that enjoy their finest gaiety in such constraint and perfection under a law of their own."[49] More generally, Nietzsche's frequently repeated point that both individuals and peoples need tables of values to guide them, even if those tables are ultimately overturned and replaced by new ones, points in the same direction.

Thus Nietzsche argues that the metaphysical self does not exist, that human beings are persistent selves made up of a multiplicity of under-souls, and further that human beings must actively work to create and maintain a hierarchy among the under-souls, though any such hierarchy is both contingent and potentially overcomeable. Those who are unable to establish such a hierarchy, who cannot give style to their characters, are tossed about by their various desires, instincts, perceptions, and thoughts. The distinction that Nietzsche draws in the *Genealogy* between the man of conscience, who is capable of creating a limited hierarchy among his under-souls, and the man without conscience, whose behavior is determined by whatever impulse arises most forcefully at the moment, neatly illustrates the importance of this issue. More generally, it is only those who are able to accept and integrate every one of their under-souls into a stable relationship who are able to live out *amor fati* and embrace the eternal return, while those who cannot harmonize their component drives will always view parts of themselves and their world with resentment.

Nietzsche versus Buddha on the Self

As I have argued, both Nietzsche and the Buddha deny that there is any metaphysical self, and the two thinkers agree that what human beings experience as their persistent selves are in fact unstable multiplicities of experiences—desires, instincts, thoughts, beliefs, sensory impressions, and so on. Both appear to believe that consciousness and the capacity for deliberative choice arise from the interactions of these constituent parts. Further, both agree that the perception of the underlying multiplicity as a single, unified, diachronically continuous self is an illusion. These significant areas of agreement have led a number of commentators to suggest that Nietzsche and the Buddha have the same view of the self.[50]

As I have suggested above, I agree that Nietzsche and the Buddha offer the same *description* of the self, but on my reading they offer radically different advice about the *attitude* we should take toward our experience of being selves. Indeed, Nietzsche himself talked about Buddhism in a number of places and believed that his own philosophy was diametrically opposed to that of the Buddha.[51] I believe that Bret Davis's reading of the conflict between the two thinkers is exactly right: "In short, while for Nietzsche there is no ego as a given, there is the task of constructing an ego, of organizing the plurality of disparate impulses by submitting them to the rule of a commanding will to power. Buddhism, on the other hand, speaks directly against the willful construction of an ego, and indeed sees the task to be that of uprooting the ruling will behind this construction."[52] The Buddha counsels precisely what Parkes above mistakenly attributed to Nietzsche: that the persistent self could eventually be abandoned.

When the two theories are compared, it becomes clear that the Buddha is right, for two reasons. First, his implicit critique of Nietzsche's position as being inevitably caught up in existential resentment seems correct *even from Nietzsche's perspective*. The experience of being a persistent self—the illusion that we are unified, diachronically continuous selves—is a voluntary lie, one that (with effort) we could come to see as false and dispensable. Nietzsche himself admits as much when he identifies the persistent self as an accomplishment that should be maintained. Both points—that it is possible to fail to develop a persistent self and that it is possible to lose it—suggest that human beings are capable of living without the illusion of being persistent selves. Thus when Nietzsche counsels us to nonetheless persist in the illusion, it appears that he is telling us to pretend that we are different than we (could) know ourselves to be. Pretending that the world is different than it really is, because we cannot accept the reality,[53] is the root of *ressentiment*.

The second reason that the Buddha's advice about how to relate to our bundle-selves is better than Nietzsche's advice is that Nietzsche is wrong to believe that letting go of the belief that one is a persistent self will make it impossible to pursue normative ideals. Indeed, the opposite is more likely to be true. Nietzsche's concern seems to be that if one were to give up the illusion of being a persistent self, one would also thereby give up the ability to commit oneself to long-term intentions and goals. In this way, his concern anticipates the criticism made of Nietzsche's own theory by Fennell, Booth, Janaway, and Staten: that a being made up only of conflicting drives is not capable of agency and thus not capable of pursuing normative ideals. I argued above that this is a mistaken criticism of Nietzsche's view, because his theory of the persistent self explains how agency can emerge from the conflicts of the under-souls. For roughly the same reasons, I believe that it is also a mistaken criticism of the Buddhist advice about how to relate to our bundle-selves. Plainly, it is accurate that a being that is human but has never attempted to create any kind of hierarchy among its various under-souls would be incapable of the kind of self-conscious agency that we associate with human subjectivity. But, aside from feral children and similar, highly unusual cases, that is never the case that confronts us. Rather, we are concerned with cases in which some such hierarchy among the under-souls has already been created through socialization and cognitive development. The question that concerns us is what the individual should now do with regard to the existing hierarchy, especially if and when the individual realizes that the hierarchy is supported by the illusion of being a unified and diachronically persistent self. Here I believe that Parkes has it exactly right: one could achieve a degree of integration of the under-souls such that one could dispense with the illusion of being a persistent self and nonetheless retain the hierarchy among the drives and the capacity for agency and choice. The post-self individual would be able to make choices and even pursue normative ideals, to the extent that their existing hierarchy of under-souls embodies or implies those ideals. What they would be unlikely to do is to conceive of themselves as under an obligation to obey normative ideals that do not resonate with their personality structure. But, of course, that's precisely the advice that Nietzsche gives to those who chafe under the slave morality because it restricts their nobility of spirit and is the animating spirit behind the metaphor of the three metamorphoses of the spirit in *Zarathustra*.[54]

The Politics of No-Self

The Buddha's and Nietzsche's different views of the self lead them to different conclusions about the role of the self and one's self-view in politics. The questions of what exactly the Buddha and Nietzsche thought about politics are the subjects of large literatures. Given the necessity of discussing their views about the self in depth above, my discussion here of the relevance of their theories of the self to politics is necessarily brief.

In the discussion of the Buddha's theory of no-self above, I mentioned that developing the right understanding of the self (as well as suffering and impermanence) is a crucial step toward enlightenment. The Buddha explicitly taught that having false beliefs about the self and its interests causes personal suffering and social conflict: "[I]t is the bonds of envy and niggardliness that bind beings so that, although they wish to live without hate, hostility, or enmity, and to live in peace, yet they live in hate, harming one another, hostile, and as enemies.... Envy and niggardliness ... arise from liking and disliking.... [which themselves arise] from thinking.... Thinking ... arises from elaborated perceptions and notions."[55] The scholar and translator Bikkhu Bodhi explains "elaborated perceptions and notions" thus: "The term seems to refer to perceptions and ideas that have become 'infected' by subjective biases, 'elaborated' by the tendencies to craving, conceit, and distorted views."[56] In other words, our self-driven desire for pleasure and happiness (the desire that has been infected by subjective biases) leads us to thinking (about how to fulfill that desire), which leads us to liking and disliking (of experiences and people that either help or hinder our pursuit of our desires), which lead us to envy and greed, which lead us ultimately to hate, harming one another, and hostility. In another teaching, repeated in many places in the early texts, the Buddha shows how adopting the right view toward the three characteristics of existence can interrupt this process: "when the perception of impermanence is developed and cultivated, it eliminates all sensual lust, it eliminates all lust for existence, it eliminates all ignorance, it uproots all conceit 'I am.' "[57]

Following this logic, human beings individually are at their best when they hold and follow the correct views regarding the three characteristics of existence, including the nonexistence of self, and the best possible human society would be one made up of such people. When we look at the one *sutta* in which the Buddha discussed the best possible human society (which may be partially fanciful), we find this inference confirmed. As explained in chapter 1, the *Cakkavatti-Sīhanāda Sutta* concerns a series of *cakkavattis*, or spiritually enlightened kings.[58] *Cakkavattis* can only emerge in a society that is already morally and socially advanced; in particular, the *sutta* makes clear that in such a society there is no poverty, theft, or violence. This suggests that the people have overcome "envy and niggardliness" through coming to have correct views about the three characteristics.

The *sutta* tells of eight successive generations of *cakkavattis*, and then of a ninth generation in which the king prefers to follow his own ideas rather than the tradition of his predecessors and the dhamma. This king fails to give to the needy, which leads to envy and theft, which leads to punishment, which in turn leads to violence, and so on, until the society is destroyed and the people reduced to living in the wilderness and killing each other like beasts. At that low point a handful of the people commit themselves to moral self-reform and manage to rebuild their society. They and their descendants work for tens of thousands of years, until once again the society contains no self-driven crime or poverty and is morally good enough to produce a *cakkavatti*, who in turn is morally good enough to adopt the proper policies. (Since the Buddhist conception of time is both cyclical and antiteleological, the implication is that eventually the society will decline again, only to be rebuilt yet again, and so on.) The highest possible stage of social development is reached when the people once again create a society largely free of envy, hatred, stinginess, and violence. Thus, just as holding onto a false view of self causes both personal suffering and social conflict, abandoning all such views leads both to personal enlightenment and to the best possible social and political system.

As I suggested above, Nietzsche sees his theory of the self as the mean between *ressentiment* (a self-view rooted in being rather than becoming) and nihilism (the no-self view). Although Nietzsche never spells out what a society based in nihilism would look like, it seems that his discussion of the Higher Men in *Zarathustra* gives us some hints.[59] In brief, the higher men have the intelligence, honesty, and courage to recognize that their previous beliefs are false and pointless but lack the imagination and faith to create new, contingent beliefs for themselves. They continue many of the outward rituals of their former faiths, for lack of any alternative, but no longer believe in or enjoy them. Lacking a guiding principle, they lack the will to live fully. I believe that we can extrapolate that a society of such people might be stable, but it would also be stagnant, drab, and lifeless. Nietzsche views such a future with horror.

In contrast, and at the other extreme, a society based in *ressentiment* would have guiding principles, but those principles would be hostile to human life. The basic motivation is to revenge oneself against a life that is too strong for one, too painful, too unfair. The characteristic move is to believe in both a metaphysical self and a transcendental source of value that will ultimately either reward or punish the self. Nietzsche suggests in a number of places that antisocial violence, theft, deceit, and so on are all generated by *ressentiment*. For example, we see this point expressed clearly in the *Genealogy*:

> Historically speaking, justice on earth represents . . . the battle, then, *against* reactive sentiment, the war waged against the same on the part of active and aggressive forces, which have partly expended their strength in trying to put a stop to the spread of reactive pathos, to keep it in check and within bounds, and to force some kind of compromise with it. Everywhere that justice is practiced and maintained, the stronger power can be seen looking for means of putting

an end to the senseless ravages of *ressentiment* amongst those inferior to it.[60]

The mean between these extremes is occupied by people strong enough to withstand life without resentment or resorting to false justifications. Nietzsche describes such people thus:

> [They are] strongly held in check by custom, respect, habit, gratitude and even more through spying on one another and through peer-group jealousy, [and], on the other hand behave towards one another by showing . . . resourcefulness in consideration, self-control, delicacy, loyalty, pride and friendship.[61]

By implication, a society made up (only) of such people would be a democratic society (an "aristocracy of equals"), since presumably no one would be willing to be told what to do, and a peaceful society, since those who are strong and capable both understand the value of social peace and are able to achieve it through self-control. (I intentionally leave aside the question of what kind of politics Nietzsche envisions in a society that contains both the strong and the weak—that fascinating and difficult issue of interpretation is beside the point for my current purposes. Rather, here I'm interested in the question of what a utopia consisting of those with Nietzsche's preferred self-view would look like.) As I argued above, the people who occupy this mean are precisely those who have overcome their earlier beliefs and have created new, contingent beliefs for themselves as a path to yet further overcoming. In the language of self-views, they are people who have adopted Nietzsche's view of the persistent self.

Thus, Nietzsche and the Buddha agree that people who continue to believe in what I have called the metaphysical self are not only mistaken but are also adopting a view that is likely to lead them to engage in antisocial behavior. Where they disagree is over how far one might go in effacing one's sense of self. The Buddha argues for letting go of it altogether, while Nietzsche argues that it should be relativized but not abandoned. The Buddha sees no-self as the basis of the best possible social order, while Nietzsche fears that that position goes too far and leads to nihilism. I have argued that the Buddha has the better argument when it comes to the likely effect on the individual of abandoning one's self-view, and I believe that the points I raised there are also relevant to the question of who has the better prediction of how changing our self-view will affect politics. On the one hand, it seems unlikely that abandoning one's self-view would lead one to be unable to make commitments or pursue ideals, since one's basic personality structure and values would already be in place. Thus it seems unlikely that the no-self view would lead to the kind of aimless nihilism that Nietzsche fears. On the other hand, pretending that one is a persistent self when one knows that one really is not threatens to preserve a destructive kernel of *ressentiment* in one's worldview. It is precisely when one cannot fully accept the truth of how life is that one falls back on resentment against it, a petulant complaint to the universe that life isn't as one would have it. By holding on to the persistent self, Nietzsche threatens to undermine the achievements he envisions arising from effacing one's belief in a metaphysical self, since there will always be one fact about existence that one can not, will not accept. That festering seed of resentment threatens to reintroduce precisely the antisocial harms that Nietzsche thought he had overcome. For both of these reasons, when it comes to politics and self-view, the Buddha was right and Nietzsche was wrong.

5

Theories of Limited Citizenship, East and West

The man who takes no part in public affairs is not unbusied . . . but useless.

Pericles, *Funeral Oration*

However, the government does not concern me much, and I shall bestow the fewest possible thoughts on it. It is not many moments that I live under a government, even in this world.

Thoreau, *Resistance to Civil Government*, 18

THE TEXTS OF BUDDHISM ARTICULATE an unusual theory of politics. On the one hand, as we saw in part I, the texts clearly express a normative political theory. They implicitly endorse enlightened monarchy as the best possible system of lay government, explicitly offer advice to kings about how to rule well and how to become (relatively) enlightened, and even offer advice about how to preserve the semirepublican system of tribal government that was (despite the advice) rapidly disappearing during the lifetime of the Buddha. They criticize contemporary kings for bad behavior, reveal that good kings have been rewarded in their next incarnations, propose a justificatory origin story for government, and offer a vision of political utopia.

But at the same time, the texts (especially the early texts) consistently deprecate the value of politics and government. The Buddha famously turned his back on his family's expectation that he would succeed his father as ruler of their tribe and refused an invitation from Māra (the tempter of Buddhist mythology) to become ruler of the known world.[1] The Buddha's most advanced lay disciple, Citta, refused a similar offer

87

from various well-intentioned gods.[2] When the Buddha discusses the best possible political system, which he envisioned arising tens of thousands of years in the future, he explicitly subordinates the king to his spiritual teacher, the future Buddha Metteyya. Even the best kings retire by abdicating the throne and becoming homeless monks, hoping to achieve enlightenment before death. The various rules governing the community of monks and nuns forbid the religious community (*sangha*) from involvement in government, including merely discussing politics. Overall, the Buddhist teachings suggest that monastics should have no involvement in politics, and lay people very little.

As we saw in chapter 1, this complex attitude toward politics has led some Western commentators, most famously Max Weber,[3] to argue that Buddhism is fundamentally antipolitical—that it counsels complete disinterest and noninvolvement in politics and government. Previously I argued that this interpretation goes too far; in particular, it seems to ignore the normative theory of government that the early texts articulate. If the Buddha really were counseling complete noninvolvement, we would not expect to find any theory of government in his teachings at all. That we do find such a theory suggests that his attitude toward politics is more complex than the crude antipolitical reading recognizes.

Rather than being merely a version of antipolitics, early Buddhism represents what I call a theory of limited citizenship. Thus the texts do articulate a normative theory of politics, while at the same time arguing that politics is ultimately not very important when compared with other aspects of human life and that right-thinking people should give politics and government very little of their time and attention.

On its face, that seems like an extremely odd attitude toward politics, one that may not turn out to be coherent or persuasive on further scrutiny. But, I argue in this chapter, the theory is both more familiar and more important than we might initially think. First, there is a tradition of theories of limited citizenship in Western political thought, in which we also find an acknowledgement that politics and government are sufficiently important that we should bother to come up with a normative theory about them, going hand-in-hand with a judgment that nonetheless politics and government are not terribly important compared with other concerns. We find this combination, I argue, (at least) in the work of Epicurus, Thoreau, and some versions of Christianity, especially that developed by the theologian John Howard Yoder.

Second, paying attention to the tension embodied in theories of limited citizenship helps us see something that is otherwise obscured in most Western political theory: when we assess the role of politics/government we are actually making two different judgments. One is about the *value* of politics/government: What are its costs and benefits, and how can we maximize the latter while minimizing the former? But the second judgment is about the relative *importance* of politics/government. Political thinkers are (understandably) prone to assuming that politics/government, whether on balance good or bad for humanity, is terribly *important*. The earliest and most obvious example is Plato, for whom the fate of one's soul is intimately tied to the success or failure of the political regime in which one lives. Almost nothing could be more important than getting politics/government right, even if it's unlikely that we will actually achieve that. At the opposite extreme we find the anarchists, for whom opposition to government is the defining issue. Government may be terribly bad according to the anarchists, but it is certainly very important. In contrast when Thoreau says "As for adopting the ways the State has provided ... I know not of such ways. They take too much time, and a man's life will be gone. I have other affairs to attend to," he reminds us that human beings rightfully have other claims on their time and attention, other goals that may trump the goals of politics/government.[4] Well-constructed political theory not only has to make an argument about the value of politics, it also has to make an argument about the relative importance of politics. Reading the texts of both the Buddhist and the Western limited citizenship traditions helps remind us of that and uncovers some preliminary guidelines for making those judgments.

Situating Theories of Limited Citizenship

Before we look at the Buddhist and Western theories of limited citizenship in depth, it will help to have some context and settled terminology. First, for the purposes of this discussion, I understand government to be the processes and institutions either authorized to make or effectively capable of making binding decisions for a geographically bounded population, including the power to enforce those decisions coercively. Politics, more broadly, is the set of practices and institutions that are concerned with the operation, staffing, maintenance, and possible modification of government, including the extreme of wanting to abolish government altogether or at least radically change it. Theories of limited citizenship are concerned (to varying degrees) with all of those issues, and, for the sake of simplicity, I refer to them collectively as politics.

Second, I argue that theories of limited citizenship make four distinct claims: (1) Politics is inevitable and often beneficial. (2) Politics is sufficiently morally and/or practically important that thoughtful individuals need normative theories to guide their political decisions, including the threshold decision of how much to engage in politics at all. (3) Nonetheless, politics is relatively unimportant when compared with other human concerns, and thoughtful individuals will give very little of their time and attention to politics. Many such theories identify one particular concern that dramatically outweighs the importance of politics, for example obedience to God. (4) Politics has relatively little power to either help individuals achieve the truly important things in life or to hinder them from achieving those things. Thus the claim is not merely that politics is an unpromising strategy for getting desirable things but that it is largely irrelevant. However, under unusual and temporary circumstances it may be necessary or desirable to become actively engaged with politics.

Given limitations of space, I assume that it's obvious how different such theories are from the mainstream of the Western political theory tradition, in which politics is typically seen as of great if not supreme importance. Despite this general consensus in Western political theory on the importance of politics, there are a number of traditions that we might think of as distant relatives of the limited citizenship theories. The oldest such tradition is the debate among the ancient Greeks between the active and contemplative lives.[5] Roskam and Brown separately examine this tradition with the goal of asking whether it develops the later (Epicurean) idea of principled withdrawal from political life, and they conclude that it largely does not (see below for more on their arguments).[6] Rather, they conclude that the arguments for the contemplative life tend to be focused on particular individuals (those with a philosophical nature) or circumstances (when government is being run badly) and not on a rejection of public life by most people under most circumstances.

Another such tradition emphasizes conscientious citizenship and begins with Socrates.[7] This tradition shares with limited citizenship theories the idea that the individual may need to disobey, resist, or even secede from politics under some circumstances, such as Socrates's quiet refusal to arrest Leon of Salamis to bring him to an unjust execution.[8] Ultimately, however, such theories are the inverse of limited citizenship: they emphasize active participation in politics until an emergency forces one out, whereas the limited citizenship theories emphasize staying away from politics until an emergency forces one in. (See below for more on Socrates as an individual.)

Although for different reasons, Stoicism comes to a similar conclusion. For the Stoics, the goal of life is tranquility, but in general they argue that politics will help one achieve tranquility (e.g., by sustaining a government capable of preventing crime and defending against invasion). Thus the Stoics conclude that the better strategy is to be involved with politics unless circumstances make abstention temporarily preferable.[9]

Another distant relative is the civil society tradition that begins with (depending on whom you ask) Hegel, Alexis de Tocqueville, Adam Ferguson, or Adam Smith.[10] By emphasizing the importance of voluntary association outside the spheres of family and state, the civil society tradition shares with the limited citizenship tradition a desire to show that politics is always in tension with other valid human concerns and institutions and that its value can be only relative, never absolute. But, by arguing that politics nonetheless always plays some important, irreplaceable role in a good human life, even though other things play similar roles, the civil society tradition ultimately embraces politics rather than relegating it to near irrelevance.

Thus, despite some areas of overlap, these traditions—contemplative life, conscientious citizenship, Stoicism, and civil society—do not ultimately come to the same conclusions as the limited citizenship tradition, which remains an outlier.

The Buddhist Theory of Politics

Chapter 1 summarizes and interprets the main early Buddhist texts relevant to politics. However, in widely scattered places in the rest of the 12,000-page canon of early texts we find additional passages that clarify the Buddha's view about the place of politics in human life. The first point along these lines is simply that the best possible human goal is achieving enlightenment; indeed, the Buddha explicitly contrasts enlightenment to possessing political power: "Better than power over all the earth, better than going to heaven and better than dominion over the worlds is the joy of the man who enters the river of life that leads to NIRVANA."[11]

A second general point is that after achieving enlightenment, the Buddha initially hesitated to teach what he had learned to others for fear that they would be unreceptive. It took the intervention of one of the gods to convince him that there were some people who would understand the dhamma (teaching) and that such people would be lost without the Buddha's help.[12] This story, repeated in many places in the early texts, shows that the Buddha's motivation in teaching was rooted in compassion—he was trying to help people who were seeking relief from the suffering of life. The political significance of this fact becomes clear when we examine the story, mentioned above, of Māra, the tempter of Buddhist mythology, trying to trick the Buddha into giving up his devotion to the spiritual path: "Then Māra the Evil One, having known with his own mind the reflection in the Blessed One's mind, approached the Blessed One and said to him: 'Venerable sir, let the Blessed One exercise rulership righteously.... [Buddha:] 'How could a person incline to sensual pleasures / Who has seen the source whence suffering springs? / Having known acquisition as a tie in the world, / A person should train for its removal.' "[13] The key point in this passage is that Māra's argument is implicitly that through being a righteous ruler, the Buddha could relieve the suffering of people who currently live under inferior rulers. The Buddha rejects this line of reasoning, explicitly on the grounds that it would distract him from his proper work and implicitly on the grounds that his spiritual teaching will be more helpful for reducing suffering than being a righteous ruler would be.

We see the same rejection of rulership as a distraction from Citta, the Buddha's most advanced lay disciple (mentioned in passing above), who on his deathbed reported the following to his family: "[P]ark devatās [minor gods], grove devatās, tree devatās, and devatās dwelling in medicinal herbs and forest giants assembled and said to me: 'Make a wish, householder, thus: "May I become a wheel-turning monarch [*cakka-vatti*] in the future!"' And I said to them: 'That too is impermanent; that too is unstable; one must abandon that too and pass on.'"[14]

The Buddha spoke frequently with the rulers of the various kingdoms in which the *sangha* was established. Many of those rulers are depicted in the early texts as deeply wicked, such as Ajātasattu of Magadha, who killed his father Bimbisāra to obtain the throne, or Viḍūḍabha of Kosala, who usurped power from his father Pasenadi through treachery and then exterminated the Buddha's own Sakya clan to avenge a personal insult (more on that story below). Yet, unless he is specifically asked for his opinion or spiritual guidance, the Buddha does not try to educate, improve, or oppose these kings, even to stop them from committing great evils (with one important exception, discussed below).

When instructing the *sangha* about how to pursue enlightenment, the Buddha laid down a number of rules and edicts that seem intended to keep the monks and nuns out of politics as completely as possible. Thus monks are forbidden to watch armies fighting,[15] to stay with an army for more than two or three nights,[16] or to watch any of an army's exercises.[17] Further, the monks are forbidden to talk about politics: "Bhikkhus, do not engage in the various kinds of pointless talk, that is, talk about kings, thieves, and ministers of state; talk about armies, dangers, and war."[18]

Further, the Buddha forbade the *sangha* from ordaining anyone as a monk who was under an existing obligation to the state (or under a legal obligation to an individual). Thus he specifically forbade ordaining active-duty soldiers, notorious thieves not in custody, thieves who have escaped from jail, thieves who have been publicly condemned, anyone who has been scourged or branded as punishment, debtors, and slaves.[19] The implication seems to be that the *sangha* should avoid interfering with the business of the state, even to help an individual achieve enlightenment. For example, the prohibition against ordaining soldiers is illustrated by a story in which some soldiers recognize that killing is wrong and abandon their posts to immediately become monks, thereby irritating their generals and the king, who asks the Buddha to ensure that it doesn't happen again.

The upshot of all of these passages appears to be that a person who is already enlightened will have nothing to do with politics (unless specifically asked for their opinion) and that someone seriously seeking enlightenment will do the same. Enlightenment is a more important goal even than genuinely righteous rule, and one can help the suffering more by pursuing enlightenment than through politics.

And yet there are several passages in which the Buddha appears to temper this strictly antipolitical message, at least for the enlightened and laypeople (the *sangha* remains strictly apolitical, perhaps because of the obvious practical dangers that it would face if it were to be perceived as a political threat by the rulers whose toleration it could not do without). Thus, if we look more closely at the Buddha's advice to the Vajjians, we can see that he encourages them to do whatever is customary for citizens in their society. Hence, he advises (in part) that they: "hold regular and frequent assemblies," "meet in harmony, break up in harmony, and carry on their business in harmony," and "do not authorise what has not been authorised already, and do not abolish what has been authorised, but proceed according to what has been authorised by their ancient tradition."[20] Since the Vajjians are in the habit of holding assemblies, they should continue to do so, and the individual citizens should participate in them in whatever way tradition dictates. We can infer a similar kind of advice for the subjects of kings, based on the restrictions discussed above about who may be ordained: do whatever the laws of the state require of you, and do not expect the *sangha* to exempt you from your obligations. (However, monks and nuns already ordained were exempt from any subsequent such obligations other than obeying the ordinary laws of the state.) We can further infer from the *Aggañña-Sutta* that citizens have a practical duty to pay their taxes and obey the laws. In these ways the Buddha seems to be counseling lay people to do what is required or expected of them by the state when it comes to politics. But, implicitly, anything beyond that would be a distraction from the time and energy needed to attain enlightenment.

More dramatically, when the stakes were both high and personal, the Buddha did directly involve himself in politics. *Jātaka* No. 465 tells us the story of King Viḍūḍabha,[21] mentioned in passing above. King Pasenadi of Kosala asked the Sakya clan to send him a girl of good birth to be his chief queen. The Sakyas didn't want to offend the king but also didn't want to send a well-born girl because that would have violated their customs. The decided to send him Vāsabhakhattiyā, a girl whose father was of noble birth and whose mother was a slave. They presented Vāsabhakhattiyā as being wholly of noble birth. Pasenadi married Vāsabhakhattiyā and made her his chief queen. She soon gave birth to Viḍūḍabha, who was his father's heir. During his childhood, Viḍūḍabha discovered the deception and vowed revenge. When he eventually became king (through treachery), he immediately set out to attack the Sakyas. The Buddha, knowing what was happening, intervened three times (peacefully) to protect his clan. But the fourth time that Viḍūḍabha set out for the attack, the Buddha did not intervene because he saw that the Sakyas could not avoid the karmic consequences of their deceit, and Viḍūḍabha massacred the Sakyas.

All of these texts together reveal a theory of limited citizenship, rather than either a theory of active citizenship or a theory opposed to politics altogether. First, the Buddha clearly argues, especially in the *Aggañña-Sutta*, that politics is both inevitable and often beneficial. There does not seem to be any practical alternative for securing basic social peace. Thus, secondly, given the practical necessity of politics, the Buddha gives us a normative theory of politics, especially in the *Aggañña-Sutta* and *Cakkavatti-Sīhanāda Sutta*. Third, and in contrast to the first two points, the Buddha clearly implies that active engagement with politics is a distraction from the more important goal of achieving enlightenment. We see that message especially in the stories of the Buddha and Citta's rejections of invitations to become righteous rulers and in the Buddha's rules prohibiting the *sangha* from even discussing politics. And yet, fourth, the Buddha does seem to advise laypeople to do whatever the state requires of them (pay the taxes, obey the laws, attend the assemblies), and he also seems to acknowledge that there may be emergencies of sufficient gravity (such as Viḍūḍabha's threat to the Sakyas) that even the enlightened will directly get involved in politics. All that adds up to a theory of limited citizenship: do what you have to do; in emergencies do more than that; but don't forget that politics are largely a distraction from the important things in life.

The Western Limited Citizenship Tradition

Why Not Socrates?

It's difficult to decide whether the Western limited citizenship tradition begins with Socrates or Epicurus, though in the end I think Epicurus is the better choice.[22] First, it's not clear whether Socrates thought that government was inevitable or beneficial, though his comments in the *Crito* about the benefits he received from the laws of Athens suggest that he would have answered yes to both questions.[23] Second, Socrates left us very little in the way of a normative theory of politics (if we treat the Socrates of the *Republic* as a mouthpiece for Plato rather than as a faithful representation of the man himself). On the other hand, and third, it's clear from his behavior that Socrates did think that contemplation and the search for truth were more important than engaging in the business of the public (at least for himself). And fourth he clearly said in the *Apology* that his *daimon* had always advised him to stay out of politics, and that he had done his duty (e.g., serving in the military[24]), but nothing above and beyond that.[25]

The problem for us—as for Socrates's philosophical heirs in the ancient world—is deciding in what direction these vague hints point. Is he suggesting a total withdrawal from conventional life, as the Cynics thought? Or rather a suspension of belief in anything not demonstrable to the senses, as the Pyrrhonian Skeptics believed? Or is he instead suggesting that we should limit our engagement in politics only until we have discovered the principles that should guide them, as Plato concluded? Perhaps he is suggesting that the goal is personal knowledge and virtue, and the question of engagement in politics is always a matter of tactical appropriateness, as the Stoics believed. Finally, of course, perhaps he is advocating a theory of limited citizenship. Because we don't know how to put together the suggestive pieces of Socrates's attitude toward the place of politics in the good life, we can't unambiguously place him either in or out of the limited citizenship tradition.

Epicurus

Thus the earliest unambiguous theorist of limited citizenship in the Western tradition appears to be Epicurus, though Roskam argues that the fragments we have from Democritus hint at some similar ideas, and Brown argues that some fragments from Euripides can be interpreted as advocating something like limited citizenship.[26] Although some scholars see Epicurus as being wholly apolitical,[27] and others read him as being actively interested in politics,[28] the majority of commentators agree that his view of politics was that the wise person would avoid it except in response to an emergency.[29] For Epicurus the goal was *ataraxia*, peace of mind, which was to be achieved through security—that is, being confident about one's future.[30] Security is best achieved through withdrawal from public life and the cultivation of a group of intimate, like-minded friends. Epicurus's main political advice was to "live unnoticed."

Active involvement in politics threatened *ataraxia* in several ways.[31] First, it threatened to put one into the public eye and thus attract the attention of others who might in some way bother one. Second, it threatened to confuse one about how security could best be achieved, promoting the false idea that security comes from external institutions and circumstances rather than from one's own philosophical insight and state of mind. Third, it threatened to waste one's time and energy, which would be better spent on reflection and cultivating friendship.

Nonetheless, Epicurus and later followers explicitly acknowledged the inevitability and value of politics.[32] Thus, Aalders argues: "[W]ithout … positive law, without the existing order, the secure life of the Epicurean philosopher would be impossible. According to the Epicurean Colotes law and political rule guarantee security and freedom from turmoil.... In behalf of the Epicurean ideal of happiness, the existing order is accepted as a necessary base."[33]

Epicurus also offers a theory of justice, thus providing a normative theory to guide politics, at least partially. For Epicurus, the social contract emerges because people can rationally perceive the mutual benefits of social cooperation, and justice is whatever serves the goal of mutual benefit.[34] While Epicurus is highly critical of metaphysical theories of justice, which see justice as having some intrinsic essence, he agrees that justice is more than merely whatever laws the people adopt. For a law to be just, it must be to the mutual benefit of the community.[35]

Brown and Schofield[36] separately point out that Epicurus in fact goes further than this, acknowledging that active involvement in politics may sometimes be necessary. Even during ordinary times, one should obey the laws and fulfill any duties imposed by the state since failing to do so would almost certainly be more troublesome than compliance.[37] In an emergency, the wise may need to become actively involved in politics (as some Epicureans did during the Roman civil war of the first century BCE) to help maintain law and order.[38] The goal is always *ataraxia* through security; engagement or avoidance of politics is merely a strategy for achieving that higher goal.

Thus we find in Epicurus the four defining features of theories of limited citizenship. First, he acknowledges that politics is inevitable and often beneficial. Second, he offers a normative theory of politics, which enables us to decide whether particular laws or institutions are just. Third, he argues that, nonetheless, politics is relatively unimportant to the good life and has little power to either help or harm us. Fourth and finally, he argues that under ordinary circumstances one should do whatever the state requires of citizens but nothing more and that under some limited and unusual circumstances it may be necessary to become actively involved with politics. Although we see bits and pieces of this theory in later thinkers (and the whole thing in later Epicureans), we don't see any non-Epicurean advocates of the whole limited citizenship theory until the nineteenth century.

Thoreau (and Possibly Emerson)

Trying to understand Thoreau's attitude toward politics is difficult.[39] On the one hand, in many places he is openly dismissive of politics. To take just one of many such passages, he writes: "What is called politics is comparatively something so superficial and inhuman, that, practically, I have never fairly recognized that it concerns me at all."[40] But, on the other hand, Thoreau wrote several works that are explicitly political ("Resistance to Civil Government," "Slavery in Massachusetts," "A Plea for Captain John Brown," "Martyrdom of John Brown," and "The Last Days of John Brown"); several that touch on important issues of the day though without explicitly discussing politics ("Paradise (to be) Regained," "The Service," "The Herald of Freedom," and "Wendell Phillips"); and several more whose themes and discussions of history are at least arguably political (*Walden* and *A Week on the Concord and Merrimack Rivers*).

In addition to the contents of those texts, we should also consider their contexts. "Resistance to Civil Government" not only records Thoreau's famous refusal to pay his poll tax on the grounds that it would go to support both slavery and the Mexican-American War, it was a text that Thoreau also delivered as a speech and published during his lifetime. "Slavery in Massachusetts" was focused on the injustice and immorality of Massachusetts's enforcement of the Fugitive Slave Act and was also delivered as a public speech. The three John Brown essays were yet again public speeches, and they defended Brown in the period immediately following the Harpers Ferry raid, when the vast majority of abolitionists were denouncing him. In all of these cases, it's hard to avoid the conclusion that Thoreau hoped, at least in part, for these essays and speeches to affect the policies of the state and federal governments and the actions of his fellow citizens. Even *Walden*, typically read as a kind of hermit's *bildungsroman*, is explicitly addressed to Thoreau's neighbors in Concord and is frequently phrased as advice about how they might better live their lives.

One of the great challenges of Thoreau interpretation has been figuring out how to reconcile these two apparently opposed strains of his thought: one that appears to reject politics tout court, and another that appears to engage in politics directly. The critical literature divides into three basic schools of thought on this issue.[41] The first sees Thoreau as ultimately either apolitical or antipolitical and treats his ostensibly political writings as aspects of his (possibly inconsistent) self-cultivation rather than as an attempt to intervene in politics per se. At the opposite end of the spectrum are critics who see Thoreau's work as being deeply and persistently political, and who see his antipolitical comments as largely pertaining to specific *modes* of being political that Thoreau rejected. Between these two schools of thought there is a third, which sees Thoreau as being primarily concerned with nonpolitical pursuits but as being pulled into politics temporarily (if repeatedly) by various crises that he could not ignore. Ultimately, I will argue that this third reading strikes the right balance between his conflicting motivations, and that it reveals him to be a theorist of limited citizenship.

The first reading of Thoreau, that he was ultimately anti- or nonpolitical, is supported by several different lines of reasoning. Arendt, Wagner, and Simon[42] each argues that Thoreau was in effect a moral solipsist and placed the purity of his own conscience above any duty to help society arrive at a practical compromise between principle and pragmatism. A second version of the reading of Thoreau as antipolitical sees Thoreau as at heart an anarchist. Buranelli, Eulau, and Diggins each see this as a failing in Thoreau's work, while Ketcham, Drinnon, and Nichols each see it as admirable (if not necessarily practical).[43] The third and final reading within this school argues that some aspect of Thoreau's beliefs or personality prevented him from acting effectively. This line of interpretation begins with Emerson's eulogy for Thoreau, in which Emerson famously said: "[I]nstead of engineering for all America, he was the captain of a huckleberry party. Pounding beans is good to the end of pounding empires one of these days; but if, at the end of years, it is still only beans!"[44] Nelson and Fergenson (separately) see Thoreau as unable to choose between seclusion and social engagement.[45] Finally Abbott ascribes Thoreau's inability to fully engage in politics to a fragile and fragmentary personality structure (one that perhaps many moderns share).[46]

At the opposite end of the critical spectrum, we find a number of thoughtful readings that see Thoreau as being deeply, persistently political, in some cases even when his writing was on its surface far removed from politics. Thus, for example, Shulman, Lauter, and McWilliams each read Thoreau as a prophet, actively warning of and bearing witness to political evil. Similarly, Cavell, Marshall, Turner, Taylor, and Walker each see Thoreau as engaged in a lifelong project of educating his fellow citizens for political life.[47] Several readers—Villa, Gougeon, and Hyde[48]—see Thoreau as starting out apolitical but driven by the collision of his principles with circumstances into becoming actively and persistently political. Finally, there are readings that see Thoreau as primarily focused on cultivating a personality capable of democratic citizenship

(Mariotti), as a defender of the waning tradition of American republicanism (Neufeldt), and as a communitarian focused on how individual identity is both rooted in and made possible by society (Worley).[49]

Many of the readings in these first two schools of Thoreau interpretation are reasonable and even persuasive. I make no claim to offer any new critical angle on Thoreau but am simply casting my lot with the third school of thought, which sees Thoreau as primarily focused on nonpolitical concerns, yet also as being occasionally and temporarily drawn into politics by various crises. This interpretation seems to me to strike the right balance between Thoreau's competing commitments. A number of critics make this point more or less in passing, as part of a broader discussion of Thoreau and his work. Thus Jenco sees Thoreau as falling between the rejection of politics of the Christian anarchists on the one hand and the embrace of them by the more socially active transcendentalists on the other.[50] Marx reads the location of Thoreau's Walden cabin—at the edge of Concord, and thus straddling the boundary between society and the wild—as representing a choice to engage with society selectively.[51] Hodder, Robinson, Cafaro, and Kritzberg agree that Thoreau did occasionally engage in politics actively but only temporarily, soon returning to his individual pursuits.[52]

Several critics focus particularly on this aspect of Thoreau's thought— his concern to limit the duties and demands of citizenship to leave room for other and more important pursuits. Ruth Lane thus emphasizes two points in her reading of Thoreau's politics: first, Thoreau's major concern was self-government, and, second, self-government requires both attention to one's own life and a very limited duty to engage with others, especially in response to an emergency or crisis (Thoreau cites helping the drowning).[53] Jonathan McKenzie interprets this combination of concerns as advice from Thoreau to mind one's own business.[54] McKenzie calls our attention to an odd passage in "Slavery in Massachusetts," where Thoreau says "I feel that, to some extent, the State has fatally interfered with my lawful business. It has not only interrupted me in my passage through Court street on errands of trade, but it has interrupted me and every man on his onward and upward path, on which he had trusted soon to leave Court street far behind."[55] This comment suggests that Thoreau hadn't been much interested in the problem of slavery until it obtruded itself into Thoreau's affairs; Thoreau's subsequent political activity (including delivering "Slavery in Massachusetts" as a speech) is a kind of self-defense. As McKenzie emphasizes, this reinforces the idea that Thoreau's involvement with politics was sporadic: "The assertion that the Fugitive Slave Law's primary crime is its interference with the daily life of a free individual strikes many readers as odd, but the remark captures the essence of Thoreau's temporary engagement with slavery and with politics."[56]

The most developed readings of Thoreau as a theorist of limited citizenship come from George Kateb, Nancy Rosenblum, and Jane Bennett. Kateb approvingly interprets Thoreau as being committed to developing and protecting democratic individuality. [57] On this view, there is a proper and necessary role for government: to look after what is expedient (that is, what is pragmatically necessary or convenient but morally neutral) and to stay out of the way of individuals pursuing what is morally obligatory. Government should neither seek to encourage virtue nor to restrain vice,[58] but should largely be confined to what citizens can agree on as mutually necessary and acceptable.[59] Citizenship requires little more than neighborliness, and Thoreau famously declared himself willing to accept such duties: "I have never declined paying the highway tax, because I am as desirous of being a good neighbor as I am of being a bad subject."[60] When politics demands more than this, one may ignore it. When politics demands or imposes what is immoral, one must resist.[61]

Jane Bennett comes to much the same conclusion, though she is more ambivalent about whether Thoreau's limited citizenship is admirable. She reads Thoreau as being afraid of good citizenship commonly understood and the compromises and conformity it requires: "In the arts of the self he develops, the first step is to identify the They as an object of suspicion; the second is to mark the specific occasions during which one's susceptibility to it is greatest. For Thoreau himself these occasions are political ones, times when he is called upon to be a good citizen."[62] The better activity is self-fashioning: "To be more than occasionally and lightly engaged by politics—its debates and struggles, even its promise of reform and social justice—is for Thoreau to be distracted from the more difficult, more worthy, and logically prior task of becoming a deliberate self."[63] Yet Thoreau does allow himself to be drawn into politics: "Occasionally in his writing Thoreau acknowledges the necessity of such participation in collective life: business and politics are not expendable activities, even for a sojourning individual."[64]

Nancy Rosenblum is even more ambivalent, both about the value of Thoreau's vision of politics and about how best to describe it. In some places in her writing about Thoreau, she seems to identify him as someone who is persistently, if idiosyncratically, engaged in politics.[65] In other places she seems to see Thoreau as squarely in the limited citizenship tradition. For example, she writes: "For Thoreau the question is always the same: how much must an individual have to do with democratic government at all? By posing the question and admitting that he sometimes almost does not recognize it at all, Thoreau indicates his ongoing relation to democracy, however tentative and intermittent, and even if government's contribution to well-being is only comparatively important."[66] Ultimately, it seems, Rosenblum sees Thoreau as torn between these impulses:

> He was not satisfied to incite disobedience to the fugitive slave law by serving as an example of what it means to consent in a democracy (he quietly stopped paying his poll tax before the law was passed, and did nothing to encourage his arrest). And he did not subscribe to a theory of justice or good government. On the other hand, he was not entirely content to cast himself as a unique victim of commercial civilization and to rebel or to seek self-protective cover in art or nature. Thoreau's militant conscience was an uneasy intermediate stance.[67]

Overall, Thoreau appears to be a good if not perfect fit for the limited citizenship tradition begun by Epicurus. As I've argued, it's clear Thoreau sees politics as inevitable and possibly beneficial (to take care of what is "expedient"), and he argues that politics is generally less important than other things, though what exactly those other concerns are Thoreau leaves vague. It's fair to say that Thoreau provides very little in terms of a normative theory of politics, though he does suggest in a number of places that neighborliness is the value that should guide social cooperation.[68] Finally, there is the question of whether people should fulfill the ordinary duties of citizenship. On the one hand, we know that Thoreau disparaged voting in "Resistance to Civil Government," but on the other hand, we know that he scrupulously paid his highway tax. This suggests that Thoreau is mostly a theorist of limited citizenship, though with some idiosyncrasies that seem appropriate to his character. (George Kateb has argued that Emerson's politics are identical in all essentials to Thoreau's.[69] If that is correct, then Emerson would also be a theorist of limited citizenship; I do not pursue that issue here.)

John Howard Yoder and *The Politics of Jesus*

The American Mennonite theologian John Howard Yoder (1927–1997) proposed an interpretation of Christianity that is based on seeing Christians as limited citizens. Yoder explicitly identified his interpretation as the mean between the completely antipolitical stance of Christian anarchism and the Constantinian/Augustinian ethic of responsibility that called on Christians to engage actively in political life.[70] Hence:

> Either one accepts, without serious qualification, the responsibility of politics, i.e. of governing, with whatever means that takes, or one chooses a withdrawn position of either personal-monastic-vocational or sectarian character, which is "apolitical." . . . If Jesus is confessed as Messiah this disjunction is illegitimate. To say that any position is "apolitical" is to deny the powerful (sometimes conservative, sometimes revolutionary) impact on society of the creation of an alternative social group, and to overrate both the power and the manageability of those particular social structures identified as "political."[71]

Commentators have also argued that Yoder's theory represents a mean between two positions within the Mennonite community during the twentieth century—the traditional "nonresistance" position, which advocated obedience to the state (within the bounds of Christian, pacifist conscience) but noninvolvement in its institutions and offices, and an emerging view that called on Mennonites to engage more fully with the broader society and state to promote their pacifist version of Christianity.[72]

It is beyond the scope of both this chapter and my competence to assess whether Yoder's interpretation of the gospels is correct, or whether he is faithful to the Mennonite tradition. Rather, I argue his vision of Christian involvement in politics, primarily as articulated in his influential 1972 book *The Politics of Jesus*, is an example of the Western limited citizenship tradition, and it represents a plausible interpretation of Christianity as calling for all believers to be only limited citizens.

Yoder's argument is straightforward, and much of it is familiar from the broader Christian tradition. Government is part of fallen humanity and exists to restrain evil by using evil against it so that God's eschatological plan for humanity can proceed. In particular, government restrains evil through the use of violence. Government will be necessary as long as people are sinful. Hence: "This order of the sword that has ruled humanity from earliest times is not God's form of justice or redemption; nevertheless it represents an expression of God's grace aimed at redemption, by keeping God's fallen creation in existence (however destructive sin itself is) with a view toward the God-intended redemption of the fallen creation." [73] Therefore, Christians have a duty to obey government in all requirements that do not violate their conscience. Government cannot be made good, since it cannot abandon the use of violence while people are still sinful. Thus: "The first thing to be clear about is that the New Testament contains no expectation of ... 'progress'; that is, there is no expectation in the New Testament that there would be a basic change, one to be evaluated positively, in the relationship between the church and the world." [74]

Jesus's life and teachings call us to build the church as a polity that works in a radically different way than government:

> If the lostness of man consists in his subjection to the rebellious powers of a fallen world, what then is the meaning of the work of Christ? Man's subordination to these Powers is what makes him human, for if they did not exist there would be no history nor society nor humanity. If then God is going to save man *in his humanity*, the Powers cannot simply be destroyed or set aside or ignored. Their sovereignty must be broken. This is what Jesus did, concretely and historically, by living among men a genuinely free and human existence. [75]

In particular Jesus calls us to abandon the use of violence in all circumstances, even to save our own lives or prevent other evils. More broadly, Jesus calls us to abandon the desire for mastery over other people and the course of history. [76] The church's social mission is to serve as an example of what a polity built on love and the rejection of violence looks like. It is not the church's job to reform government or to take responsibility for the functioning of government: "The church is not fundamentally a source of moral stimulus to encourage the develop-ment of a better society—though a faithful church should also have this effect—it is for the sake of the church's own work that society continues to function. The meaning of history—and therefore the significance of the state—lies in the creation and the work of the church."[77] Rather, it is the church's job to be an example of a better society and to tell the government (and anyone else) when it is doing wrong and how it could do right. The church will only be able to do this if the church is itself, as a polity, avoiding wrong and doing right: "The church must be a sample of the kind of humanity within which, for example, economic and racial differences are surmounted. Only then will she have anything to say to the society that surrounds her about how those differences must be dealt with."[78]

Christians may not take roles in government that involve them in the use of force. Fulfilling the ordinary duties of citizenship, such as voting, paying taxes, obeying general laws, and even holding some noncoercive offices does not contradict this duty, though serving in elected office probably would and serving in the military definitely would:

> The elective process, and in a general sense even the legislative process . . . may thus best be understood not as final and respon-sible participation in the making of government decisions about how the sword of the state is to be used, and still less as morally blame-worthy involvement in executing those decisions; but rather as one relatively effective way the subject population has of making its likes and dislikes known.[79]

Unlike with the other thinkers discussed in this essay, there isn't much debate about what Yoder said or meant; the debate is primarily over whether he was right.[80] For my purposes in this chapter, we can largely bypass that question (see below for a brief discussion), since right or wrong it's clear that Yoder is an advocate of limited citizenship. First, he argues that politics is necessary and even beneficial in its own sphere. Second, he argues that politics is important enough that we need a normative theory regarding it and provides one: politics is God's way of controlling evil through evil to allow the church the social peace necessary to demonstrate a different way of living. Third, he argues that, nonetheless, politics is relatively unimportant compared with other goals, specifically living as Jesus instructed us to live. Thus for most Christians most of the time, time and energy should go toward making the church the best possible witness of a polity based on love and not toward participating in or trying to reform secular politics, other than by fulfilling the ordinary duties of citizenship. And yet, fourth, when government does wrong, Christians should point out its errors, and part of the point of the existence of the church is to engage in an ongoing, public debate with government about how human beings should relate to one another. The worse the political situation, the more actively the church should engage the powers that be and show them the errors of their ways.

Conclusion: Is This an Adequate Theory of Citizenship?

Despite their relatively marginal place in the political theory tradition, theories of limited citizenship have been extensively criticized. Three criticisms are especially common and important: parasitism, irrelevance, and irresponsibility. The parasitism criticism charges that limited citizens want the benefits of social cooperation and government without doing the work or risking the moral compromises that those benefits entail. This criticism dates back to Plutarch's essay against the Epicurean Colotes: "among so many philosophers [the Epicureans] alone (one might say) enjoy the advantages of civilized life without paying their share."[81]

The basic response to this criticism is expressed by Schofield, in defense of Epicureanism: "There will always be plenty of people who want fame and power at whatever the cost, as Epicurus seems to have conceded. So unless there is a general collapse of public order or a threat to the body politic, there is as a matter of fact no need for the rational person, intent on his own security, to enter the political arena."[82] Essentially the same response is available to the Buddha, Thoreau, and Yoder. All of them acknowledge that emergencies may require even the wise to engage actively with politics, and all of them seem to believe that in ordinary times there will always be someone more than willing to shoulder the burden of politics for (misguided) reasons of their own.

The charge of irrelevance asserts that limited citizenship is a self-defeating strategy, since withdrawing from the public sphere reduces the chances of the right views prevailing. The basic response to this criticism is to argue that it rests on a mistaken understanding of causality. Thus the Buddha would reply that the suffering of the world arises primarily from individual errors rather than from collective or political errors, that no policy choices would be likely to improve that situation, and that both teaching and setting an example of individual spiritual change would be more likely to improve the world. Epicurus and Thoreau basically agree with the Buddha. Yoder's response is different, since his view rests on the eschatological belief that ultimately the wicked will be punished and the righteous will be rewarded, and thus the morally urgent question is obedience to God rather than attention to the problems of politics.

Third, the criticism of irresponsibility argues that by refusing to engage actively in politics, limited citizens are actually making things worse than they otherwise might be, since they are ceding the field to people with fewer (or worse) compunctions. Here the Buddha and Yoder have roughly the same reply, which is that the criticism rests on a mistaken normative evaluation. Once one is trapped in *saṃsāra* or sin without any desire to escape, one is already living as badly as possible. Yes, some versions of sin and *saṃsāra* may be more or less pleasant than others, but that is not the relevant issue. If our primary concern is helping people make moral/spiritual progress, the relative goodness or badness of the political situation is largely irrelevant. Epicurus and Thoreau might agree with that response, but they have another as well: they have no moral duty to help others avoid the ordinary problems of life (as opposed to an unusual emergency, like drowning), so long as they are not complicit in creating or aggravating those problems.

There are two other criticisms that are less obvious but also important: one about privilege, and one about *paideia*. The first argues that those who seek to be limited citizens are typically privileged individuals who are seeking to enjoy their position and avoid responsibility either for maintaining the system that benefited them or for changing the system from which their privilege was ill-gotten. Hence Slavoj Žižek says: "'Western Buddhism' . . . enables you to fully participate in the frantic pace of the capitalist game while sustaining the perception that you are not really in it; that you are well aware of how worthless this spectacle is; and that what really matters to you is the peace of the inner Self to which you know you can always with-draw."[83] This criticism is easier for some theorists to respond to than it is for others. The Buddha and Yoder can acknowledge that Žižek is probably right, but also argue that they are acting in the service of a higher moral obligation and that in the end the benefits that will come from their actions outweigh the harms that they might indirectly and unintentionally contribute to (both forbid intentional harms or obvious complicity with evil). Thoreau and Epicurus have a harder time defending themselves against Žižek's criticism, since they both avoid making claims about broader moral laws and are in essence asking to be left alone to pursue their personal preferences. I think their best strategy is to argue that this disagreement with Žižek amounts to a case of value pluralism. Žižek makes a valid and compelling argument, but both Epicurus and Thoreau believe that their preferred course of action represents a more compelling value choice: doing what one thinks is best with one's life is morally more important than solving the problems of the world into which one was born, and being happy if selfish is better than being unhappy but altruistic. The question is whether we can rank these competing value preferences, and it seems to me that Epicurus and Thoreau have a good argument that we cannot.[84] Thus Žižek's argument is not defeated so much as set aside as valid yet less important than other valid arguments.

The other less obvious criticism is that refusing to take an active role in politics might interfere with or even prevent the development of some essential human virtues in the abstaining individual. Beginning with Plato, there is a long tradition that believes that one cannot be fully human (or perhaps maximally excellent) unless one engages actively with politics. For example, the *Republic* argues that no individual in the polis can fulfill their potential unless everyone is playing the social role appropriate for them—even would-be philosopher-kings would be unable to achieve their highest capacity for wisdom and knowledge if they had to spend some of their time tending crops or defending the polis from outside aggression rather than engaging in contemplation. I want to suggest that this criticism is also an example of an irreconcilable conflict between value preferences. The pro-politics party argues that the virtues that can be cultivated only through politics are more important than the virtues that can be cultivated only by eschewing politics in favor of some other important pursuit like meditation, while the limited-citizenship party argues the opposite. Absent a noncontroversial rank ordering of the relevant moral values, there is no principled way to choose between the competing options, and neither choice can be shown to be universally morally preferable.

Further, it's important to recognize that every theory of citizenship acknowledges that human beings rightfully have other concerns: minimally, the need to eat, sleep, maintain bodily health, and to seriously consider the moral quality of one's actions; more typically: the need to earn a living in some way that is likely not to be political, the need to have intimate relationships and families, the need to have friends, the need to have leisure and variety in life, and so on. In fact, most theories of citizenship envision citizens spending a very small amount of their time and energy on politics. And of course in most societies, most of the time, the vast majority of citizens do nothing more than what the limited citizenship theorists ask to be allowed to do: obey the laws, pay the taxes, vote in the elections (or comparable minimal duty of engagement), and otherwise mind their own affairs. Really the question is not about what one does as a citizen, but about what one believes oneself obligated to do. Do citizens have a moral duty to engage in politics, to believe themselves personally responsible for the fate of the polity, to seriously consider holding office, to make politics one of their major concerns and political activity one of their major expressions of duty? This is where the limited citizenship thinkers draw the line and argue that some and perhaps all people have other obligations that trump their political obligations, other things that have a prior claim on their time, attention, and care.

Should everyone be a limited citizen? Obviously politics as we know it would not be possible under those circumstances. But it's worth asking what could lead to such an apparent crisis. If everyone were to become a Buddhist monk, or a morally earnest and self-sufficient essayist, presumably many of the problems that government currently exists to remedy would either not exist or be dramatically reduced in severity. Under those circumstances, society might be able to endure politics operating on a much smaller scale. On the other hand, if there were not enough people who were inclined to active participation in politics, and yet the familiar social problems persisted, then the wise would arguably follow their own advice and become more actively involved in politics to prevent social collapse (the case is clearer for the Buddha and Epicurus, less so for Thoreau and Yoder). Yet if it became clear that even the efforts of the wise could not save society, then probably the wise would once again withdraw to help themselves and/or others survive the inevitable catastrophe by focusing on the things that matter most in human life: enlightenment, *ataraxia*, self-knowledge, or living as Jesus lived whatever the circumstances.

Ultimately, the argument for limited citizenship comes down to an assertion about how to rank various values that cannot be put into practice simultaneously. It seems unlikely that there is any argument that could convince everyone who initially prefers a different rank ordering of values that limited citizenship is morally praiseworthy. That's the problem with moral pluralism—even when everyone involved agrees that all the various options instantiate genuine moral goods (I assume for the sake of argument that everyone agrees that the goals of the limited citizenship theorists are morally valuable), it may nonetheless be impossible to find a principled basis for preferring one ranking over others.[85] Given that problem, the question to ask is whether limited citizenship is morally defensible. Is it coherent? Does it aim at genuine, morally valuable goals? Is it able to respond to criticisms? Does it rest on premises that are obviously false or that are held in bad faith? On those criteria, limited citizenship is a defensible conception of how people should engage in politics. For those who have some sympathy with the rank ordering of values that limited citizenship rests on, or who prefer to leave individuals free to rank values as they see fit, limited citizenship will be appealing, even admirable. As Thoreau writes:

> I please myself with imagining a State at last which can afford to be just to all men, and to treat the individual with respect as a neighbor; which even would not think it inconsistent with its own repose if a few were to live aloof from it, not meddling with it, nor embraced by it, who fulfilled all the duties of neighbors and fellow men.[86]

6

Buddhism, Naturalistic Ethics, and Politics

EVEN A CASUAL READER OF Buddhist texts would quickly conclude that they contain some kind of ethical theory. There is copious advice about how best to live one's life, and there are extensive discussions of good and bad actions, merit and demerit, and so on. But determining exactly what the texts' ethical theory is requires more thought, and, predictably, modern scholars disagree sharply on these issues.

Because of the great complexity and variety of Buddhist ethical arguments over the past 2,500 years, this chapter looks only at the ethical theory of the early texts. As with chapter 1, the idea here is that it will be helpful to be clear about what the early texts say, since all Buddhists recognize the early texts as being authentic and authoritative. After that we can get down to arguing about how later texts did or did not replace, supplant, reinforce, or otherwise modify the early texts (given limits on time and space I leave that later discussion for another occasion).

Everyone agrees that the early Buddhist ethical theory is a version of ethical naturalism. Thus early Buddhism rejects the idea that ethical or moral truths arise from or depend on anything supernatural. There is no god whose will distinguishes right from wrong, no mysterious moral law whose dictates we must merely obey. Rather, whatever the status of our ethical and moral beliefs, they are rooted in the natural facts of the universe. That alone would make early Buddhist ethics of interest to political theorists, since naturalistic theories of ethics have been controversial in Western thought since Plato and remain the focus of intense debate.[1]

But once we get past the issue of naturalism, interpretations of early Buddhist ethics vary widely.[2] There are several major debates ongoing in the field, particularly whether early Buddhist ethics are better understood as consequentialist or a version of virtue ethics (almost no one argues for deontology),[3] whether the typical lay aspiration of achieving a good rebirth makes a single ethical system with the typical monastic aspiration to avoid being reborn at all, or whether those goals represent two separate ethical systems;[4] whether people who achieve enlightenment during their lifetimes are in some sense beyond morality; and generally how to relate early Buddhist ethics to more familiar Western categories and concerns.[5]

The issue that I focus on is metaethics. It is my contention that the best reading of the early texts reveals what I call a Hypothetical theory of ethics.[6] (I borrow the language from Kant's distinction between Categorical Imperatives, which are moral duties incumbent upon every rational being, and Hypothetical Imperatives, which are duties that one owes only because one has undertaken some voluntary commitment, like making a promise.) On this interpretation, early Buddhist ethics is essentially descriptive, explaining the natural consequences of varying courses of action and recommending some as being instrumentally wise, but not judging some courses of action as being absolutely better or worse than others. That reading of early Buddhist ethics should be of interest to political theorists for several reasons. First, it ties into existing debates in political theory and philosophy about naturalistic versus nonnaturalistic ethics, and whether either approach can be made coherent. Second, it would make Buddhism the only major religion to have a Hypothetical rather than a Categorical approach to ethics. That suggests that a Hypothetical ethics could succeed in the real world and not only in the seminar room. Third, it ties into an existing tradition in Western thought of trying to articulate political ethics in an entirely naturalistic or immanent idiom, avoiding appeals to the supernatural or the mystical. That tradition has its roots in Epicurus and Lucretius, continues through Spinoza, and is represented today by thinkers such as Gilles Deleuze and Félix Guattari, Michael Hart and Antonio Negri, and William Connolly. Understanding the Buddhist theory of ethics and comparing it with similar Western theories allows us to assess the relative strengths and weaknesses of the two approaches.

Early Buddhist Ethics

When we act based on greed, hatred, and delusion, we cultivate a character based on those ways of approaching the world. Such actions are governed by *kamma* (Sanskrit: *karma*) and will lead us to be reborn again and again, always into an existence that was somehow chosen by our previous actions. If our actions are ethically good (but driven by desire) they generate merit (*puñña*), while desire-driven, ethically bad actions generate demerit (*apuñña* or *pāpa*). Upon the death of the body, the complex combination of one's generated *puñña* and *apuñña/ pāpa* determines one's next birth.

Kamma (which literally means "action") is understood to be a natural phenomenon that operates by natural laws. There is no Book of Life, no Rhadamanthus to judge one after death.[7] Rather, one's actions incline one toward a future birth in which one reaps what one has sown. For example, someone who has lived by murder (and thus cultivated the mind of an animal rather than that of a rational person), might be drawn toward rebirth as an animal. Since the law of the jungle is eat or be eaten, life as an animal is likely to be full of anxiety, dread, pain, and premature death. As Buddhists sometimes put the point, one is punished or rewarded *by* one's deeds, not *for* them. Here the justice is poetic rather than juridical.[8]

A typical first step on the Buddhist path is to attempt to generate only *puñña* and thus secure a good rebirth. However, the ultimate goal is to stop generating *puñña* and *apuñña* altogether, by acting in a way that is not driven by desire. If one can achieve that goal (typically through intensive meditation and coming to understand *dhamma* (Sanskrit: *dharma*), the law of nature or truth about the universe), one will slowly exhaust whatever *puñña* and *apuñña* had been generated in previous lives. When one no longer has any of these "fruits" of action, and one no longer generates any new kammatic fruits, then one has escaped from *saṃsāra*, the cycle of birth, death, and rebirth. Upon death such a person (called an *arahat*; Sanskrit: *arhat*) will not be born again but will pass into *nibbāna* (Sanskirt: *nirvāṇa*). The Buddha was famously vague about what *nibbāna* entails, other than that it is the permanent end of all suffering.

One potent source of confusion and debate in early Buddhist ethics is the fact that the Buddha frequently used the terms *kuśala* and *akuśala* to evaluate actions. *Kuśala* means "skillful," and *akuśala* is its opposite, "unskillful." This particular choice of words makes the ethical theory appear Hypothetical and descriptive, while the use of *puñña* and *apuñña* makes it appear to be Categorical.

Early Buddhist Metaethics

The question of the metaethics of early Buddhism is the subject of ongoing scholarly debate. Are the early texts arguing that achieving *nibbāna* is morally good, and/or that all people have a moral duty to achieve it? Or are they instead offering Hypothetical advice about how to end one's suffering, if one were inclined to do such a thing, but without offering a Categorical judgment about the desirability of that goal?

Categorical Readings

The two most prominent English-language scholars of Buddhist ethics are Peter Harvey and Damien Keown, both of whom argue that early Buddhist ethics is Categorical. Harvey's argument for this reading is a bit vague, though it draws on two different considerations. The first is the nature of *kamma*, which Harvey interprets as reflecting objective moral norms: "An important point to note, here, is that an action's being good does not consist in its having pleasant karmic results. Rather, it is seen as having pleasant karmic results because it is itself good or whole-some."[9] Conversely: "[F]or Buddhism, an act is seen to have unpleasant karmic results because it is *wrong*; it is not seen as 'wrong' *because* it happens to produce bad karmic results."[10] A second consideration is that early Buddhism does, on Harvey's reading, contain a concept of moral obligation: "A moral life is not seen as a bald 'ought,' but as an uplifting source of happiness, in which the sacrifice of lesser pleasures facilitates the experiencing of those which are more enriching and satis-fying, for both oneself and others. Nevertheless, duty is not a concept foreign to Buddhism; it is simply that what one *should* do is also seen as what is enriching and rewarding."[11] Those interpretations add up to a Categorical reading: "Buddhism ... has ethical norms which all should follow."[12]

Damien Keown gives a more detailed argument, largely based on the usage of several key ethical terms in the Pāli texts, and comes to the same conclusion:

> On the issue of Relativism and Absolutism we note that Buddhism steers a middle course and acknowledges variation within a structured pattern of the pursuit of human good. The good for man is not arbitrary—it is governed by the facts of human nature and the inalienable characteristics of the world we inhabit, such as impermanence and change. A position of extreme relativism is therefore ruled out. Yet within these confines forms of life may vary to some degree, a fact acknowledged by the Buddha, and the basic goods may be participated in in a variety of ways: the absolutism is, accordingly, attenuated and qualified. This does not mean that none of the precepts are absolutes, only that not all of them are.[13]

In other work, Keown interprets *dhamma* as universal law governing both the physical and the moral worlds: "The ultimate foundation for Buddhist ethics is Dharma. Dharma has many meanings, but the underlying notion is of a universal law which governs both the physical and moral order of the universe. Dharma can best be translated as 'natural law,' a term that captures both its main senses, namely as the principle of order and regularity seen in the behaviour of natural phenomena, and also the idea of a universal moral law whose requirements have been revealed by enlightened beings such as the Buddha."[14]

He also responds to the point, made by several of the Hypothetical readings (see below) that the various ethical precepts of early Buddhism are adopted voluntarily:

> In common with deontology, Buddhism has rules and precepts that approach the status of moral absolutes. Early sources tirelessly repeat that certain acts, such as taking life, are not to be performed under any circumstances, and rules of this kind are typical of deontological ethics. We can note in passing that as evidence against a deontological

reading, the point is often made that since the precepts are voluntarily assumed—unlike the commandments of Christianity—Buddhism does not impose moral obligations on anyone. However, this overlooks the fact that Dharmic obligations exist whether or not one formally acknowledges or accepts them.[15]

Finally, he addresses the general character of early Buddhist ethics:

> It is *relativistic* in the sense that it includes scope for flexibility where appropriate, but not in the sense of holding that moral norms (as distinct from customs and etiquette) are merely a function of local cultural and historical circumstances. It is *absolutistic* in holding that certain things are always immoral (greed and hatred, for instance) and that certain things are always good (such as compassion and non-violence). On the question of *objectivity* . . . Buddhist ethical teachings are thought to be objectively true and in accordance with the nature of things.[16]

Thus, on the Categorical-reading side, we find arguments from the general tenor of the texts, from the meaning and scope of *dhamma*, from the workings of *kamma*, from the alleged presence of the notion of moral duty in the early texts, and from analysis of the actual usage of key terms in the early texts.

Ambivalent Readings

Two interpretations of early Buddhist ethics, one from P. D. Premasiri and one from Shundo Tachibana, don't fit neatly into the Hypothetical/ Categorical distinction. Both readings assert that the Buddha offered a Categorical theory, but both describe that Categorical theory in Hypothetical language. These readings are especially helpful because they show the difficulty of establishing what kind of theory the early texts put forward. Hence, Premasiri writes:

> The implication of all this is that according to early Buddhism moral judgements need defence, and moral discourse is a species of rational discourse. What we need to bring in defence of moral judgements

are facts about the world and ourselves which have a relation to the consequences turning out to be happy (*sukha*) or unhappy (*dukkha*). Thus when Buddhism judges murder to be a bad action it bases this judgement on one or more of a number of factual premises such as: (1) that it springs from *lobha* [greed], *dosa* [hatred], and *moha* [delusion], or any one of those mental conditions which impede the agent's progress towards the highest happiness; (2) that it has harmful kammic consequences to the agent in this life itself or in a future life; (3) that it has harmful consequences to the agent which may not fall under the law of kamma, but resulting from the laws of his country etc.; (4) that it causes pain to a person or persons other than the agent and thus leads to socially harmful consequences. All these matters are, according to Buddhism, to be settled by observation of natural facts and there is no question of intuiting a non-natural property of goodness as the intuitionist philosophers attempted to maintain.[17]

Shundo Tachibana's Categorical reading of the early texts is very similar. Tachibana argues that the enlightened person is no longer bound by moral norms (while also emphasizing that such a person is simply incapable of committing immoral acts). He also argues that the function of moral norms is primarily to be a form of training to enable a spiritual seeker to achieve higher, super-moral states of being. Yet, like Premasiri, he insists that the early Buddhist ethical norms really do identify absolute moral truths. He writes: "Buddhism as a characteristically ethical teaching cannot be bold enough to admit the total abolition of moral distinction for any persons. What we expect here is that good will decidedly be good, and evil will decidedly be evil, in the case of the wise or the ignorant, the Buddha, the Arahan [*Arahat*], or other men."[18] But he then goes on to say: "Thus the Bhikkhu [monk], the Brāhmaṇa [spiritually knowledgeable person], the Buddha ... are described as being above good and evil things, pleasant and unpleasant, and so on. Such attainment is the result of high mental culture prosecuted through the activity of perfect moral consciousness.... He is not immoral, but we may say that he is supermoral.... [T]he relative ideas therefore of good and evil, pleasure and pain, agreeableness and disagreeableness, right and wrong, are all annihilated for him."[19]

Hypothetical Readings

Many practitioners and scholars see the ethical teachings of early Buddhism as being Hypothetical. In some cases, this reading is simply presented as an assessment of the overall tenor of the early texts, with no further argument. For example, the American Buddhist teacher Gil Fronsdal writes: "Buddhism understands virtue and ethics pragmatically, based not on ideas of good and bad, but rather on the observation that some actions lead to suffering and some actions lead to happiness and freedom."[20] In that same vein, another American Buddhist teacher, Joseph Goldstein, writes: "The Buddha outlined five areas of basic morality that lead to a conscious life. These training precepts are given to all students who wish to follow the path of mindfulness. They are not given as absolute commandments; rather, they are practical guidelines to help us live in a more harmonious way and develop peace and power of mind."[21]

Although it's possible that this interpretation is a product of the adaptation of Buddhism in the West, we do find similar conclusions from scholars and practitioners in the East. For example, Sri Lankan Buddhist scholar Hema Goonatilake writes: "It is ... to be understood that precepts are rules of training and not commandments from God, the Buddha, or anyone else. It is only an undertaking by one, to oneself, if one is convinced that it is a good practice to observe."[22] Similarly, speaking about the narrower but crucial question of *kamma*, K. N. Jayatilleke writes: "Karma as a natural law in Buddhism is not different in principle from a law in the natural sciences. In fact, it would be misleading to call it a 'moral law' since it does not constitute a divine command, a categorical imperative or a norm."[23]

Some scholars offer a more detailed argument to defend the Hypothetical reading, though making such an argument is difficult. Precisely because the early Buddhist ethical theory is naturalistic, there are no references in the texts to the ultimate source of ethical norms. Nonnaturalistic ethical theories wear their hearts on their sleeves, explicitly identifying and justifying the source of their norms. In contrast, naturalistic theories point to various natural facts to support their arguments about how one should act, often making it difficult to discern whether they are making Categorical or Hypothetical arguments (as we saw above with the readings from Premasiri and Tachibana).

Melford Spiro and Winston King, like Shundo Tachibana, separately argued that early Buddhism saw obedience to ethical norms as a preliminary training for higher spiritual achievement and that human beings who had achieved enlightenment during their lifetime were no longer bound by moral rules (though there were also incapable of acting in a way that would be considered immoral by the unenlightened). If their interpretations are correct (which is the source of ongoing controversy),[24] Buddhist ethics is Hypothetical rather than Categorical. A set of norms that is obligatory for some people but not others simply isn't what we usually mean by a moral theory but is consistent with the idea that ethical norms are instrumental rather than absolute. Spiro's version of this argument is as follows:

> Hence, Buddhist morality, like Buddhist meditation, is primarily a technique for mind-training. To be sure, moral and immoral behavior have karmic consequences, but compliance with moral norms should not be based on a concern with these consequences; this is to base behavior on impure intentions. . . . For nibbanic Buddhism, morality is primarily a form of spiritual discipline; it is a means to the attainment of a certain psychological state which is the first condition for the achievement of nirvana.[25]

King's interpretation is more explicitly Hypothetical. Hence he writes: "Thus in common with atheistic humanism Buddhism proclaims that there is no metaphysical backing for moral values nor any great overall purpose by which man should be guided and to which he should conform his ways."[26] Although elsewhere King acknowledges that there are elements of both Categorical and Hypothetical ethical theories in the texts,[27] he ultimately concludes that the dominant message is Hypothetical: "[Buddhism] prefers to say that the Precepts are counsel to the wise, based on the fact that their observance brings blessed (kammic) consequences both in this life and lives to come, and their non-observance produces grief, pain and misfortune. Thus one may take or leave the good advice for he is not *commanded* to accept it."[28]

Thus King and Spiro offer another kind of argument in favor of a Hypothetical reading: if it is true that people who have achieved enlightenment (or are relatively far along the path) are no longer bound by moral norms, then the overall ethical theory of early Buddhism is instrumental rather than absolute.

David Bastow offers yet another argument for a Hypothetical reading:

> This brings us to the . . . question, of whether these principles are moral; whether the Way can be described as a set of moral injunctions, and the goal as a moral ideal. It seems in fact that little depends on such a classification. . . .[The principles] are not incumbent on every man; the Buddha does not say that it is a man's duty to undertake the Way. His attitude is rather that any recluse who having heard the Truth follows some other kind of religious life must be stupid or blind. Similarly a householder's life may be of profit, but much greater and sweeter is the profit of the Way.[29]

Bastow's interpretation offers another kind of relevant evidence: in all those 12,000-plus pages, the Buddha never explicitly says that living according to the Way is a moral duty or obligation, nor that someone who decides not to is morally bad or evil (as opposed to foolish, blind, short-sighted, etc.).

David Kalapuhana argues that early Buddhist epistemology is very similar to William James's version of pragmatism, emphasizing the practical and instrumental and avoiding the metaphysical. Given that epistemology, Kalapuhana argues, early Buddhist ethics must be Hypothetical and instrumental rather than absolute:

> With the above definitions of perception and conception, the determination of the truth or falsity of a percept, the meaningfulness or meaninglessness of a concept, shifts from the traditional criterion of essence to that of function or consequence. Within the framework of such a pragmatic definition there cannot be a place for a rigid fact-value distinction. Thus, the revolutionary attempt to accommodate empirical psychology in philosophical discourse by the Buddha in the sixth century B.C. and by William James in modern Western philosophy provided a totally different foundation for moral philosophy.[30]

Kalapuhana concludes: "It is well known that the nonsubstantialist Buddha denied any form of absolute existence (*atthitā*). When the *is* gets defused, so does the *ought*.... The ought is therefore not an absolute command or necessity, but a pragmatic call to recognize the empirical existence and adopt solutions to whatever problems are associated with it."[31] Thus Kalapuhana offers an additional argument for a Hypothetical reading: it is more consistent than a Categorical reading with the broader epistemology implied by the early texts.

Finally, Charles Goodman offers a Hypothetical reading based on the structure of Pāli, the language of the early texts:

> Pāli texts often talk about what we *should* do, expressing their recommendations in the form of gerundives or optatives. But they seem not to have a way of talking about what we are *obligated* or *morally required* to do. . . . [T]hey see people as required to obey the moral rules that they have explicitly and voluntarily promised to obey. . . . Someone who has not promised to follow these rules is not required to follow them. On the other hand, life without the rules is still subject to the Law of Karma, and the grim consequences of performing the actions that would be forbidden by the rules can give people prudential reasons to choose to accept the rules as binding on them.[32]

Thus we have several kinds of argument supporting the Hypothetical reading: (1) it is consistent with the overall tenor of the early texts; (2) it arises from a (disputed) distinction between *kamma*-focused ethics and *nibbāna*-focused ethics; (3) the early texts never assert a moral duty to follow the Way; (4) the Buddha's allegedly instrumental epistemology necessarily relativizes his ethical claims; and (5) the language in which the early texts were written does not allow the expression of moral duties.

Problems of Naturalism

One further consideration weighing in favor of a Hypothetical reading is that ethical theories that seek to be both naturalistic and morally realist (that is, asserting that there exist moral truths that are absolute and objective) run into the objection raised most famously by David

Hume and G. E. Moore that there appears to be some kind of logical mistake in deriving normative conclusions from nonnormative descriptions, an "ought" from an "is."[33] Without endorsing the specific arguments raised by Hume or Moore (which remain controversial),[34] it seems that their objections reflect at least three of our stubborn intuitions about ethics. The first is embodied in Hume's criticism: describing natural facts feels like a different intellectual activity than asserting moral norms. Thus when we describe facts and then assert that norms arise from them, many people feel as if an essential premise has been skipped over—we can't quite see where the norm comes from. The second intuition is roughly the converse of Hume's and is basically Moore's point: when we describe moral norms in terms of descriptive facts, the description seems incomplete, as if we haven't fully captured what we meant by the norms. Hence a description of all the natural facts associated with murder doesn't necessarily reveal the *wrongness* of murder. The third intuition is that the identification of only some natural facts with norms seems arbitrary—we aren't able to give an account of why some (combinations of) natural facts give rise to norms while others do not.

Where does this leave us? It seems clear that the early texts contain aspects of both Categorical and Hypothetical ethical systems. For example, they appear to condemn murder in Categorical terms but conversely describe failure to follow the path to enlightenment as unskillful or foolish rather than morally wrong. (It's worth noting that the Vedic tradition, from which Buddhism arose, was not hesitant to use explicitly Categorical language to describe one's failure to live rightly.) In my view, as is often true with a large, complex textual tradition, there are no knock-down arguments in favor of one reading or another, of either a Hypothetical or a Categorical reading of early Buddhist ethics (or for or against naturalistic realism in ethics generally). Instead, we have to proceed with what appears to us to be the best reading, based on a thoughtful consideration of the evidence and contending interpretations. In my view, the Hypothetical reading seems to best capture the overall tenor of the texts, to explain the Buddha's use of *kuśala* and *akuśala* to evaluate some ethical choices, to harmonize with the description of achieving *nibbāna* as being in some sense beyond moral goodness, and to be in sync with the Buddha's rejection of mysticism and the inexplicable. Further, only the Hypothetical reading seems to me to be appropriately consistent with the *anicca* doctrine that all things are impermanent. If ethical truths were Categorical, they would be the only things in the universe that were permanent and had unchangeable essences, yet the Buddha consistently and explicitly says that we have no knowledge of any things with those qualities. Thus, the rest of this essay assumes that Buddhist ethics is Hypothetical and then examines what consequences that might have for politics.

Pragmatism, Naturalism, and Politics

One perennial concern about Hypothetical ethical theories is that they won't have the normative force necessary to constrain people's behavior, either in terms of individual action or in terms of social/political action. As we saw in chapter 1, early Buddhism advocates a political system of enlightened monarchy, bound by a set of ethical guidelines that require the king to rule in the collective interest of the society. As we saw in chapter 3, in the mid-nineteenth century the crisis of colonialism and globalization forced every Buddhist country to abandon monarchy and instead embrace some version of republicanism. Although the ratio-nalizations of this change differed among countries, a common theme was the idea that, under the conditions of modernity, republican insti-tutions could fulfill the ethical requirements for government as well as or better than monarchical institutions. Today there are no abso-lute monarchies in Buddhist countries, all of which have more-or-less republican governments. Thus one central question for contemporary Buddhists is whether the Hypothetical ethical theory found in the texts of early Buddhism is adequate to ground, justify, and constrain repub-lican government and civil institutions.

A handful of Western political theorists have tried to ground poli-tics in Hypothetical ethical systems in recent scholarship using the term "immanent" rather than Hypothetical. Such immanent theories are naturalistic, in that they reject any role for the supernatural and also morally irrealist, in the sense that they are trying to provide reasons to act in one way or another, rather than absolute or objective norms that one is in some way obliged to follow. In both of those respects, they are very similar to the ethical thinking of early Buddhism as I have interpreted it. Comparing the ethical system of early Buddhism to the most successful immanence theories should help us assess the relative strengths and weaknesses of both strains of thought.

In other work, I've argued that it's helpful to think of immanence theories as tending toward three types or flavors.[35] The first tendency is toward *declaration*. Declarations are affirmative, even apodictic, claims about how the world is and what follows from that description. Spinoza's *Ethics* is a good example of this tendency—it offers a comprehensive ontology and metaphysics, along with arguments about what follows from those premises, while remaining an immanence theory by resolutely denying that there are any principles or agents in the universe other than those that emerge contingently. The second tendency is toward *description*. Descriptive theories say: here's how I think of the world; it's been helpful to me; perhaps you'll find it helpful too. Probably the best example of this tendency is Pyrrhonian skepticism, with its insistence that even its own claims cannot be known to be true, but that many people have found acting *as if* they were true helpful.[36] The third tendency, which is roughly in between declaration and description, is *invitation*. Invitations say: here's what I believe; I can't prove my claims definitively, but here are some elements of my beliefs that I think you are likely already to agree with, and here are some reasons why you might come to agree with more of my beliefs after some reflection. I see early Buddhism as an example of an invitation, with its initial claim that most people naturally come to see that life contains much suffering, its claim to have a method of relieving that suffering, and its emphasis on the point that each person must investigate that claim for him- or herself.

Each tendency comes with its own characteristic problems. Declarations run into essentially the same problems as nonnaturalistic theories—making contestable assumptions, claiming more than they can prove (especially in terms of deriving normative judgments from descriptive facts), and hypostatizing the contingent into the necessary. At the opposite extreme, descriptions run the risk of being seen as poetry rather than philosophy. That is, to the extent that a politics of immanence is purely an optional perspective, one for which no truth-claims are made, it is open to the objection that while it may be of great help to its adherents, there is no reason to think that it will be widely enough adopted to be of broader social significance. Finally, precisely because they take a midway position between declaration and description, invitations suffer from both sets of problems. When they make affirmative claims, they act like declarations. When they affirm their own contestability, they act like descriptions. Yet, I argue that invitation theories are the most likely to succeed. In brief, they maximize the benefits of partial agreement, while reducing what's at stake where disagreement remains.

William Connolly's Immanence Politics

William Connolly's version of immanence is an example of an invitation theory. For purposes of analysis, we might say that Connolly's theory starts with some basic ontological commitments. Connolly identifies himself as an immanent naturalist. For him, naturalism means that there is no god or supernatural force at work in the universe. Thus he writes: "By naturalism I mean the faith that nature and human culture survive without the aid (or obstruction) of a divine force."[37] This means both that there is no god to either save or damn us but also that there is no transcendent source of normative values or judgments that we must consult.[38]

Connolly not only admits but also celebrates the fact that these ontological or metaphysical commitments are contestable. Part of the motivation for that position is his point, made in a number of books including *Why I Am Not a Secularist*, *Pluralism*, and *Capitalism and Christianity: American Style*, that everyone has basic commitments whose truth or necessity they cannot prove. In recent work, he refers to these basic commitments as an existential faith: "By existential faith I mean an elemental sense of the ultimate character of being."[39] And he argues that everyone has some kind of existential faith: "To be human is to be inhabited by existential faith. There is no vacuum in this domain, though there might very well be ambivalence, uncertainty, and internal plurality."[40] Connolly emphasizes that existential faiths are not merely discursive beliefs, but are also organizations of bodily experience and habit, which exist on registers below that of discursive consciousness.[41] And those faiths are deeply contestable, since they rest upon beliefs and assumptions for which there is not (and may not ever be) evidence that is overwhelmingly conclusive.

On my reading, Connolly celebrates this contestability (even of his own deepest beliefs) for a handful of related reasons. First, the contestability of existential faiths is itself an instance of the immanence of the universe, the way in the which the universe is always full of more possibilities (and actualities) than we can systematize or account for. As Nietzsche, one of Connolly's acknowledged inspirations, argues, there are only two ways to respond to this overwhelming fecundity of the universe: love or resentment. Like Nietzsche, Connolly chooses love. A second reason that Connolly embraces the contestability of immanent naturalism is because of his views on identity. As laid out most fully in his *Identity/Difference,* Connolly subscribes to the view that identity is always fashioned through differentiation and distinction. If that approach is even roughly correct, then the fact that there are others who contest my most fundamental commitments is constitutive of me as a self. From this perspective, plurality is both a problem and the condition of possibility for identity. There are no nonplural solutions to the problems of plurality. A third reason that Connolly celebrates the contestability of immanent naturalism is because he believes that the shared experience of having our most cherished beliefs challenged may itself become a basis for cooperation and respect across difference.[42]

More generally, Connolly's approach to the plurality of modern politics is to seek a fair settlement among existing identities/constituencies while also remaining attuned to the possible emergence of new identities, rights, demands, and needs. These two elements are what Connolly refers to as *pluralism* and *pluralization.*[43] To achieve these two goals, which are related but also in tension with each other, Connolly suggests that two sensibilities or ethics (he also calls them civic virtues) would be especially helpful: agonistic respect and critical responsiveness. In a recent formulation, he writes about agonistic respect: "An ethos of agonistic respect grows out of mutual appreciation for the ubiquity of faith to life and the inability of contending parties, to date, to demonstrate the truth of one faith over other live candidates. It grows out of reciprocal appreciation for the element of contestability in these domains. The relation is agonistic in two senses: you *absorb the agony* of having elements of your own faith called into question by others, and you *fold agonistic contestation* of others into the respect that you convey toward them."[44] If agonistic respect is about attending to existing differences, critical responsiveness is about being attuned to new ones, whose development and emergence will always necessarily be disruptive and disorienting. He writes: "Critical responsiveness takes the form of *careful listening and presumptive generosity* to constituencies struggling to move from an obscure or degraded subsistence below the field of recognition, justice, obligation, rights, or legitimacy to a place on one or more of those registers."[45]

These ethics are explicitly optional—they are ways of approaching the world that Connolly believes are helpful to achieving social cooperation given conditions of both plurality and pluralization, but there is no moral imperative to adopt them, and no assurance that the experience of difference will somehow spontaneously generate them. To some extent we can draw them from existing belief systems and institutions, and to some extent we must create them for ourselves through micropolitical techniques of self-fashioning (following Nietzsche and Foucault), through arguing for our ideals, through creating partial alliances with others with whom we have some shared beliefs, and through political struggle to enact our preferred policies. Connolly describes this difficult balancing act of simultaneously holding one's own beliefs, engaging in a respectful agonism with people who hold other beliefs, and all the while remaining open to the emergence of unforeseen new identities and beliefs, as developing a "bicameral" understanding of ourselves.[46]

In contrast to this hopeful vision of what we might achieve, the great dangers are existential resentment and evil. Existential resentment— what Connolly also sometimes calls the drive for existential revenge[47]— arises when the contingency of both identity and existence threatens to overwhelm us, and we respond by trying to fix identity, trying to police difference, and with resentment against a world that contains such maddening indeterminacy. When resentment reaches an extreme level, it becomes evil: "The tendency to evil within faith is this: The instances in which the faith of others incites you to anathematize it as inferior or evil can usher into being the demand to take revenge against them for the internal disturbance they sow, even if they have not otherwise limited your ability to express your faith."[48] Importantly, evil is a possibility for *every* faith, not just for those whose explicit commitments call for the curtailing of difference.

Connolly acknowledges the problem of making an optional world-view useful and offers concrete reasons to believe that others might be drawn to it. He writes:

> But what could attract multiple constituencies to such an agenda? Negotiation of such an ethos of pluralism, first, honors the embedded character of faith; second, gives expression to a fugitive element of care, hospitality, or love for difference simmering in most faiths; third, secures specific faiths against persecution; and fourth, offers the best opportunity for diverse faiths to coexist without violence while supporting the civic conditions of common governance.[49]

As I suggested earlier, as an invitation theory, Connolly's approach is subject to two different sets of objections. On the one hand, to the extent that he affirms substantive claims and commitments, like a declaration theory, he has to make assertions that reasonable people could contest, which thus reduces the utility of his theory as a solution to the problem of political coordination. On the other hand, to the extent that he emphasizes the contestability of his claims and commitments, he risks making his theory merely a description—an optional perspective on the world that only the already like-minded would likely support.

However, we might instead conclude that invitation theories are wily, in that they attempt to maximize agreement while minimizing disagreement. By making ontological and ethical claims, Connolly moves away from the purely poetic pole of description. By acknowledging the contestability of those claims, he carefully avoids the tendency of declarative theories to claim more than they can prove. By putting himself between those two extremes, Connolly has crafted a true invitation—a theory that stakes some claims, acknowledges its limits, and points out reasons why people who initially disagree with some or all of it might nonetheless either come to agree with (some of) it, as well as reasons why cooperation might still be possible despite continued disagreement. His approach shows how immanence theories can defuse possible problems, for example, by staking positive claims but acknowledging their contestability, and then using the shared pain of acknowledging the contestability of one's views as the basis for a possible experience of unity and similarity among people otherwise separated by their ideas.

As Connolly himself points out, there's no guarantee that this approach will work, but his efforts to manage the problems of immanence theories suggest that his style of theorizing may stand the best chance of succeeding.

Conclusion: The Fruits of Comparative Political Theory

When the texts of early Buddhism were composed and recorded (fourth to first centuries BCE), Buddhism was a relatively small sect. It had no political power and was instead dependent on the patronage and protection of sympathetic rulers (over whom it had some limited, hortatory influence). Its theory of politics was limited, offering general advice but otherwise staying out of public life. Further, as a monastic faith, early Buddhism could largely preach to the converted—the various sermons were usually directed at people who had already embraced Buddhism or who were at least willing to seriously consider its arguments.

When, in the mid-nineteenth century, the various Buddhist countries began to abandon monarchy in favor of republicanism, one of the motivating reasons was the recognition that Buddhism needed an approach to politics that could cope with plurality, both externally, as Buddhist countries sought to respond to colonialism, and internally, as non-Buddhist religious minorities sought independence, autonomy, or simply some voice in the political system. As a religion, Buddhism can preserve its traditionally passive stance toward non-Buddhists: they are invited to come see for themselves whether Buddhism has something to offer. But as the basis of a political system, Buddhism needs a more robust theory about how to deal with differences in belief and about how to manage a pluralistic society. Most Buddhist countries have simply adopted republican institutions and practices from the West. They may be compatible with Buddhism, but they are not obviously rooted directly in Buddhist beliefs and goals.

Connolly's immanence politics offers one direction that Buddhists could go in developing a more adequate political theory for modernity. Although there are substantial differences between the two theories, they share some important features: both rest on a naturalistic or immanent view of the universe; both acknowledge the interdependence of personal ethical/spiritual development and maintenance of an adequate system of political/social cooperation; both recognize the need to stake some ontological and ethical claims, while also acknowledging that no claims are so self-evident that all people are logically compelled to accept them; both make claims about the best way to live, and make (Hypothetical) distinctions between right and wrong; both acknowledge that ethical and political theorizing has to start with some existentially basic claims or assumptions, which no theory can fully justify; both seek to build alliances where possible, to maximize the effectiveness of agreement while minimizing the disruption of disagreement; finally, both demonstrate that a naturalistic, Hypothetical approach to ethics and political theory is both theoretically defensible and practically useful.

7

Buddhist Political Theory
in the Twenty-first Century

HOW DO WE NOW COMBINE parts I and II, the descriptive reading of the Buddhist political texts with my interpretive argument about what is of importance and value in them? I choose to begin by addressing head-on the most cynical position: today there is no Buddhist political theory at all, merely Western political theory with a decorative veneer of Buddhism; worse, the Buddhist political theory that existed prior to 1850 is not only utterly dead but deserves to be since it championed a political system that no one in a democratic age would advocate. All told, on this view, Buddhist political theory may be of interest to historians, but it has neither interest nor value for contemporary political thinkers.

As I have suggested in several places so far, I believe that this cynical dismissal of Buddhist political theory is quite wrong. The theory of government of early and traditional Buddhism—enlightened but more-or-less-absolute monarchy—is certainly a system that has no appeal in the twenty-first century. But that's true of virtually every theory of politics that political theorists study—no one is advocating that we create Locke's version of monarchy, Plato's ideal city, or even Hannah Arendt's polis of action and judgment. Political theory isn't an effort to find a perfect government ready-made or a thinker we can treat as the source of all wisdom, but rather an exercise in thinking broadly and critically about a certain set of issues related to politics. The early and traditional Buddhist political texts and ideas are of ongoing value and interest for just the same reasons that we continue to read Machiavelli's *Prince*—because they depict a unique approach to permanent problems of human collective life.

Further, a typical move in political theory is to attempt to identify a set of principles that underlie a particular text or tradition, separate them from their particular historical context, and ask whether they have some broader application. That is, we separate a political theory (underlying principles) from a theory of government (the particular application of those principles in a particular historical context). Buddhist political theory rests on the three principles discussed at length in part II—the idea that there is no self; a deflationary assessment of the importance of politics (the idea of limited citizenship); and a naturalistic, irrealist theory of ethics (which for ease I will continue to refer to as a Hypothetical theory). That political theory remains interesting and valuable for two main reasons: first, it continues to underlie Buddhist politics and political theorizing today, suggesting that perhaps it is the Western institutions of Buddhist-majority countries that are the veneer laid over a profoundly Buddhist approach to politics, and providing a clear and strong basis for Buddhist political theorizing in the future; second, it both overlaps and conflicts with many debates within contemporary Western political theory, thus providing an opportunity to examine familiar ideas in a new context and an opportunity to see limitations that are otherwise obscured by cultural myopia. In short, Buddhist political theory is not only alive and well, it is also an invaluable partner for Western political theory.

The Three Core Components

In part II we looked at how the three core components of Buddhist political theory relate to particular debates and thinkers in the Western tradition. Here I examine how they relate to the Western tradition more broadly, to show how they are both related to and yet distinctly different from Western approaches to these issues, and how Western thinkers can't afford to overlook Buddhism's perspective.

Theory of Limited Citizenship

It is overwhelmingly clear from the early texts that the goal of Buddhism is individual transformation (though there is considerable debate about whether one ought to save oneself as soon as possible or intentionally submit to continued rebirths to help save others first). As we discussed earlier, the content of the Buddha's first sermon after achieving enlightenment was the Four Noble Truths, the core of the religion, which explain (1) that life is suffering, (2) that suffering is caused by clinging, (3) that one could stop suffering if one stopped clinging, and (4) that one could stop clinging by living according to the Noble Eightfold Path.[1] The entire focus is on how individuals can make spiritual progress to escape the cycle of reincarnation and suffering.

That raises the question of the relative importance of politics to soteriology. Is politics integral to early Buddhism, such that individual transformation is significantly affected by the political system under which one lives? Or is politics of secondary importance, such that it has a relatively small or even negligible effect on individual spiritual progress? As Joanna Macy correctly argues, politics must have some effect on salvation, because the theory of *paticcasamuppāda*, or dependent co-arising argues that every condition is the result of all previous causes in the universe.[2] If politics exists, it has some effect on individuals and their struggle for enlightenment.

As we saw in chapter 5, the early texts themselves make clear that politics has a relatively small effect on salvation and that politics is relatively unimportant in human life. Further, a closer reading of the *Cakkavatti-Sīhanāda Sutta* offers substantial evidence against the idea that political factors are essential to achieving enlightenment. The *Cakkavatti-Sīhanāda Sutta* clearly places the historical Buddha's own era, when people lived to be 100 (that is the typical human life span mentioned in the early texts), as being far inferior to the era in which a *cakkavatti* rules and also as being on the downslope toward things getting worse.[3] Thus, it is apparently possible to achieve enlightenment (as the Buddha and many members of the early *sangha* did) without living under the rule of a *cakkavatti*, whom the *Cakkavatti-Sīhanāda Sutta* implies appears only in the eras when people live to be 80,000 years old. Conversely, the text makes clear that the vast majority of people alive during the reigns of the nine successive *cakkavattis* did not achieve enlightenment. This indicates that while living under an enlightened ruler is helpful, it is not enough alone to lead one to enlightenment.

At the nadir of human existence, when people live for only ten years, it is some of the people themselves who decide that they must improve their behavior, not a *cakkavatti* or even an inferior king. Thus it appears that the people are capable of moral self-reform and do not require the help of a king, either good or bad. Indeed, the next *cakkavatti* won't appear until the people become so good that they once again live for 80,000 years, which won't be for tens of thousands of years. During that entire period, the people will continue to improve without the guidance of a *cakkavatti*, though admittedly they will presumably have inferior kings to help them (though, interestingly, the inevitable errors of those less-than-righteous kings appear to be unable to derail the overall society's moral progress). Thus, while the text overtly appears to say that the actions of the *cakkavatti* (i.e., the political environment) determine whether the society is morally good or not, the structure of the story suggests that it is the moral goodness of the people/society that makes the emergence of a *cakkavatti* possible in the first place. The *cakkavatti* then clearly does have some influence on whether that moral goodness will be maintained, but it also appears that political leaders are powerless to improve a society that is already deteriorating or to undermine a society that is steadily improving, and that truly excellent political leaders don't emerge in morally bad times.

Therefore, even the *Cakkavatti-Sīhanāda Sutta* appears to say that while social and political factors are relevant to the spiritual progress of individuals, they are not determinative. A bad social environment cannot stop people who are determined from making moral progress (witness the survivors of the generation that lives to ten), and a generally good social environment cannot stop people from deteriorating morally (witness the generation that lives to 80,000 due to their general moral goodness, but begins to behave immorally after the failed-*cakkavatti*'s errors). Further, the quality of government and social policies appears largely to *follow* from the goodness of the people, rather than to *lead* it.

Thus, while politics obviously plays some role in human life and has some effect on how easy or difficult the individual finds it to achieve enlightenment, politics is neither a central help nor a central hindrance to salvation. Politics simply isn't that relevant to the truly important things in life; at most it plays a supporting role.

While it's certainly true that we see bits and pieces of this theory in the Western tradition, as we discussed in chapter 5, no one Western theory includes all of them or puts them together in this way. Thus, for example, we certainly see something like a theory of limited citizenship in some Western thinkers, such as in Thoreau's point that he came to the world to live in it rather than to improve it, and in Augustine's pessimism about the possibility of avoiding evil when involved in politics.[4] Yet both Thoreau and Augustine argue that there are some circumstances—rare for Thoreau, common for Augustine—under which one must nonetheless take an active role in the political life of the community. We see nothing like that in the early Buddhist texts. *Someone* has to run the society, but it needn't be *you*, and there will always be someone else eager to do it, usually for all the wrong reasons.

More common in the Western tradition is the idea that participation in government is pragmatically necessary, morally obligatory, and/or the only path to full development of one's capabilities. We see this theme in the earliest works, such as in Plato's implicit argument in the *Republic* that no class of citizens can fully develop its nature without the cooperation of the other classes through politics, and in Aristotle's overt argument in the *Politics* that individual perfection and the good life can be achieved only in the polis.[5] That same theme recurs throughout the Western tradition, in Augustine's argument that Christians have a moral duty to participate in politics despite the likelihood that they will sin in the process, in Locke's assumption that political participation is the only rational course of action, in Marx's assertion that human beings can only achieve their full potential through active participation in a democratic and egalitarian society, in Arendt's valorization of the life of action in the public sphere, in the value pluralists' argument that plurality requires a kind of constant political engagement, and in the civic republican emphasis on self-cultivation through political participation.[6] It is virtually always true that the cure proposed for anomie, alienation, sectarian conflict, disempowerment, and other political ills is ... more politics!

Given the Western tradition's emphasis on more and more politics, it's tempting to treat the Buddhist argument that politics isn't so very important as being an irresponsible quietism or the response of an elite that can shelter itself from the consequences of bad policies. Indeed, as we saw in chapter 5, Slavoj Žižek argues just that.[7] Yet this response misses the fact that the Buddha's depreciation of politics successfully captures the experience of many modern-day citizens. The Buddha's advice is to participate in the political system in whatever ways are required and/or typical—obey the laws, pay your taxes, and vote for the candidates you think will enact the best policies. But don't expect politics to dramatically improve the society. Change ultimately comes additively, from the many personal transformations of individual citizens. Yes, it matters what happens in the world of politics, but what happens in the mind of each individual matters more, not just for those individuals personally (contra Žižek) but for the society as a whole as well. To paraphrase Rousseau, good laws cannot make good citizens, and bad citizens cannot make good laws. Only improving citizens can create improving laws. Although patterns of political participation and engagement vary widely among societies, this idea—that one should not expect fundamental social change to be led by the political system—is a familiar feature of the politics of many contemporary democracies. To the extent that this deflationary view reflects the views of (some) modern citizens, the Buddhist theory of politics seems to be a better fit for them than much of the Western theory tradition, whose optimism about politics strikes many modern citizens as quaint.

Hypothetical Theory of Ethics

The early texts depict an unusual moral universe, one that requires some interpretation and unpacking. First, as mentioned in the summary of the *Aggañña-Sutta* in chapter 1, the universe has neither beginning nor end, only endless cycles of expansion and contraction. Buddhism offers no theory about where the universe came from or what its ultimate fate might be—in that way, it focuses on soteriology and avoids eschatology.[8] Similarly, the universe is apparently spontaneously repopulated with sentient beings during each expansion. Buddhism does not posit a creator god or power, and actively works to depict the chief Vedic god, Brahma/Brahman, as just one more sentient being—an unusually powerful one, but not the creator of any aspect of the universe.[9] Indeed, the Buddha teaches that the gods who think themselves to be creators have merely forgotten their own origins, limitations, and mortality.[10]

As we discussed in chapter 6, the fundamental force in the Buddhist universe is *kamma*. In the Buddhist texts *kamma* is widely explained as merely being cause and effect—every action leads to some reaction. There is no cosmic judge or accountant who tallies up one's *kamma* and sends one to one's next incarnation; rather, one's *kamma* creates a disposition or quality of character that leads one naturally and inevitably to a uniquely suitable next life. While the early texts do sometimes talk of future incarnations as being rewards or punishments,[11] we should understand that language metaphorically—people in essence choose their own next incarnations through their actions.

Sentient beings are caught in the cycle of continuous rebirth called *saṃsāra*. Achieving enlightenment allows one to escape from *saṃsāra*, and after the death of their body an enlightened person enters *nibbāna*, about which the Buddha was exceedingly vague. Various people tried to get the Buddha to clarify whether *nibbāna* was a state of existence or nonexistence, and so on, but he refused all such requests. All he said explicitly was that *nibbāna* was beyond suffering and beyond birth and death.[12] Human beings are uniquely well positioned to achieve enlightenment. The implication seems to be that subhuman incarnations are so filled with either misery or the struggle for survival that it is exceedingly difficult to behave in a way that will lead either to a better incarnation or directly to enlightenment, and that conversely the superhuman incarnations (as gods, demigods, and so on) often lead beings to be both complacent and arrogant, such that spiritual progress stalls or relapses.[13]

As I argued in chapter 6, this is a Hypothetical moral theory. There is no transcendent source of rules or laws, no judge, no reward or punishment, no telos. Everything that happens in this universe follows knowable natural laws. Thus, for example, one's next birth is the natural consequence of one's current, freely chosen actions (though those actions are themselves influenced by one's actions in previous lives). While each sentient being must inevitably make moral choices about his or her behavior, there is no outside authority that judges one. In a sense, the natural and the normative are coextensive, in that the effects of good or bad *kamma* are both natural facts about the universe and the basis of moral evaluation. For that reason, the Buddhist moral theory is very similar to the later theories developed by Hobbes and Spinoza.[14] Finally, it's worth noticing that the Buddhist moral universe is made up *only* of Hypothetical imperatives—if you wish to escape *saṃsāra* and the suffering it entails, act in this particular way. Otherwise you are free to continue being reincarnated forever, though of course the Buddha thinks that that is such an unappealing option that no rational person would choose it. But, importantly, that would be a weak or foolish choice, not an evil one.

We see this point illustrated in the Buddha's insistence that each individual must test for him- or herself whether the Buddha's teachings are true and helpful. The Buddha articulated this point in response to a question from the Kalamas about how they could know which of the various religious wanderers who visited them (including the Buddha) were right. The Buddha's answer was:

> Now, look you, Kālāmas. Be ye not misled by report or tradition or hearsay. Be not misled by proficiency in the collections, nor by mere logic or inference, nor after considering reasons, nor after reflection on and approval of some theory, nor because it fits becoming, nor out of respect for a recluse who holds it. . . . But if at any time ye know of yourselves: These things are profitable, they are blameless, they are praised by the intelligent: these things when performed and undertaken, conduce to profit and happiness,—then, Kālāmas, do ye, having undertaken them, abide therein.[15]

Here, too, we see important connections to Western political theory. Many thinkers in the West, from Epicurus to Hume to Nietzsche to Connolly, have been attracted by the idea that our moral ideas and judgments do not represent objective facts or truths about the universe but are instead a kind of instrumental advice (albeit especially important and compelling advice). However, despite the wide interest in this idea in the West, it has always been an abstract idea, something that philosophers considered, rather than a serious possibility for living one's daily life. Buddhism offers the chance for Western thinkers to see this idea played out in the real life of individuals and whole communities. (That is not to say that all Buddhists have adopted this view of Buddhist ethics—many clearly have not—but rather to say that at least some have, and that their example is invaluable as a basis for seeing what such an ethics looks like in practice.)

Theory of No-Self

As we discussed in chapter 4, in his second sermon after achieving enlightenment, the *Anattalakkhaṇa Sutta,* the Buddha taught that there is no self.[16] As I suggested earlier, this theory is unique when compared with Western theories. A number of thinkers have suggested that the self may be an illusion, from Kant and Hume to Nietzsche, Derek Parfitt, Antonio Damasio, and others.[17] But no one in the Western tradition has argued that the self is an illusion *that we could get rid of* nor the further claim that we would all be better off if we did get rid of it.

Yet, not surprisingly, the Western philosophical tradition contains several different strands of thought about the self, which are more or less close to the Buddhist position. The view that is the furthest from the Buddhist no-self theory is the Greek and Christian idea that human beings are or possess selves and that those selves are indestructible, immortal natural essences (i.e., souls). A view that takes one step toward the Buddhist position is the idea that human beings are or possess selves, but that those selves arise more-or-less contingently from the functioning of the body and/or mind. In this group we get thinkers like William James, who argues that the self is ultimately merely a way of talking about some aspects of the body, like Kant, who argues that the mind's perception of a single, unified self is merely the logically necessary but empirically unverifiable corollary of the mind's perception of external objects extended in space and time, and finally like the contemporary "embodied mind" school of thought, which builds off of phenomenology to suggest that our experience of being selves may be rooted in both bodily and cognitive processes.[18] The closest that Western thinking about the self gets to the Buddhist perspective comes in the work of Hume, who suggests that the self is an illusion, but one that we cannot get rid of, and Nietzsche, who suggests that the self is an illusion that we might turn to our own purposes.[19] One influential line of contemporary Western thought (which roughly corresponds with "postmodernism") has built on the insights of Hume, Kant, and

Nietzsche to argue that identity is either largely or wholly contingent or constructed.[20]

Given this range of ideas, we can see, first, that while the Buddhist no-self position goes further in one direction than any influential Western theory, there are similarities between the two traditions, and, second, that the Buddhist position extends one of the Western approaches to its logical conclusion.[21] The *anattā* doctrine would not be shocking to Hume, Kant, or Nietzsche, though none of them would be prepared to embrace it, and it, at the same time, represents the logical next step for contemporary theories of the constructed and contingent nature of identity. Thus the Buddhist theory is not so foreign that it could not enter into conversation with Western theories, and it presents the opportunity to extend more familiar theories in their natural direction of development. For both reasons, it is simultaneously distinct from Western theories and an appealing alternative (or supplement) to them.

Further, the Buddhist theory adds a welcome alternative to Western theories of the self by explaining how autonomy is possible without either assuming an essential self or denying the causal influences of super-personal social forces. When we assume that there is an essential self, the question of autonomy gets posed as a metaphor based on physics—we assume that the self is capable of arriving at a final determination about how to act and then worry that various intervening forces, both psychological and social, may prevent the self from acting in that way. We see the self as having a certain momentum and then wonder whether the opposing forces will stop it in its tracks. Although it's not obvious on its face, we use the same semiconscious metaphor when we assume that the self is more or less the product of external social forces. On this view, because the particular self is the result of the effects of many different forces, it is not identical with any one of them and thus may have interests or needs that are in opposition to some or all of them. In that way, it has unique interests that it might be able to assert interstitially, provided that it is not entirely blocked by those various forces, either as they have been internalized as part of the self (i.e., guilt) or as they continue to exist outside the self (i.e., as the police, public opinion, and so on). On this view, autonomy consists in the self being able to assert and pursue its idiosyncrasy despite being hemmed in by normalizing and homogenizing forces.

Once again, we have a semiconscious metaphor of opposing forces—the self-determination of the individual versus the obstructions of various aspects of power. And once again the problem of autonomy is cast as a problem of the relative strength (or perhaps wiliness) of the contending forces.

The Buddhist no-self position dissolves this problem by denying that there is a self that has a single, determinate interest or agenda that it is pursuing. Even the theory that sees the self as socially constructed nonetheless argues that the self is a *something*, albeit a constructed something. The Buddhist position flatly denies this. There is no something that comes to a final and potentially effective decision about how to act, and that thus stands as a moving object opposed to other moving objects and forces. Rather than being an object, what we think of as the self is a space, a forum, in which competing forces, both external and internal, interact. The space or forum itself has no interests or goals. The actions of the human being are ultimately determined by reconciliation of the various forces—the adding together of forces pushing in the same direction, the canceling out of opposing forces, the veering off-course of one force influenced by another, and so on. In essence, this is the same theory of decision-making as that embraced by those who see the self as socially constructed, but without the anxiety. On this view, human beings can act against social forces when the reconciliation of the various forces inclines them in that way. Among the active forces are all the familiar internal ones like memory, consciousness, emotion, intention, knowledge, and so on. The Buddhist point is simply that nothing helpful is added by saying that sometimes the reconciliation of forces is good (autonomous) and sometimes it is bad (heteronomous)—it merely is what it is. If particular outcomes cause either that human being or others to suffer, there will be feedback that will itself become a force in future reconciliations, and perhaps the future behavior of that person will be different. There isn't anything else useful to be said. Thus, if what we mean by autonomy is that the individual human being can sometimes act against some of the external forces that influence it, then human beings do have autonomy. If what we mean is that the human being's actions consistently reflect that person's self, either being an intrinsic essence or a constructed essence, then we do not have autonomy because we do not have such selves. In this way, the Buddhist theory of the self manages to defang what is otherwise an insoluble problem by undermining one of its shaky premises.

The Value of Buddhist Political Theory

On my interpretation, each of these three core ideas—no-self, limited citizenship, and Hypothetical ethics—is interesting and valuable in its own right. But it is the combination of the three, which imply and require each other, that makes up Buddhist political theory and makes it unique. We can uncover this unity however we enter the triangle—if there is a self, then it makes sense to ask whether it is a bearer of rights and duties, which may then find (unique?) expression and development through politics and citizenship; alternatively, if citizenship and political participation are important in their own right, there must be a reason for that intrinsic importance, which seems likely to be rooted in some benefit to the individual conceived not merely as a contingent assemblage of stuff but as an ongoing project of subjectivity and agency, and that normative judgment of value and importance implies a system of moral principles and judgments whose force is Categorical rather than Hypothetical; or, approaching it from a third perspective, if there are realist normative truths, there must be permanent aspects of personal identity for human beings to be the agents/subjects/objects of those truths, and the question of whether the collective lives of such subjects is consistent with those moral truths becomes an urgent matter of concern. In other words, the ideas of the self, normative ethics, and normatively obligatory politics imply and rest on one another in the Western tradition. One of the great benefits of studying Buddhist political theory is to see that triad clearly and to at least consider the possibility of abandoning it wholesale (or at least more seriously examining whether it could be disaggregated). Conversely, Buddhist political theory also reveals that those of us who find the idea of the self problematic, or are attracted to irrealist theories of ethics, or who find the Western emphasis on the importance of politics to be implausible or unattractive (not to mention tedious) are unconsciously also flirting with adopting the other elements of the Buddhist vision. Thus both for the individual elements and for the insight that the three elements are intimately connected, Western theorists cannot afford to ignore Buddhist political thought.

Finally, by way of conclusion, I argue not only that Buddhist political theory remains relevant today (it does), nor merely that it is of ongoing importance for Western-trained political theorists (it is), but also that it is a good political theory, one that deserves serious consideration as a guide to how we should structure our collective lives.

For a political theory to even be a contender for substantive evaluation as good or bad it must meet a handful of threshold criteria. First, it must be *normative*, in the sense that it must rest on (or imply) normative principles that are sufficient both to ground the theory's own judgments and to provide the basis for speculating and drawing inferences about how the theory applies to novel questions or circumstances. Second, it must be *coherent*, in the sense that it must not contradict itself regarding its own major claims or important implications. Third, it must be *comprehensive*, in the sense that it can explain or account for the entire range of human behavior. Fourth, it must be *political*, in the sense that it must be capable of addressing the questions of how people ought to structure the collective aspects of their lives.

Buddhist political theory meets these threshold criteria. It provides appropriate normative principles, though it insists that normative judgments are Hypothetical rather than Categorical, instrumental rather than absolute. It is coherent and comprehensive and is appropriately political. It does not justify only one system of government but provides criteria for distinguishing among systems that are acceptable and systems that are unacceptable, and also for creating a (partial) ranking among acceptable systems.

Whether one thinks that a theory that meets those threshold criteria is good is ultimately a matter of whether it comports with one's other normative beliefs. Buddhism does comport with my other normative beliefs, and thus I believe that it is a good theory (and so should you, since of course my normative beliefs are the correct beliefs). Buddhism is right to hold that moral judgment is Hypothetical rather than Categorical or absolute, and right to conclude that no serious problems arise from recognizing that fact. Further, Buddhism is right in believing that there is no self and that the mistaken belief in the self is the source of many personal and social problems. Finally, Buddhist political theory is right that the goal of life is enlightenment (understood either as transcendence of mundane existence, or, more prosaically, as something very close to the Stoics' *ataraxia*, or life without anxiety). Given that there are no absolute moral obligations, each individual is free to live as he or she pleases. The only thing that each of us can control is our own feelings, our own attitude toward our experience. Thus it makes sense to live to make our experience of our experience as pleasant as possible. It's impossible to make our experience uniformly pleasant or pleasurable, for reasons well articulated by the Buddha above. The best we can hope for is equanimity/*ataraxia*, and Buddhism provides clear and helpful instructions about how to achieve or at least approach that both individually and in terms of how we organize our collective activity.

NOTES

Introduction

1. For an excellent (if now somewhat dated) bibliography of major recent work, see March, "What Is Comparative Political Theory?," 532.

2. I have been able to identify only a handful of works in political science since 1970 that offer a substantive discussion of Buddhist ideas: Barnhart, "An Overlapping Consensus"; Beatty, "Radical Change"; Bell, "Review: The Limits of Liberal Justice"; Black, "The Axial Period"; Fitzgerald, "Gratitude and Justice"; Glass, "The Yogin & the Utopian"; Hartshorne, "Beyond Enlightened Self-Interest"; Kelly and Reid, *Asian Freedoms*; Lipset, *Political Philosophy*; Marty and Appleby, *Fundamentalisms and the State*; McCarthy, *The Political Theory of Tyranny*; Peek, "Buddhism, Human Rights, and the Japanese State"; Pollis, "Cultural Relativism Revisited"; Seery, "Moral Perfectionism and Abortion Politics"; Dallmayr, *Comparative Political Theory*; Žižek, "From Western Marxism to Western Buddhism"; Myint, "Buddhist Political Thought."

3. "I find it most useful to periodize Buddhist history not in relationship to presumed events, institutions or periods within it but to what can be known by modern academic observers, and how. The first or *early* period lasts from the time of the Buddha (whenever that was) to that of Aśoka. Some of Aśoka's inscriptions mention Greek kings, who can be dated with confidence, and so his reign, *c.* 268–239 BC, provides the first really secure historical data we have for Buddhism.... [T]he consensus of scholarship has been to accept the approximate accuracy of the statement in the *Dīpavaṃsa* and *Mahāvaṃsa* ... that the Pali Canon was written down

for the first time in the second half of the first century BC" (Collins, *Nirvana*, 53–54). Bechert, "Sangha, State, Society, 'Nation,'" 85.

4. See Cousins, "The Dating of the Historical Buddha."

5. See Moore, "Political Theory Today."

6. For a helpful discussion of the different activities called political theory, see March, "What Is Comparative Political Theory?," 533–34.

7. Cousins, "The Dating of the Historical Buddha."

8. The *Dhammacakkappavattana Sutta*. See Bodhi, *Connected Discourses*, 56:11, 1843–47.

9. The *locus classicus* of this view is the *Dhamma-niyama Sutta* of the *Anguttara-Nikāya* (III:134); see *Book of the Gradual Sayings*, IV, 264–65.

10. Bodhi, *Connected Discourses*, 22:56, 895–97.

11. This theory is laid out in many places in the early texts. One clear example is the *Mahātaṇhāsankhaya Sutta* (Bodhi, *Middle Length Discourses*, 354–55). For further discussion, see Bodhi, *Middle Length Discourses*, 30–31.

12. On my reading, the early texts are not consistent on the question of freewill. On the one hand, the theory of dependent arising (*paticcasamuppāda*) strongly suggests some version of determinism. On the other hand, there would be no point in the Buddha teaching people unless his teaching might lead them to act differently than they otherwise would have. (And his teaching cannot be perfectly determinative of their future actions or else his initial hesitation to teach would make no sense.) Thus, it seems that people must have freewill, even though the implicit physics and metaphysics of Buddhism suggest that they may not. For an excellent overview of the freewill debate in Buddhist scholarship, see Gowans, *Buddhist Moral Philosophy*.

13. For example, see Rahula, *What the Buddha Taught*; Mitchell, *Buddhism*.

Chapter 1

1. See Bartholomeusz and De Silva, *Buddhist Fundamentalism*; Harris, *Buddhism and Politics in Twentieth-Century Asia*; Tambiah, *Buddhism Betrayed*; Spiro, *Buddhism and Society*; Harris, *Buddhism, Power and Political Order*; Suksamran and Ling, *Political Buddhism in Southeast Asia*; Bartholomeusz, *In Defense of Dharma*; Sarkisyanz, *Buddhist Backgrounds of the Burmese Revolution*; French, *The Golden Yoke*. A good, recent overview of the current role of Buddhism and Buddhists in the national politics of various countries can be found in Friedlander, "Buddhism and Politics." Similarly, a good overview of the role of Buddhism/Buddhists in the postclassical period can be found in Harris, *Buddhism and Politics in Twentieth-Century Asia*. See also Houtart, "Buddhism and Politics in South-East Asia: Part One"; Houtart, "Buddhism and Politics in South-East Asia: Part Two"; Suksamran and Ling, *Political Buddhism in Southeast Asia*.

2. Chakravarti, *The Social Dimensions of Early Buddhism*; Schmithausen, "Aspects of the Buddhist Attitude Towards War."

3. Chakravarti, *The Social Dimensions of Early Buddhism*; Collins, *Selfless Persons*; Collins, *Nirvana*.

4. Tachibana, *The Ethics of Buddhism*; Keown, *Contemporary Buddhist Ethics*; Keown, *The Nature of Buddhist Ethics*; Saddhatissa, *Buddhist Ethics*; Sizemore and Swearer, *Ethics, Wealth, and Salvation*.

5. Hershock, *Buddhism in the Public Sphere*; Edwards, *The Compassionate Revolution*; Jones, *The New Social Face of Buddhism*; McLeod, *Mindful Politics*.

6. Scholars use several different terms to identify the same aspect of Buddhism: what is written in the Pāli Canon (PC), and in some cases in the major commentaries on the PC. Thus Damien Keown calls this "classical Buddhism" (Keown, "Are There Human Rights in Buddhism?," 17.) Heinz Bechert calls this literature "canonical," as does Ilana Silber (Bechert, "Sangha, State, Society, 'Nation' "; Silber, "Dissent through Holiness"). Balkrishna Gokhale calls it "early" Buddhism (Gokhale, "Dhamma as a Political Concept.")

7. "Ancient Buddhism represents in almost all practically decisive points the characteristic polar opposite of Confucianism as well as of Islam. It is a specifically unpolitical and anti-political status religion, more precisely, a religious 'technology' of wandering and of intellectually-schooled mendicant monks" (Weber, *The Religion of India*, 206).

8. Hence: "Certain it was that there was no real *salvation* to be found in the sociohistorical context or in the improvement of its forms. This means that Buddhism on the whole has surveyed political forms with supreme indifference. Or perhaps it might be stated better thus: Buddhism took the monarchical form of secular society that it found in India for granted and was not concerned enough to worry about changing it" (King, *In the Hope of Nibbana*, 177–78).

9. See Macy, "Dependent Co-Arising"; Ling, "Kingship and Nationalism in Pali Buddhism"; Warder, *Indian Buddhism*; Jayasuriya, "Buddhism, Politics, and Statecraft"; Jayatilleke, "Principles of International Law."

10. See King, *In the Hope of Nibbana*.

11. See Macy, "Dependent Co-Arising."

12. See Harris, *Buddhism and Politics in Twentieth-Century Asia*; Spellman, *Political Theory of Ancient India*; Gard, *Buddhist Influences*; Ghoshal, *History of Indian Political Ideas*; Gard, "Buddhism and Political Authority"; Gokhale, "Dhamma as a Political Concept"; Gokhale, "Early Buddhist Kingship"; Gokhale, "The Early Buddhist View of the State"; Tambiah, *The Buddhist Conception of Universal King*.

13. For a discussion of the relevant literature, see Collins, "The Discourse on What Is Primary"; Huxley, "When Manu Met Mahāsammata."

14. Walshe, *Long Discourses*, 409–10.

15. Walshe, *Long Discourses*, 412.

16. Walshe, *Long Discourses*, 413.

17. Walshe, *Long Discourses*, 413.

18. Walshe, *Long Discourses*, 413.

19. Walshe, *Long Discourses*, 414.
20. Bodhi, *Connected Discourses*, 56:11, 1843–47.
21. Coomaraswamy argues that the wheel, the *dhamma cakka*, is related to pre-Buddhist images that represent the revolution of the year, especially the movement of the sun, and that it is intended to represent the totality of existence (Ananda Kentish Coomaraswamy, *The Origin of the Buddha Image*, 25–34). In Buddhist iconography, the wheel more narrowly symbolizes the dhamma—the truth of the world, and/or the truth of the Buddha's teaching.
22. Walshe, *Long Discourses*, 279–90.
23. Walshe, *Long Discourses*, 396–97.
24. Walshe, *Long Discourses*, 397–98.
25. Walshe, *Long Discourses*, 399–400.
26. Walshe, *Long Discourses*, 402.
27. See Obeyesekere, Reynolds, and Smith, *The Two Wheels of Dharma*.
28. See Gokhale, "Early Buddhist Kingship."
29. See Strong, *The Legend of King Aśoka*.
30. Walshe, *Long Discourses*, 231–32.
31. See the Janavasabha Sutta at Walshe, *Long Discourses*, 291–300.
32. Macy, "Dependent Co-Arising."
33. Gokhale, "Early Buddhist Kingship"; Sharma, *Republics in Ancient India: C. 1500 B.C.–500 B.C.*
34. Cowell, *The Jataka*, no. 385, p. 174.
35. Kulatissa Jayatilleke argues that *Jātaka* 432 may permit the use of force to overthrow bad kings (Jayatilleke, "Principles of International Law," 527–28). The relevant passage reads:

> "Let town and country folk assembled all give ear
> Lo! Water is ablaze. From safety cometh fear.
> The plundered realm may well of king and priest complain.
> Henceforth protect yourselves. Your refuge proves your bane."
>
> When they heard what he said, people thought, "The king, though he ought to have protected others, threw the blame on another. After he had with his own hands placed his treasure in the tank, he went about looking for the thief. That he may not in future go on playing the part of a thief, we will kill this wicked king." So they rose up with sticks and clubs in their hands, and then and there beat the king and the priest till they died. But they anointed the Bodhisatta and set him on the throne." (Cowell, *The Jataka*, III:306)

On my reading, this passage is ambiguous. It may justify overthrowing a king because he is a bad ruler, but it may instead justify punishing an exposed thief, even though he happens to be the king.

36. Huxley, "The Buddha and the Social Contract."
37. Collins, "The Lion's Roar."
38. For an example of the explanation of the relationship between the two texts see Harris, *Buddhism and Politics in Twentieth-Century Asia*, 4; quote from Gokhale, "The Early Buddhist View of the State," 736.
39. Gokhale, "Dhamma as a Political Concept," 254. See also Gard, "Buddhism and Political Authority," 45.
40. See Locke, *Second Treatise of Government*, §6.

Chapter 2

1. This chapter is heavily indebted to the work of Stanley Tambiah, Steven Collins, Andrew Huxley, and Richard Gard. In particular, see: Collins, "The Discourse on What Is Primary"; Collins, "The Lion's Roar"; Collins and Huxley, "Post-Canonical Adventures"; Gard, *Buddhist Influences*; Gard, *Buddhist Political Thought; a Bibliography*; Gard, *Buddhist Political Thought; a Study of Buddhism in Society*; Gard, "Buddhism and Political Authority"; Huxley, "How Buddhist"; Huxley, "The Reception of Buddhist Law"; Huxley, "Buddhism and Law"; Huxley, "The Buddha and the Social Contract"; Huxley, *Thai Law, Buddhist Law*; Huxley, "When Manu Met Mahāsammata"; Huxley, "Buddhist Law"; Huxley, "Rajadhamma Confronts Leviathan"; Tambiah, *World Conqueror and World Renouncer*; Tambiah, *The Buddhist Conception of Universal King*; Tambiah, "King Mahāsammata."
2. Collins, *Nirvana*, 53–54; Bechert, "Sangha, State, Society, 'Nation,'" 85.
3. "As far as I know there are no Buddhist traditions, literary or otherwise, of kings being 'democratically' elected, of 'social contract' in the sense propounded by Rousseau, of justifiable 'rebellion' or 'just war' against a king who has broken a social contract" (Tambiah, "King Mahāsammata," 107).
4. This analysis draws from Tambiah, "King Mahāsammata"; Collins and Huxley, "Post-Canonical Adventures"; Gard, "Buddhism and Political Authority"; Gard, *Buddhist Political Thought; a Bibliography*; Gard, *Buddhist Political Thought; a Study of Buddhism in Society*.
5. See Tambiah, "King Mahāsammata," 109.
6. *The Mahāvastu*, I, 293–302.
7. *The Mahāvastu*, I, 225–34.
8. For example, see the discussion between Mahā-Kāśyapa and Mahā-Kātyāyana at *The Mahāvastu*, I, 84 ff.
9. See Tambiah, "King Mahāsammata," 111. The *Saddhamma-pakāsinī*, a sixth-century CE commentary on the canonical *Paṭisambhidā-magga* and attributed to Mahānāma, also identifies Mahāsammata as having been one of the Buddha's prior incarnations. See Collins and Huxley, "Post-Canonical Adventures," 624.
10. Buddhaghosa, *Visuddhimagga*, translated by Bhikkhu Ñāṇamoli, XIII.54, p. 412.

11. See Tambiah, "King Mahāsammata," 112, and Collins and Huxley, "Post-Canonical Adventures." The *Mahāsammatavaṃsa/Rājavaṃsa*, a Burmese text from the sixteenth century, largely reproduces the *Mahāvaṃsa* lineage connecting the Buddha and Mahāsammata. See Collins and Huxley, "Post-Canonical Adventures," 628.

12. *Mahāvaṃsa*, 10.

13. See Geiger's comparison of these two genealogies, as well as that given in the Tibetan *Dulva* (*Mahāvaṃsa*, 273).

14. A later Sri Lankan text (or possibly series of texts), the *Rājāvaliya*, dated by Collins and Huxley to between the fourteenth and nineteenth centuries, also provides a genealogy of early Sri Lankan kings tying them to the Buddha's Sākya clan (and thus to both the Buddha and Mahāsammata). See Collins and Huxley, "Post-Canonical Adventures," 631–32.

15. See Collins and Huxley, "Post-Canonical Adventures," 626.

16. See Tambiah, "King Mahāsammata," 114.

17. King Ruang, *Three Worlds*, 147.

18. Ruang, *Three Worlds*, 148.

19. Ruang, *Three Worlds*, 148.

20. Ruang, *Three Worlds*, 149.

21. Ruang, *Three Worlds*, 149.

22. Ruang, *Three Worlds*, 150.

23. Ruang, *Three Worlds*, 150.

24. Ruang, *Three Worlds*, 324.

25. See Tambiah, "King Mahāsammata," 113, and Collins and Huxley, "Post-Canonical Adventures."

26. Ratanapañña Thera, *The Sheaf of the Garlands*, 31.

27. Tambiah, "King Mahāsammata"; Huxley, "The Reception of Buddhist Law"; Huxley, "The Buddha and the Social Contract"; Huxley, *Thai Law, Buddhist Law*.

28. The title is the translation given by Lozang Jamspal, *The Range of the Bodhisattva*; Jamspal, *The Range of the Bodhisattva*, xv.

29. On the meaning of the term, see Jamspal, *The Range of the Bodhisattva*, 143.

30. Jamspal, *The Range of the Bodhisattva*, 42.

31. Jamspal, *The Range of the Bodhisattva*, 48.

32. Jamspal, *The Range of the Bodhisattva*, 52–53.

33. *Suhṛllekha* is Nagarjuna, *Nagarjuna's Letter to a Friend*; see Gard, "The Saṅgha: Buddhist Society and the Laity."

34. See Halkias, "The Enlightened Sovereign."

35. Asvaghosha, *The Buddha-Karita*.

36. Asvaghosha, *The Buddha-Karita*, ch. II.

37. Aśvaghoṣa, *The Saundarananda*.

38. Aśvaghoṣa, *The Saundarananda*, 3.

39. See Gard, "The Saṅgha: Buddhist Society and the Laity."

40. Āryadeva, "Āryadeva's Four Hundred Stanzas on the Middle Way [Catuḥśataka]," 118 (hereafter "Four Hundred Stanza's").

41. Āryadeva, "Āryadeva's Four Hundred Stanzas," 120.

42. Āryadeva, "Āryadeva's Four Hundred Stanzas," 122.

43. Āryadeva, "Āryadeva's Four Hundred Stanzas," 123.

44. Āryadeva, "Āryadeva's Four Hundred Stanzas," 124.

45. Āryadeva, "Āryadeva's Four Hundred Stanzas," 146.

46. This text is called by more than one name. Gard calls it *Kāruṇikarāja-Prajñāpāramitā-sūtra*; see Gard, "The Saṅgha: Buddhist Society and the Laity." Orzech translates that as *The Prajñāpāramita Sūtra For Humane Kings Who Wish to Protect Their States*; see Orzech, "Puns on the Humane King," 18.

47. For a brief history, see Orzech, "Puns on the Humane King."

48. De Visser, *Ancient Buddhism in Japan*, 132–33.

49. See Gard, "Buddhism and Political Authority," 44.

50. *Golden Light Sutra*, 32.

51. *Golden Light Sutra*, 57–58.

52. *Golden Light Sutra*, 58.

53. See Nichiren, "The Writings of Nichiren Daishonin," Chapter 2.

54. Gard also mentions in passing a number of other Mahāyāna texts that are relevant to politics, though without elaborating. These include: *Rāṣṭrapālaparip ṛcchā (pāla-sūtra)*, Āryaśura's *Jātakamālā*, and Śāntideva's *Śikṣāsamuccaya* and *Bodhicaryāvatāra* (c. eighth century CE) (Gard, "The Saṅgha: Buddhist Society and the Laity"). Specifically in the Japanese tradition, he also mentions Nichiren's *Kai-moku-sho*. Unfortunately, my knowledge of these texts is too limited to allow me to evaluate Gard's suggestion that they are in some sense political.

55. See *Mahāvaṃsa*, appendix A.

56. See also Bechert, "Aspects of Theravāda Buddhism," 21–23.

Chapter 3

1. Regarding the response to colonialism, see Harris, *Buddhism and Politics in Twentieth-Century Asia*, 15–17.

2. "Moreover the form of kingship envisioned in canonical and later legal sources, as we have now had ample cause to note, no longer seems to match the constitutional arrangements currently operative in Southeast Asia's two remaining Theravada monarchies, Cambodia and Thailand" (Harris, "Something Rotten," 227).

3. Bechert, "Aspects of Theravāda Buddhism"; Bechert, "S.W.R.D. Bandaranaike"; Sarkisyanz, "Buddhist Background of Burmese Socialism." Collins points out that "Buddhist modernism" as a concept was coined by Alexandra David-Neel in 1911 (Collins, *Nirvana*, 55, n.72).

4. Bechert, "Aspects of Theravāda Buddhism," 25.

5. Bechert, "Sangha, State, Society, 'Nation,'" 91, internal citation omitted.

6. "The ideals of democracy were searched for and found by the modernists within Buddhist tradition, e.g., in the structure of the early Buddhist *Sangha*" (Bechert, "S.W.R.D. Bandaranaike").

7. Sarkisyanz, "Buddhist Background of Burmese Socialism," 94.

8. Smith, *Religion and Political Development*, 10–11.

9. Macy, "Dependent Co-Arising"; Ling, "Kingship and Nationalism in Pali Buddhism"; Jayasuriya, "Buddhism, Politics, and Statecraft"; Jayatilleke, "Principles of International Law"; Ratnapala, *Buddhist Democratic Political Theory and Practice*; Warder, *Indian Buddhism*.

10. Smith, *Religion and Political Development*, 198.

11. Smith, *Religion and Political Development*, 226.

12. Gard, "Buddhism and Political Authority," 66–67.

13. Kyi, *Freedom from Fear*, 173.

14. *Book of the Gradual Sayings*, I, 170–75.

15. Gyatso, "Buddhism and Democracy," n.p.

16. See, for example, the rise of "engaged Buddhism"; Queen and King, *Engaged Buddhism*.

17. See Thiên Dô, "The Quest for Enlightenment," and "Buddhism and Secular Power in Twentieth-Century Korea"; on Korea see Sørensen, "Buddhism and Secular Power in Twentieth-Century Korea."

18. See Kawanami, "Japanese Nationalism and the Universal *Dharma*"; Pardue, *Buddhism*, ch. 5; Borchert, "Buddhism, Politics, and Nationalism."

19. For good overviews and an introduction to the literature, see Harris, *Buddhism, Power and Political Order*; Harris, *Buddhism and Politics in Twentieth-Century Asia*.

20. On Buddhism and politics in Bhutan, see Mathou, "Political Reform in Bhutan"; Gallenkamp, *Democracy in Bhutan*; Wangchuk, "The Middle Path"; Aris, *The Raven Crown*; Mathou, "How to Reform a Traditional Buddhist Monarchy."

21. Aris, *Raven Crown*, 96.

22. "The Constitution of the Kingdom of Bhutan."

23. See the transcripts at http://www.constitution.bt/html/making/speeches.htm. But see also:

> Among the laity, my main informants, the emphasis was on a vocabulary of moral conduct with their legal cases treated as removed directly from religious values. Yet, when I suggested to Bhutanese that Buddhism was not important to the emerging laws and legal system, this was vigorously denied and I was informed that Buddhism was at the core of the laws. Examining the emergence of the modern legal system and laws passed by the National Assembly established in 1953, it is clear that from the 1950s to 1980s as the state sought to develop the country, laws were mainly imported. In the following period, from approximately 1991 onwards, there has been a conscious engagement by the judiciary and the emerging cadre of legally educated

lawyers to integrate the laws with a broader understanding of Bhutanese values. The core of these values, often referred to as "Bhutanese culture," lie in Buddhism. (Whitecross, "Separation of Religion and Law," 708)

24. Mathou, "Political Reform in Bhutan," 617.

25. Mathou, "Political Reform in Bhutan," 613, n.2.

26. Mathou, "How to Reform a Traditional Buddhist Monarchy," 7.

27. On the relationship between Buddhism and government in Burma, especially in the modern period, see Smith, *Religion, Politics, and Social Change in the Third World*; Harris, "Something Rotten"; Huxley, "Rajadhamma Confronts Leviathan"; Matthews, "The Legacy of Tradition and Authority"; Sarkisyanz, "Buddhist Background of Burmese Socialism"; Sarkisyanz, *Buddhist Backgrounds of the Burmese Revolution*.

28. The translation is from Harris, "Something Rotten," 221.

29. The translation is from Harris, "Something Rotten," 221.

30. See Huxley, "Rajadhamma Confronts Leviathan," 27.

31. Sarkisyanz, *Buddhist Backgrounds of the Burmese Revolution*.

32. On Buddhism and politics in modern Cambodia, see Suksamran, *Buddhism and Political Legitimacy*; Gyallay-Pap, "Reconstructing the Cambodian Polity"; Harris, "Something Rotten."

33. See Gyallay-Pap, "Reconstructing the Cambodian Polity," esp. 81–82.

34. Gyallay-Pap, "Reconstructing the Cambodian Polity"; Suksamran, "Buddhism, Political Authority, and Legitimacy."

35. See Harris, "Something Rotten."

36. Suksamran, "Buddhism, Political Authority, and Legitimacy," 137.

37. On Buddhism and politics in Laos, see Stuart-Fox, "Laos"; Stuart-Fox, "Marxism and Theravada Buddhism"; Grabowsky, "Buddhism, Power and Political Order in Pre-Twentieth Century Laos"; Suksamran, *Buddhism and Political Legitimacy*.

38. Stuart-Fox, "Laos"; Stuart-Fox, "Marxism and Theravada Buddhism"; Suksamran, *Buddhism and Political Legitimacy*.

39. "Constitution of the Kingdom of Laos."

40. Stuart-Fox, "Laos," 154.

41. Suksamran, *Buddhism and Political Legitimacy*, 83–84.

42. On Buddhism and politics in Sri Lanka, see Bechert, "Sangha, State, Society, "Nation,'"; Bechert, "S.W.R.D. Bandaranaike"; Bechert, "Aspects of Theravāda Buddhism"; Smith, *Religion and Legitimation of Power in Sri Lanka*; Tambiah, *World Conqueror and World Renouncer*.

43. Bechert, "S.W.R.D. Bandaranaike," 201.

44. Hence: "In my view some of the major issues relating to the religious pursuit and political action in both early and historical Buddhism are incapable of unambiguous and clear resolutions; rather, the text themselves portray dialectical tensions, polarities and complementarities, in the treatment of basic issues" (Tambiah, *World Conqueror and World Renouncer*, 402).

45. Tambiah, *Buddhism Betrayed?*, 5–7.
46. On the relationship between Buddhism and politics in Thailand, see Tambiah, *World Conqueror and World Renouncer*; Swearer, "Centre and Periphery"; Harris, "Something Rotten"; Reynolds, "Sacral Kingship and National Development"; Keyes, "Buddhist Politics"; Suksamran, "Buddhism, Political Authority, and Legitimacy."
47. See Chakrabongse, *Lords of Life*, 260–63.
48. See Keyes, "Buddhist Politics."
49. Chakrabongse, *Lords of Life*, 289–90.
50. Chakrabongse, *Lords of Life*, 276.
51. Chakrabongse, *Lords of Life*, 309–14.
52. Keyes, "Buddhist Politics."
53. See Chakrabongse, *Lords of Life*.
54. On the relationship between Buddhism and politics in Tibet, see Harris, "Something Rotten," 232; Gyatso, *My Land and My People*, 231; Gyatso, "Buddhism, Asian Values, and Democracy," 4; Harris, *Buddhism and Politics in Twentieth-Century Asia*, 11 ff. Schwartz, "Renewal and Resistance"; Gyatso, "Buddhism and Democracy," n.p.
55. Gyatso, "Buddhism, Asian Values, and Democracy," 4.
56. Gyatso, *My Land and My People*, 231.

Chapter 4

1. See Martin and Barresi, *Personal Identity*.
2. One instance of this frequently repeated teaching is SN 22:45 in Bodhi, *Connected Discourses*, 884–85.
3. See Rahula, *What the Buddha Taught*; Mitchell, *Buddhism: Introducing the Buddhist Experience*.
4. For two contemporary, thorough explications of this view, see Albahari, "Against No-*Ātman* Theories of *Anattā*"; Pérez Remón, *Self and Non-Self in Early Buddhism*. For a critical overview of earlier literature, see the introduction to Collins, *Selfless Persons*.
5. Bodhi, *Connected Discourses*, 22:59, 901–02.
6. Bodhi, *Connected Discourses*, 22:56, 895–97.
7. This analysis is influenced by Collins, *Selfless Persons*.
8. Bodhi, *Connected Discourses*, 901.
9. Bodhi, *Connected Discourses*, 902.
10. Bodhi, *Connected Discourses*, 902.
11. Bodhi, *Middle Length Discourses*, Alagaddūpama Sutta; MN 22; 232–33.
12. Bodhi, *Connected Discourses*, 22:89, 943.
13. Bodhi, *Connected Discourses*, 22:89, 945.
14. Bodhi, *Connected Discourses*, 22:89, 945.
15. Bodhi, *Middle Length Discourses*, 137–38.

16. Bodhi, *Middle Length Discourses*, Alagaddūpama Sutta; MN 22:23, 231.
17. In the work published by Nietzsche:
    Nietzsche, *Human, All Too Human*, §II, 366, p. 294.
    Nietzsche, *Daybreak*, §105, p. 06, §09, p. 10.
    Nietzsche, *Gay Science*, §290, p. 32.
    Nietzsche, *Zarathustra*, §I:4, pp. 61–62.
    Nietzsche, *Beyond Good and Evil*, §12, pp. 43–44, §16, p. 46, §17, p. 47, §19, p. 49, §34, p. 66, §54, p. 81.
    Nietzsche, *Genealogy*, §I:13, p. 28.
    Nietzsche, *The Anti-Christ*, TI III:5, p. 169; VI:3, p. 78.
    Because I cannot claim to have mastered all the unpublished materials, I cite here the places in the *Will to* Power where Nietzsche discusses these issues, as well as other unpublished comments of which I am aware.
    Nietzsche, *Will to Power*, §229, p. 132, §259, pp. 149–50, §370–71, pp. 199–200, §476–93, pp. 263–72, §517–19, pp. 280–81, §531, pp. 288–89, §547–56, pp. 294–302, §561, p. 303, §569, p. 307, §631–32, pp. 336–37, §635, p. 338, §660, p. 348–49, §966, pp. 506–07.
    Schlechta, *Nietzsches Werke in Drei Bände*, 487–88, 540–41.
    Nietzsche, Colli, and Montinari, *Sämtliche Werke*, 9:6[70].
18. Note that this list contains only work that discusses Nietzsche's views on the self at some length. A number of other sources mention the issue in passing: Booth, "Nietzsche on 'the Subject as Multiplicity'"; Cox, "The 'Subject' of Nietzsche's Perspectivism"; Davey, "Nietzsche and Hume"; Davey, "Nietzsche, the Self, and Hermeneutic Theory"; Kirkland, "Nietzsche's Honest Masks"; Fennell, "Nietzsche Contra 'Self-Reformulation'"; Gemes, "Postmodernism's Use and Abuse of Nietzsche"; S Hales, "Recent Work on Nietzsche"; Hales and Welshon, *Nietzsche's Perspectivism*; Hanson, "Searching for the Power-I"; Loy, "Beyond Good and Evil?"; Morrison, *Nietzsche and Buddhism*; Morrison, "Response to Graham Parkes' Review"; Parkes, "Nietzsche and Early Buddhism"; Parkes, "Nietzsche and Nishitani"; Parkes, "Nietzsche and Zen Master Hakuin"; Poole, "Nietzsche: The Subject of Morality"; Schmitt, "Nietzsche's Psychological Theory"; Parkes, "The Overflowing Soul"; Strong, "Texts and Pretexts"; Welshon, "Nietzsche's Peculiar Virtues and the Health of the Soul"; Zuckert, "Nature, History and Self"; Sokoloff, "Nietzsche's Radicalization of Kant"; Conway, "The Birth of the Soul"; Nehemas, "'How One Becomes What One Is'"; Haar, "La Critique Nietzscheenne De La Subjectivite"; Mistry, *Nietzsche and Buddhism*; Janaway, *Self and World in Schopenhauer's Philosophy*; Steinhart, *On Nietzsche*; Janaway, *Beyond Selflessness*, 213–22; Staten, *Nietzsche's Voice*; Hales, "Recent Work on Nietzsche"; Thiele, *Friedrich Nietzsche and the Politics of the Soul*; Stack, *Lange and Nietzsche*; Corngold, "The Question of the Self"; Richardson, *Nietzsche's System*; Nehemas, *Nietzsche: Life as Literature*.
19. Nietzsche, *Genealogy*, §I:13, p. 28.
20. Nietzsche, *Beyond Good and Evil*, §12, p. 43.

21. Nietzsche, *Zarathustra*, §I:4, p. 61.
22. Nietzsche, *Beyond Good and Evil*, §12, pp. 43–44.
23. Nietzsche, *Beyond Good and Evil*, §19, p. 49.
24. Nietzsche, *Will to Power*, §259, p. 149.
25. Nietzsche, *Will to Power*, §490, p. 270.
26. Nietzsche, *Will to Power*, §492, p. 271.
27. Fennell, "Nietzsche Contra 'Self-Reformulation'"; Janaway, "Nietzsche, the Self, and Schopenhauer," 137; Janaway, *Beyond Selflessness*; Booth, "Nietzsche on 'the Subject as Multiplicity'"; Staten, *Nietzsche's Voice*.
28. Hales and Welshon, *Nietzsche's Perspectivism*.
29. Hales and Welshon, *Nietzsche's Perspectivism*, 181.
30. Miller, "The Disarticulation of the Self in Nietzsche"; Strong, "Texts and Pretexts."
31. Miller, "The Disarticulation of the Self in Nietzsche," 260.
32. See Parkes, "The Overflowing Soul"; Parkes, *Composing the Soul*; Parkes, "Nietzsche and Zen Master Hakuin"; Parkes, "Nietzsche and Early Buddhism"; Parkes, "Reply to Robert Morrison." See also van der Braak, *Nietzsche and Zen*.
33. Parkes, "Nietzsche and Early Buddhism," 264.
34. Morrison, "Response to Graham Parkes' Review."
35. Morrison, "Response to Graham Parkes' Review."
36. Gemes, "Postmodernism's Use and Abuse of Nietzsche," 344–45.
37. Thiele, *Friedrich Nietzsche and the Politics of the Soul*, especially 91; Nehemas, *Nietzsche: Life as Literature*, ch. 6.
38. Davis, "Zen after Zarathustra."
39. This is the view of Masao Abe and William R. LaFleur, *Zen and Western Thought*; Davey, "Nietzsche and Hume"; Davey, "Nietzsche, the Self, and Hermeneutic Theory"; Davis, "Zen after Zarathustra"; Gemes, "Postmodernism's Use and Abuse of Nietzsche"; Hanson, "Searching for the Power-I"; Loy, "Beyond Good and Evil? A Buddhist Critique of Nietzsche"; Mistry, *Nietzsche and Buddhism*; Morrison, *Nietzsche and Buddhism*; Morrison, "Response to Graham Parkes' Review"; Schmitt, "Nietzsche's Psychological Theory"; Zuckert, "Nature, History and Self"; Hales and Welshon, *Nietzsche's Perspectivism*; Thiele, *Friedrich Nietzsche and the Politics of the Soul*; Nehemas, *Nietzsche: Life as Literature*.
40. Davey, "Nietzsche and Hume," 24.
41. Hales and Welshon, *Nietzsche's Perspectivism*, 174.
42. Hales and Welshon, *Nietzsche's Perspectivism*, 182; internal citation omitted.
43. Abe and LaFleur, *Zen and Western Thought*; Gemes, "Postmodernism's Use and Abuse of Nietzsche"; Hanson, "Searching for the Power-I"; Loy, "Beyond Good and Evil? A Buddhist Critique of Nietzsche"; Mistry, *Nietzsche and Buddhism*; Morrison, *Nietzsche and Buddhism*; Morrison, "Response to Graham Parkes' Review"; Schmitt, "Nietzsche's Psychological Theory"; Zuckert, "Nature, History and Self"; Thiele, *Friedrich Nietzsche and the Politics of the Soul*; Nehemas, *Nietzsche: Life as Literature*.

44. "We feel ourselves to be effective subject-identities because in this form we experience our greatest sense of unified power. The subject-feeling is essentially an assertive act, the result of our organic being as multiplicity of drives asserting itself against other power centres or subjects" (Davey, "Nietzsche and Hume," 23).

45. See Gemes, "Postmodernism's Use and Abuse of Nietzsche," especially 339; "Nietzsche seeks a solution to the crisis of modern life in the individual or 'self,' but not as that individual presently exists. The individual as he exists is, in all his particularity, the product of accident, history over which he himself had no control. There is no meaning or reason for his particular existence in these external causes. Only he himself can give these accidents meaning by finding a way of living which justifies the past" (Zuckert, "Nature, History and Self," 70; internal citation omitted).

46. Hanson, "Searching for the Power-I."

47. "Nietzsche ends up celebrating an impossible ideal, the heroic-ego which overcomes its sense of lack, because he does not see that a heroic ego is our fantasy project for overcoming lack" (Loy, "Beyond Good and Evil? A Buddhist Critique of Nietzsche," n.p.). Also: "What he considered the crown of his system-eternal recurrence-is actually its denouement. Having seen through the delusion of Being, Nietzsche could not let it go completely, for he still sought a Being within Becoming" (Loy, "Beyond Good and Evil? A Buddhist Critique of Nietzsche," n.p.).

48. Davis, "Zen after Zarathustra."

49. Nietzsche, *Gay Science*, §290, p. 32.

50. This group includes Parkes, van der Braak, Mistry, Hales and Welshon, and Morrison (all cited elsewhere).

51. There is a small comparative literature on Nietzsche and Buddhism: Amadae, "Nietzsche's Thirst for India"; Conche, "Nietzsche Et Le Bouddhisme"; Dumoulin, "Buddhism and Nineteenth-Century German Philosophy"; Elman, "Nietzsche and Buddhism"; Hare, "Nietzsche's Critique of Buddhism"; Rudolph, "Nietzsche's Buddhism"; Frazier, "A European Buddhism"; Davis, "Zen after Zarathustra"; Hales, "Recent Work on Nietzsche"; Hales and Welshon, *Nietzsche's Perspectivism*; Hanson, "Searching for the Power-I"; Loy, "Beyond Good and Evil? A Buddhist Critique of Nietzsche"; Morrison, *Nietzsche and Buddhism*; Morrison, "Response to Graham Parkes' Review"; Parkes, "Nietzsche and Early Buddhism"; Parkes, "Nietzsche and Nishitani"; Parkes, "Nietzsche and Zen Master Hakuin"; Bazzano, "Buddha Is Dead"; Abe and LaFleur, *Zen and Western Thought*; Mistry, *Nietzsche and Buddhism*; Parkes, *Nietzsche and Asian Thought*; Hales and Welshon, *Nietzsche's Perspectivism*; Welbon, *The Buddhist Nirvana and Its Western Interpreters*.

52. Davis, "Zen after Zarathustra," 112.

53. On my reading, Nietzsche believes that "reality" is merely a more foundational story about the world, with no better claim to being True. See Friedrich Nietzsche, "On Truth and Lies."

54. See Nietzsche, *Zarathustra*, 54–56.

55. The passage quoted is from the *Sakkapañha Sutta* (DN 21), reproduced in Bodhi, *In the Buddha's Words*, 35–36.

56. Bodhi, *In the Buddha's Words*, n.p. n.14.

57. Bodhi, *Connected Discourses*, 22:102, 961.

58. Walshe, *Long Discourses*, 395–405.

59. Nietzsche, *Zarathustra*, 257–86.

60. Nietzsche, *Genealogy*, 49.

61. Nietzsche, *Genealogy*, 22.

Chapter 5

1. Bodhi, *Connected Discourses*, 4:20, 209–10.

2. Bodhi, *Connected Discourses*, 41:10, 1330.

3. Weber, *The Religion of India*, 206.

4. Thoreau, *Political Writings*, 9.

5. See Brown, "Politics and Society"; Brown, "False Idles"; Roskam, *Live Unnoticed*; Joly, *Le Thème Philosophique Des Genres De Vie Dans L'antiquité Classique*.

6. Roskam, *Live Unnoticed*; Brown, "False Idles"; Brown, "Politics and Society."

7. See Villa, *Socratic Citizenship*.

8. Plato, *The Collected Dialogues of Plato*, Apology, 32c-d.

9. See Schofield, "Epicurean and Stoic Political Thought."

10. See Kotkin, *Uncivil Society*, 8; see Shils, "The Virtue of Civil Society."

11. *The Dhammapada*, 61.

12. Walshe, *Long Discourses*, 260–62.

13. Bodhi, *Connected Discourses*, 4:20, 209–10.

14. Bodhi, *Connected Discourses*, 41:10, 1330.

15. *The Book of the Discipline*, II, 375.

16. *The Book of the Discipline*, II, 377.

17. *The Book of the Discipline*, II, 380.

18. Bodhi, *Connected Discourses*, 1843.

19. *The Book of the Discipline*, IV, 92–95.

20. Walshe, *Long Discourses*, 231–32.

21. Cowell, *Arythe Jataka*, 91–98.

22. On Socrates, see Brown, "False Idles."

23. Plato, *The Collected Dialogues of Plato*, Crito 50a–53a.

24. Plato, *The Collected Dialogues of Plato*, Apology 28d–e.

25. Plato, *The Collected Dialogues of Plato*, Apology 31d.

26. Joly argues that although there is an older tradition of identifying types of lives (active, contemplative, hedonistic), Epicureanism represents a novel combination

of attitudes (hedonism married to asceticism, and contemplation turned to the end of practical morality). See Joly, *Le Thème Philosophique Des Genres De Vie Dans L'antiquité Classique*, 142–43; Roskam, *Live Unnoticed*, 27–28; Brown, "False Idles."

27. See Joly, *Le Thème Philosophique Des Genres De Vie Dans L'antiquité Classique*, 141.

28. See Farrington, *The Faith of Epicurus*, especially 77ff. For a scathing criticism of this reading, see Aalders, *Political Thought*, 44.

29. See Schofield, "Epicurean and Stoic Political Thought"; Brown, "Politics and Society"; Brown, "False Idles"; Aalders, *Political Thought*; Roskam, *Live Unnoticed*.

30. See Schofield, "Epicurean and Stoic Political Thought."

31. See: Schofield, "Epicurean and Stoic Political Thought," esp. 441–42.

32. See Schofield, "Epicurean and Stoic Political Thought"; Brown, "Politics and Society."

33. Aalders, *Political Thought*, 41.

34. See Schofield, "Epicurean and Stoic Political Thought," 440.

35. See Brown, "Politics and Society," 179.

36. Brown, "Politics and Society"; Brown, "False Idles"; Schofield, "Epicurean and Stoic Political Thought," esp. 442–43.

37. Roskam, *Live Unnoticed*, esp. 147–48.

38. Brown, "Politics and Society," 181.

39. Although many readers have detected affinities between Thoreau and Buddhism, there is very little evidence that Buddhism directly affected Thoreau's thought. See Scott, "Rewalking Thoreau and Asia." My thanks to Jonathan McKenzie for his generous help in educating me about Thoreau's political views and the critical literature about them.

40. Thoreau, *Political Writings*, 119–20.

41. There is a long history of interpretation of Thoreau's views on politics. For a critical reading of the literature up to the 1970s see Meyer, *Several More Lives to Live*; Simon, "Thoreau and Anarchism." Within the world of political theory, Thoreau scholarship was rejuvenated in the 1980s due to two articles: Nancy L. Rosenblum, "Thoreau's Militant Conscience," and George Kateb, "Democratic Individuality and the Claims of Politics." I focus on the scholarship that informed those comparatively recent works and the later scholarship that responds to them.

42. Arendt, *Crises of the Republic*, esp. 60; Wagner, "Lucky Fox at Walden"; Simon, "Thoreau and Anarchism."

43. Buranelli, "The Case against Thoreau"; Buranelli, "The Verdict on Thoreau"; Eulau, "Wayside Challenger"; Diggins, "Thoreau, Marx, and the 'Riddle' of Alienation"; Ketcham, "Some Thoughts on Buranelli's Case against Thoreau"; Drinnon, "Thoreau and John Brown," 157; Nichols, "Thoreau on the Citizen and His Government," 24.

44. Emerson, "Eulogy [for Henry David Thoreau] May 9, 1862," n.p.

45. Nelson, "Thoreau and John Brown," 144; Fergenson, "Thoreau, Daniel Berrigan," 104.

46. Abbott, "Henry David Thoreau."

47. Cavell, *The Senses of Walden*, 85–86, 88; Lauter, "Thoreau's Prophetic Testimony"; Marshall, "Freedom through Critique," 395; Shulman, "Thoreau, Prophecy, and Politics"; Taylor, *America's Bachelor Uncle*; Turner, *A Political Companion to Henry David Thoreau*; Turner, "Performing Conscience"; Walker, "Thoreau on Democratic Cultivation"; Wilson Carey McWilliams, *The Idea of Fraternity in America*.

48. Villa, *Socratic Citizenship*, 54; Gougeon, "Thoreau and Reform"; Hyde, "Henry Thoreau, John Brown, and the Problem of Prophetic Action."

49. Mariotti, *Thoreau's Democratic Withdrawal*; Neufeldt, "Henry David Thoreau's Political Economy"; Worley, *Emerson, Thoreau, and the Role of the Cultural Critic*.

50. Jenco, "Thoreau's Critique of Democracy," 73.

51. Marx, *The Machine in the Garden*, 246.

52. Hodder, *Thoreau's Ecstatic Witness*; Robinson, *Natural Life*; Cafaro, *Thoreau's Living Ethics*; Kritzberg, "Thoreau, Slavery, and Resistance."

53. Lane, "Standing 'Aloof' from the State."

54. McKenzie, "How to Mind Your Own Business," 426–27.

55. Thoreau, *Political Writings*, 135.

56. McKenzie, "How to Mind Your Own Business," 430.

57. Relevant works are "Democratic Individuality and the Claims of Politics"; "Democratic Individuality and the Meaning of Rights"; *The Inner Ocean*; and, *Patriotism and Other Mistakes*, all by Kateb.

58. Kateb, *The Inner Ocean*, 88.

59. Kateb, *Patriotism and Other Mistakes*, 254.

60. Thoreau, *Political Writings*, 17.

61. Kateb, "Democratic Individuality and the Meaning of Rights," 194.

62. Bennett, *Thoreau's Nature*, 2.

63. Bennett, *Thoreau's Nature*, 5.

64. Bennett, *Thoreau's Nature*, 10.

65. Relevant works are Rosenblum, *Another Liberalism*; "Thoreau's Militant Conscience"; "Thoreau's Democratic Individualism"; and *Liberalism and the Moral Life*; Thoreau, *Political Writings*. Rosenblum, "Thoreau's Democratic Individualism," 15.

66. Rosenblum, "Thoreau's Democratic Individualism," 30.

67. Rosenblum, "Thoreau's Militant Conscience," 84.

68. Kateb, *Patriotism and Other Mistakes*, 254. See also Jenco, "Thoreau's Critique of Democracy," 85.

69. Kateb, *Patriotism and Other Mistakes*, 252.

70. For an overview of Yoder's treatment of this issue, see Weaver, "After Politics."

71. Yoder, *The Politics of Jesus*, 111.

72. See Weaver, "After Politics."

73. Yoder, *Discipleship as Political Responsibility*, 18.

74. Yoder, *Discipleship as Political Responsibility*, 35.

75. Yoder, *The Politics of Jesus*, 147.

76. Yoder, *The Politics of Jesus*.

77. Yoder, *The Christian Witness to the State*, 13.

78. Yoder, *The Politics of Jesus*, 154.

79. Yoder, *The Christian Witness to the State*, 26–27.

80. Major secondary literature on Yoder: Weaver, "After Politics"; Kroeker, "Is a Messianic Political Ethic Possible?"; Wright, *Disavowing Constantine*; Hauerwas et al., *The Wisdom of the Cross*; Nugent, *The Politics of Yahweh*; Nation, *John Howard Yoder*; Zimmerman, *Practicing the Politics of Jesus*; Ollenburger, *A Mind Patient and Untamed*; Doerksen, *Beyond Suspicion*; Dula and Huebner, *The New Yoder*; Doerksen and Koop, *The Church Made Strange*; Carter, *Politics of the Cross*; Dorrien, *Social Ethics*; Scriven, *The Transformation of Culture*; Bergen and Siegrist, *Power and Practices*. Secondary literature within political theory that includes serious discussion of Yoder: Coles, *Beyond Gated Politics*; Coles, "Wild Patience"; Heilke, "On Being Ethical."

81. Plutarch, "Reply to Colotes," p. 309, 1127a.

82. Schofield, "Epicurean and Stoic Political Thought," 442–43; internal citation omitted.

83. Žižek, "From Western Marxism to Western Buddhism," n.p.

84. For an argument that no such commensuration is possible even in principle, see Moore, "Pluralism, Relativism, and Liberalism."

85. See Moore, "Pluralism, Relativism, and Liberalism"; Moore, "Wittgenstein, Value Pluralism, and Politics"; Moore, "Immanence, Pluralism, and Politics."

86. Thoreau, *Political Writings*, 14.

Chapter 6

1. For a recent overview of the state of the debate, see Nuccetelli and Seay, *Ethical Naturalism: Current Debates*.

2. For an excellent overview of the literature, see Gowans, *Buddhist Moral Philosophy*.

3. For consequentialist readings, see Goodman, *Consequences of Compassion*; Siderits, "Buddhist Reductionism." For virtue ethics readings, see Keown, *The Nature of Buddhist Ethics*; Keown, *Buddhist Ethics*; Whitehill, "Buddhism and the Virtues"; Whitehill, "Buddhist Ethics in Western Context." For one effort to link Buddhist ethics to Kantian deontology, see Berman, "Metaphysics of Morality."

4. See Keown, *The Nature of Buddhist Ethics*; Keown, *Buddhist Ethics*; Spiro, *Buddhism and Society*; King, *In the Hope of Nibbana*; Bastow, "Buddhist Ethics."

5. See Goodman, *Consequences of Compassion*; Harvey, *An Introduction to Buddhist Ethics*; Jayatilleke, *Ethics in Buddhist Perspective*; Kalupahana, *Ethics in Early Buddhism*; Keown, *Contemporary Buddhist Ethics*; Keown, *The Nature of Buddhist*

Ethics; Keown, *Buddhist Ethics*; King, *In the Hope of Nibbana*; Premasiri, "Moral Evaluation in Early Buddhism"; Siderits, "Buddhist Reductionism"; Spiro, *Buddhism and Society*; Tachibana, *The Ethics of Buddhism*; Whitehill, "Buddhist Ethics in Western Context: The Virtues Approach"; Whitehill, "Buddhism and the Virtues."

6. Two recent, excellent sources on the debate over this issue are Gowans, *Buddhist Moral Philosophy*, and Davis, "Moral Realism and Anti-Realism."

7. The early texts do refer to a being called Yama, who is the Vedic judge of the underworld, and whose minions inflict punishment on the wicked. However, Yama is generally treated in early Buddhism as a poetic fiction—a personification of *kamma*, rather than a real being.

8. See Harvey, *An Introduction to Buddhist Ethics*, 16–17.

9. Harvey, *An Introduction to Buddhist Ethics*, 17.

10. Harvey, *An Introduction to Buddhist Ethics*, 59.

11. Harvey, *An Introduction to Buddhist Ethics*, 51.

12. Harvey, *An Introduction to Buddhist Ethics*, 51.

13. Keown, *The Nature of Buddhist Ethics*, 231.

14. Keown, *Buddhist Ethics*, 289–93.

15. Keown, *Buddhist Ethics*, 621–26.

16. Keown, *Buddhist Ethics*, 696–703.

17. Premasiri, "Moral Evaluation in Early Buddhism," 42.

18. Tachibana, *The Ethics of Buddhism*, 53.

19. Tachibana, *The Ethics of Buddhism*, 55.

20. Fronsdal, *The Issue at Hand*, 37.

21. Goldstein and Kornfield, *Seeking the Heart of Wisdom*, 8–9.

22. Goonatilake, "Women and Family in Buddhism," 235. I became aware of this quote from Florida, "Buddhism and Abortion," 139.

23. Jayatilleke, "Principles of International Law," 483. Elsewhere Jayatilleke appears to offer a categorical reading: "So the ethical theory of Buddhism is one of ethical universalism, which recognises the relativity of and the subjective reactions regarding moral values without denying their objectivity to be measured in terms of the motives with which the acts are done as well as their psychological, social and karmic consequences. It is teleological rather than deontological in character" (Jayatilleke, *Aspects of Buddhist Social Philosophy*, 31).

24. Their readings have been extensively assessed and criticized by Keown, *The Nature of Buddhist Ethics*.

25. Spiro, *Buddhism and Society*, 47.

26. King, *In the Hope of Nibbana*, 38.

27. "It must be said in the beginning that the problem of absolute and relative value in Buddhist ethics is no simple one. For there are strong currents of both relativism and absolutism to be found here, and their intermingling and transposition make their relationship a complex matter. Sometimes one is persuaded

that all is relativistic, especially in the Kamma-rebirth context. But again, as we have seen, there is in Theravada Buddhism at least, a strong sense that even the basic Five Precepts are absolute moral laws of the universe.... And finally we must mention again the ethic-transcending flavor of Nibbana, with an absolutism of its own, that pervades the total situation" (King, *In the Hope of Nibbana*, 70).

28. King, *In the Hope of Nibbana*, 140.

29. Bastow, "Buddhist Ethics," 205–06.

30. Kalupahana, *Ethics in Early Buddhism*, 43.

31. Kalupahana, *Ethics in Early Buddhism*, 45.

32. Goodman, *Consequences of Compassion*, 52.

33. "In every system of morality, which I have hitherto met with, I have always remark'd, that the author proceeds for some time in the ordinary way of reasoning, and establishes the being of a God, or makes observations concerning human affairs; when of a sudden I am supriz'd to find, that instead of the usual copulations of propositions, *is*, and *is not*, I meet with no proposition that is not connected with an *ought*, or an *ought not*. This change is imperceptible; but is, however, of the last consequence. For as this *ought*, or *ought not*, expresses some new relation or affirmation, 'tis necessary that it shou'd be observ'd and explain'd; and at the same time that a reason shou'd be given, for what seems altogether inconceivable, how this new relation can be a deduction from others, which are entirely different from it" (Hume, *A Treatise of Human Nature*, 302); see Moore, *Principia Ethica*. Keown recognizes this potential problem: "a critic may point out that in teaching that Dharma denotes both what *is* and what *ought to be*, Buddhism seems to commit what ethicists in the West call the 'naturalist fallacy' of deducing an 'ought' from an 'is'" (Keown, *Buddhist Ethics: A Very Short Introduction*, 709–13).

34. For a helpful recent overview of the state of the debate between naturalist and nonnaturalist theories of ethics, see Nuccetelli and Seay, *Ethical Naturalism*.

35. See Moore, "Immanence, Pluralism, and Politics."

36. See Sextus Empiricus, *Selections from the Major Writings on Scepticism, Man, & God*.

37. Connolly, *Capitalism and Christianity*, 79.

38. "Of course an immanent naturalist does not anchor morality in transcendent commands or universal laws generated by a consummate subject" (Wenman, "Agonism, Pluralism, and Contemporary Capitalism," 213).

39. Connolly, *Pluralism*, 25.

40. Connolly, *Pluralism*, 26.

41. "An existential faith does find expression on the epistemic field of doctrine and belief, but its intensities extend below that field as well. It thus has a *horizontal dimension*, in that its beliefs about such issues as divinity, morality, and salvation are professed and refined through comparison to alternative beliefs advanced by others. And it has a *vertical dimension*, in that the doctrinal

element is confessed and enacted in ways that express embodied feelings, habits of judgment, and patterns of conduct below direct intellectual control" (Connolly, *Pluralism*, 25).

42. "My view, to put it briefly, is that the most noble response is to seek to transmute cultural antagonisms between transcendence and immanence into debates marked by agonistic respect between the partisans, with each set acknowledging that its highest and most entrenched faith is legitimately contestable by the others.... The pursuit of such an ethos is grounded in the assumption that residing *between* a fundamental image of the world as either created or uncreated and a specific ethico-political stance resides a *sensibility* that colors how that creed is expressed and portrayed to others" (Connolly, *Pluralism*, 47).

43. See Connolly, *The Ethos of Pluralization.*

44. Connolly, *Pluralism*, 123–24.

45. Connolly, *Pluralism*, 126.

46. Connolly, *Pluralism*, 2–5.

47. For example, Connolly, *Capitalism and Christianity.*

48. Connolly, *Pluralism*, 27.

49. Connolly, *Pluralism*, 64–65.

Chapter 7

1. The *Dhammacakkappavattana Sutta*, Bodhi, *Connected Discourses*, 56:11, 1843–47.

2. See Macy, "Dependent Co-Arising." This theory is laid out in many places in the early texts. One clear example is the *Mahātaṇhāsankhaya Sutta*, Bodhi, *Middle Length Discourses*, 354–55. For a further discussion, see Bodhi, *Middle Length Discourses*, 30–31.

3. This is indicated by a shift in verb tense. The periods from Daḷhanemi and his successors up to a generation that lives for 250 years are all described in the past tense, while the generation that lives for ten years and all succeeding generations are described in the future tense.

4. Thoreau, *Walden and Civil Disobedience*, 396; Augustine, *Political Writings*, 147–48.

5. Aristotle, *Politics*, 1252a1, p. 7.

6. Regarding Augustine, see *Political Writings*, 147–48. Regarding Locke, see for example: "If man in the state of nature be so free, as has been said; if he be absolute lord of his own person and possessions, equal to the greatest, and subject to no body, why will he part with his freedom?.... To which it is obvious to answer, that though in the state of nature he hath such a right, yet the enjoyment of it is very uncertain, and constantly exposed to the invasion of others: for all being kings as much as he, every man his equal, and the greater part no strict observers of equity and justice, the enjoyment of the property he has in this state is very unsafe, very unsecure" (Locke, *Second Treatise of Government*, §123, 65–66). Regarding

Marx, see for example this comment in the early essay "Private Property and Communism":

> Communism as the positive transcendence of private property, or human self-estrangement, and therefore as the real appropriation of the human essence by and for man; communism therefore as the complete return of man to himself as a social (i.e., human) being—a return become conscious, and accomplished within the entire wealth of previous development. This communism, as fully-developed naturalism, equals humanism, and as fully developed humanism equals naturalism; it is the genuine resolution of the conflict between man and nature and between man and man—the true resolution of the strife between existence and essence, between objectification and self-confirmation, between freedom and necessity, between the individual and the species. Communism is the riddle of history solved, and it knows itself to be this solution. (Marx and Engels, *The Marx-Engels Reader*, 84)

Arendt's discussion of action is most fully worked out in section V of *The Human Condition* ("Action"). For the value pluralists, see Berlin, *Four Essays on Liberty*; Crowder, "From Value Pluralism to Liberalism"; Crowder, "Pluralism and Liberalism"; Crowder, *Liberalism and Value Pluralism*; Crowder, "From Value Pluralism to Liberalism"; Crowder, "Two Concepts"; Gray, "Where Pluralists and Liberals Part Company"; Gray, *Enlightenment's Wake*; Gray, "Two Liberalisms of Fear"; Galston, *Liberal Pluralism*; Galston, *Liberal Purposes*; Galston, "Pluralism and Pluralism and Liberal Democracy"; Galston, *The Practice of Liberal Pluralism*.

7. Žižek, "From Western Marxism to Western Buddhism."
8. See the *Brahmajāla Sutta* in Walshe, *Long Discourses*, 67–90.
9. See the *Kevaddha Sutta* in Walshe, *Long Discourses*, 175–80. See also the *Brahmajāla Sutta* in Walshe, *Long Discourses*, esp. 75–77.
10. See the *Brahmajāla Sutta* in Walshe, *Long Discourses*, esp. 75–77.
11. For example, see the *Devadūta Sutta* in Bodhi, *Middle Length Discourses*, 1029–36.
12. There are many references to *nibbāna* throughout the Pāli Canon. For a helpful anthology with commentary, see Pasanno and Amaro, *The Island*.
13. See Bodhi, *Connected Discourses*, 56:47, 1871–72.
14. See, for example, the discussion of the natural consequences of behavior in chapter 31 of Hobbes's *Leviathan*, 253–54; see Spinoza, *Ethics*.
15. *Book of the Gradual Sayings*, I, 173.
16. Bodhi, *Connected Discourses*, 22:59, 901–02. This is the view of the overwhelming majority of Buddhists and scholars. For example, see Rahula, *What the Buddha Taught*; Mitchell, *Buddhism: Introducing the Buddhist Experience*. However, a small minority of practitioners and scholars have argued that the Buddha merely denied

that a self could be found in particular aspects of experience and did not directly teach that there is no self at all. For two contemporary, thorough explications of this view, see Albahari, "Against No-*Ātman* Theories of *Anattā*"; Pérez Remón, *Self and Non-Self in Early Buddhism*. For an overview of earlier literature, see the introduction to Collins, *Selfless Persons*.

17. See the discussion of the transcendental unity of apperception in Kant, *Critique of Pure Reason*, A115–30; Hume, *A Treatise of Human Nature*, Book I, Part IV, Section VI: "Of Personal Identity"; Nietzsche, *Genealogy*. For more on this reading, see Mistry, *Nietzsche and Buddhism*; Parfit, *Reasons and Persons*; see also Siderits, *Personal Identity*; Damasio, *The Feeling of What Happens*; see Albahari, *Analytical Buddhism* for an argument that William James, Owen Flanagan, and Daniel Dennett make similar denials of the reality of the self.

18. See for example ch. 10 of James, *Principles of Psychology*. See the discussion of the transcendental unity of apperception at Kant, *Critique of Pure Reason*, A115–30, pp. 41–50. For a current list of major work in this area, see Wilson and Foglia, "Embodied Cognition."

19. Hume, *A Treatise of Human Nature*, Book I, Part IV, Section VI: "Of Personal Identity." See Nietzsche, *Genealogy*. For more on this reading, see Mistry, *Nietzsche and Buddhism*.

20. For a helpful critical overview, see White, *Sustaining Affirmation*.

21. The Invisible Committee makes a polemical claim that we could do without a self and that we would be better off without one but without any sustained argument. See The Invisible Committee, *The Coming Insurrection*.

BIBLIOGRAPHY

Aalders, G. J. D. *Political Thought in Hellenistic Times*. Amsterdam: Adolf M. Hakkert, 1975.

Abbott, Philip. "Henry David Thoreau, the State of Nature, and the Redemption of Liberalism." *The Journal of Politics* 47, no. 1 (1985): 182–208.

Abe, Masao, and William R. LaFleur. *Zen and Western Thought*. Honolulu: University of Hawaii Press, 1985.

Albahari, Miri. "Against No-*Ātman* Theories of *Anattā*." *Asian Philosophy* 12, no. 1 (2002): 5–20.

Albahari, Miri. *Analytical Buddhism: The Two-Tiered Illusion of Self*. Basingstoke, England; New York: Palgrave Macmillan, 2006.

Amadae, S. M. "Nietzsche's Thirst for India: Schopenhauerian, Brahmanist, and Buddhist Accents in Reflections on Truth, the Ascetic Ideal, and the Eternal Return." *Idealistic Studies* 34, no. 3 (2004): 239–62.

Arendt, Hannah. *Crises of the Republic*. San Diego; New York; London: Harcourt Brace Jovanovich, 1969.

Arendt, Hannah. *The Human Condition*. 2nd ed. Chicago: University of Chicago Press, 1998.

Aris, Michael. *The Raven Crown: The Origins of Buddhist Monarchy in Bhutan*. Repr. with corrections. Chicago: Serindia, 2005.

Aristotle. *Politics*. Translated by Ernest Barker. Oxford; New York: Oxford University Press, 1995.

Āryadeva. "Āryadeva's Four Hundred Stanzas on the Middle Way [Catuḥśataka]." Ithaca, N.Y.: Snow Lion, 2008.

Aśvaghoṣa. *The Saundarananda*. Translated by E. H. Johnston. Delhi: Motilal Banarsidass, 1928.

Asvaghosha. *The Buddha-Karita*. Translated by E. B. Cowell. The Sacred Books of the East. Edited by F. Max Müller. Vol. XLIX. Oxford: Clarendon Press, 1894.

Augustine. *Political Writings*. Translated by Michael W. Tkacz and Douglas Kries. Indianapolis: Hackett, 1994.

Barnhart, Michael G. "An Overlapping Consensus: A Critique of Two Approaches." *The Review of Politics* 66, no. 2 (2004): 257–83.

Bartholomeusz, Tessa J. *In Defense of Dharma: Just-War Ideology in Buddhist Sri Lanka*. London; New York: Routledge, 2002.

Bartholomeusz, Tessa J., and Chandra R. De Silva, eds. *Buddhist Fundamentalism and Minority Identities in Sri Lanka*. Albany: State University of New York Press, 1998.

Bastow, David. "Buddhist Ethics." *Religious Studies* 5, no. 2 (1969): 195–206.

Bazzano, Manu. "Buddha Is Dead: Nietzsche and the Dawn of European Zen." Portland, Ore.: Sussex Academic Press, 2006.

Beatty, Joseph. "Radical Change and Rational Argument." *Ethics* 87, no. 1 (1976): 66–74.

Bechert, Heinz. "Aspects of Theravāda Buddhism in Sri Lanka and Southeast Asia." In *The Buddhist Heritage*, edited by Tadeusz Skorupski. Buddhica Britannica, 19–27. Tring: Institute of Buddhist Studies, 1989.

Bechert, Heinz. "S.W.R.D. Bandaranaike and the Legitimation of Power through Buddhist Ideals." In *Religion and Legitimation of Power in Sri Lanka*, edited by Bardwell L. Smith, 199–211. Chambersburg, Penn.: ANIMA Books, 1978.

Bechert, Heinz. "Sangha, State, Society, 'Nation'": Persistence of Traditions in 'Post-Traditional' Buddhist Societies." *Daedalus* 102, no. 1 (1973): 85–95.

Bell, Daniel A. "Review: The Limits of Liberal Justice." *Political Theory* 26, no. 4 (1998): 557–82.

Bennett, Jane. *Thoreau's Nature: Ethics, Politics, and the Wild*. Modernity and Political Thought. Thousand Oaks; London; New Delhi: Sage, 1994.

Bergen, Jeremy M., and Anthony G. Siegrist, eds. *Power and Practices: Engaging the Work of John Howard Yoder*. Waterloo, Ontario; Scottdale, Penn.: Herald Press, 2009.

Berlin, Isaiah. *Four Essays on Liberty*. Oxford; New York: Oxford University Press, 1969.

Berman, Michael. "A Metaphysics of Morality: Kant and Buddhism." *Canadian Journal of Buddhist Studies* 2 (2006): 61–81.

Black, Antony. "The 'Axial Period': What Was It and What Does It Signify?" *The Review of Politics* 70, no. 1 (2008): 23–39.

Bodhi, Bhikkhu. *The Connected Discourses of the Buddha: A Translation of the Saṃyutta Nikāya*. Boston: Wisdom, 2000.

Bodhi, Bhikkhu, ed. *In the Buddha's Words: An Anthology of Discourses from the Pāli Canon*. Kindle ed. Somerville, Mass.: Wisdom, 2005.

Bodhi, Bhikkhu. *The Middle Length Discourses of the Budda: A Translation of the Majjhima Nikāya*. Translated by Bhikkhu Ñāṇamoli and Bhikkhu Bodhi. 3rd. ed. Boston: Wisdom, 2005.

The Book of the Discipline. Translated by I. B. Horner. VI vols. Oxford: Pali Text Society, 1940.

The Book of the Gradual Sayings (Anguttara-Nikāya) or More-Numbered Sayings. Translated by E. M. Hare. V vols., Oxford: Pali Text Society, 1935.

Booth, David. "Nietzsche on 'the Subject as Multiplicity.'" *Man and World* 18 (1985): 121–46.

Borchert, Thomas. "Buddhism, Politics, and Nationalism in the Twentieth and Twenty-First Centuries." *Religion Compass* 1, no. 5 (2007): 529–46.

Brown, Eric. "False Idles: The Politics of the 'Quiet Life.'" In *A Companion to Greek and Roman Political Thought*, edited by Ryan K. Balot, 485–500. Malden, Mass.; Oxford: Wiley-Blackwell, 2009.

Brown, Eric. "Politics and Society." In *The Cambridge Companion to Epicureanism*, edited by James Warren, 179–96. Cambridge; New York: Cambridge University Press, 2009.

Buddhaghosa. *Visuddhimagga*. Translated by Bhikkhu Ñāṇamoli. Kandy: Buddhist Publication Society, 2010. C. fifth century CE.

Buranelli, Vincent. "The Case against Thoreau." *Ethics* 67, no. 4 (1957): 257–68.

Buranelli, Vincent. "The Verdict on Thoreau." *Ethics* 70, no. 1 (1959): 64–65.

Cafaro, Philip. *Thoreau's Living Ethics: Walden and the Pursuit of Virtue*. Athens, Ga.; London: University of Georgia Press, 2004.

Carter, Craig. *The Politics of the Cross: The Theology and Social Ethics of John Howard Yoder*. Grand Rapids, Mich.: Brazos Press, 2001.

Cavell, Stanley. *The Senses of Walden*. Expanded ed. San Francisco: North Point Press, 1981. 1972.

Chakrabongse, H.R.H. Prince Chula. *Lords of Life: The Paternal Monarchy of Bangkok, 1782–1932*. New York: Taplinger, 1960.

Chakravarti, Uma. *The Social Dimensions of Early Buddhism*. Delhi; New York: Oxford University Press, 1987.

Coles, Romand. *Beyond Gated Politics: Reflections for the Possibility of Democracy*. Minneapolis: University of Minnesota Press, 2005.

Coles, Romand. "The Wild Patience of John Howard Yoder: "Outsiders" and the 'Otherness of the Church.'" *Modern Theology* 18, no. 3 (2002): 305–31.

Collins, Steven. "The Discourse on What Is Primary (Aggañña-Sutta): An Annotated Translation." *Journal of Indian Philosophy* 21 (1993): 301–93.

Collins, Steven. "The Lion's Roar on the Wheel-Turning King: A Response to Andrew Huxley's 'The Buddha and the Social Contract.'" *Journal of Indian Philosophy* 24 (1996): 421–46.

Collins, Steven. *Nirvana and Other Buddhist Felicities: Utopias of the Pali Imaginaire*. Cambridge Studies in Religious Traditions. New York: Cambridge University Press, 1997.

Collins, Steven. *Selfless Persons: Imagery and Thought in Theravāda Buddhism*. New York: Cambridge University Press, 1982.

Collins, Steven, and Andrew Huxley. "The Post-Canonical Adventures of the Mahāsammata." *Journal of Indian Philosophy* 24 (1996): 623–48.

Conche, Marcel. "Nietzsche et le Bouddhisme." *Le cahier du collège international de philosophie* 4 (1987): 125–44.

Connolly, William. *Identity\Difference: Democratic Negotiations of Political Paradox.* Ithaca, N.Y.; London: Cornell University Press, 1991.

Connolly, William E. *Capitalism and Christianity, American Style.* Durham: Duke University Press, 2008.

Connolly, William E. *The Ethos of Pluralization.* Minneapolis; London: University of Minnesota Press, 1995.

Connolly, William E. *Pluralism.* Durham; London: Duke University Press, 2005.

Connolly, William E. *Why I Am Not a Secularist.* Minneapolis: University of Minnesota Press, 1999.

"The Constitution of the Kingdom of Bhutan." 2008. http://www.nationalcouncil.bt/en/business/constitution_of_bhutan/

"Constitution of the Kingdom of Laos, May 11, 1947: Text as revised and adopted by the National Congress in its Session of September 29, 1956," Vientiane, 1957.

Conway, Daniel W. "The Birth of the Soul: Toward a Psychology of Decadence." In *Nietzsche and Depth Psychology,* edited by Jacob Golomb, Santaniello Weaver, and Ronald Lehrer, 51–71. Albany: State University of New York Press, 1999.

Coomaraswamy, Ananda Kentish. *The Origin of the Buddha Image & Elements of Buddhist Iconography.* Louisville, Ky.: Fons Vitae, 2006.

Corngold, Stanley. "The Question of the Self in Nietzsche during the Axial Period (1882–1888)." In *Why Nietzsche Now?,* edited by Daniel O'Hara, 55–98. Bloomington: Indiana University Press, 1981.

Cousins, L. S. "The Dating of the Historical Buddha: A Review Article." *Journal of the Royal Asiatic Society* Series 3, 6, no. 1 (1996): 57–63.

Cowell, E. B., ed. *The Jataka: Or, Stories of the Buddha's Former Births.* Vol. III. Cambridge: Cambridge University Press, 1897.

Cowell, E. B., ed. *The Jataka: Or, Stories of the Buddha's Former Births.* Vol. IV. Cambridge: Pali Text Society, 1901.

Cox, Christoph. "The "Subject" of Nietzsche's Perspectivism." *Journal of the History of Philosophy* 35, no. 2 (1997): 269–91.

Crowder, George. "From Value Pluralism to Liberalism." *Critical Review of International Social and Political Philosophy* 1, no. 3 (1998): 2–17.

Crowder, George. *Liberalism and Value Pluralism.* London; New York: Continuum, 2002.

Crowder, George. "Pluralism and Liberalism." *Political Studies* 42 (1994): 293–305.

Crowder, George. "Two Concepts of Liberal Pluralism." *Political Theory* 35, no. 2 (April 2007): 121–46.

Dallmayr, Fred, ed. *Comparative Political Theory: An Introduction.* Houndmills, England: Palgrave, 2010.

Damasio, Antonio. *The Feeling of What Happens.* New York: Harcourt, 1999.

Davey, Nicholas. "Nietzsche and Hume on the Self and Identity." *Journal of the British Society for Phenomenology* 18, no. 1 (1987): 14–29.

Davey, Nicholas. "Nietzsche, the Self, and Hermeneutic Theory." *Journal of the British Society for Phenomenology* 18, no. 3 (1987): 272–84.

Davis, Bret W. "Zen after Zarathustra: The Problem of the Will in the Confrontation between Nietzsche and Buddhism." *The Journal of Nietzsche Studies*, no. 28 (2004): 89–138.

Davis, Gordon F. "Moral Realism and Anti-Realism Outside the West: A Meta-Ethical Turn in Buddhist Ethics." *Comparative Philosophy* 4, no. 2 (2013): 24–53.

De Visser, M. W. *Ancient Buddhism in Japan*. Vol. 1. Leiden: Brill, 1935.

The Dhammapada. Translated by Juan Mascaró. London; New York: Penguin Books, 1973.

Diggins, John P. "Thoreau, Marx, and the 'Riddle' of Alienation." *Social Research* 39, no. 4 (Winter 1972): 571–98.

Dô, Thiên. "The Quest for Enlightenment and Cultural Identity: Buddhism in Contemporary Vietnam." In *Buddhism and Politics in Twentieth-Century Asia*, edited by Ian Harris, 254–83. New York; London: Pinter, 1999.

Doerksen, Paul G. *Beyond Suspicion: Post-Christendom Protestant Political Theology in John Howard Yoder and Oliver O'Donovan*. Eugene, Ore.: Wipf & Stock, 2009.

Doerksen, Paul G., and Karl Koop, eds. *The Church Made Strange for the Nations: Essays in Ecclesiology and Political Theology*, Princeton Theological Monograph Series. Vol. 171. Eugene, Ore.: Pickwick, 2011.

Dorrien, Gary. *Social Ethics in the Making: Interpreting an American Tradition*. Malden, Mass.: Wiley-Blackwell, 2009.

Drinnon, Richard. "Thoreau and John Brown." In *Thoreau in Our Season*, edited by John H. Hicks, 154–68. Amherst, Mass.: University of Massachusetts Press, 1962.

Dula, Peter, and Chris K. Huebner, eds. *The New Yoder*. Eugene, Ore.: Cascade Books, 2010.

Dumoulin, Heinrich. "Buddhism and Nineteenth-Century German Philosophy." *Journal of the History of Ideas* 42, no. 3 (1981): 457–70.

Edwards, David. *The Compassionate Revolution: Radical Politics and Buddhism*. New Delhi: Viveka Foundation, 2001.

Elman, Benjamin A. "Nietzsche and Buddhism." *Journal of the History of Ideas* 44, no. 4 (1983): 671–86.

Emerson, Ralph Waldo. "Eulogy [for Henry David Thoreau] May 9, 1862." http://thoreau.eserver.org/emerson2.html.

Eulau, Heinz. "Wayside Challenger: Some Remarks on the Politics of Henry David Thoreau." *The Antioch Review* 9, no. 4 (1949): 509–22.

Farrington, Benjamin. *The Faith of Epicurus*. New York: Basic Books, Inc., 1967.

Fennell, J[on M.]. "Nietzsche Contra 'Self-Reformulation.'" *Studies in Philosophy and Education* 24, no. 2 (2005): 85–111.

Fergenson, Laraine. "Thoreau, Daniel Berrigan, and the Problem of Transcendental Politics." *Soundings* 65, no. 1 (1982): 103–22.

Fitzgerald, Patrick. "Gratitude and Justice." *Ethics* 109, no. 1 (1998): 119–53.

Florida, Robert. "Buddhism and Abortion." In *Contemporary Buddhist Ethics*, edited by Damien Keown, 137–68. Richmond, Surrey: Curzon Press, 2000.

Frazier, A. M. "A European Buddhism." *Philosophy East & West* 25, no. 2 (1975): 145–60.

French, Rebecca Redwood. *The Golden Yoke: The Legal Cosmology of Buddhist Tibet*. Ithaca, N.Y.; London: Cornell University Press, 1995.

Friedlander, Peter. "Buddhism and Politics." In *Routledge Handbook of Religion and Politics*, edited by Jeffrey Haynes, 11–25. London; New York: Routledge, 2009.

Fronsdal, Gil. *The Issue at Hand*. Redwood City, Calif.: Insight Meditation Center, 2001.

Gallenkamp, Marian. *Democracy in Bhutan: An Analysis of Constitutional Change in a Buddhist Monarchy*. Institute for Peace and Conflict Studies Research Papers. New Delhi, India: Institute for Peace and Conflict Studies, 2010.

Galston, William A. *Liberal Pluralism: The Implications of Value Pluralism for Political Theory and Practice*. Cambridge: Cambridge University Press, 2002.

Galston, William A. *Liberal Purposes*. Cambridge: Cambridge University Press, 1991.

Galston, William A. "Pluralism and Pluralism and Liberal Democracy." *Perspectives on Politics* 4, no. 4 (2006): 751–53.

Galston, William A. *The Practice of Liberal Pluralism*. Cambridge; New York: Cambridge University Press, 2005.

Gard, Richard A. "Buddhism and Political Authority." In *The Ethic of Power: The Interplay of Religion, Philosophy, and Politics*, edited by Harold D. Lasswell and Harlan Cleveland, 39–70. New York: Harper & Brothers, 1962.

Gard, Richard A. *Buddhist Influences on the Political Thought and Institutions of India and Japan*. Claremont, Calif.: Society for Oriental Studies at Claremont, 1949.

Gard, Richard A. *Buddhist Political Thought; a Bibliography*. [Outlines and Bibliographical Index, SAIS, Summer Session, 1952]. Washington, DC: School of Advanced International Studies, 1952.

Gard, Richard A. *Buddhist Political Thought; a Study of Buddhism in Society*. Bangkok: Mahamakuta University, 1956.

Gard, Richard A. "The Saṅgha: Buddhist Society and the Laity." In *Buddhism*, edited by Richard A. Gard, 191–231. New York: Washington Square Press, 1962.

Gemes, Ken. "Postmodernism's Use and Abuse of Nietzsche." *Philosophy and Phenomenological Research* 62, no. 2 (March 2001): 337–60.

Ghoshal, Upendra Nath. *A History of Indian Political Ideas: The Ancient Period and the Period of Transition to the Middle Ages*. Oxford: Oxford University Press, 1959.

Glass, James M. "The Yogin & the Utopian: Nirvana & the Discovery of Being." *Polity* 5, no. 4 (1973): 427–50.

Gokhale, Balkrishna Govind. "Dhamma as a Political Concept in Early Buddhism." *Journal of Indian History* 46, no. 2 (1968): 249–61.

Gokhale, Balkrishna Govind. "Early Buddhist Kingship." *The Journal of Asian Studies* 26, no. 1 (1966): 15–22.

Gokhale, Balkrishna Govind. "The Early Buddhist View of the State." *Journal of the American Oriental Society* 89, no. 4 (1969): 731–38.

Goldstein, Joseph, and Jack Kornfield. *Seeking the Heart of Wisdom: The Path of Insight Meditation.* Boston; London: Shambhala, 2001.

Goodman, Charles. *Consequences of Compassion: An Interpretation and Defense of Buddhist Ethics.* New York: Oxford University Press, 2009.

Goonatilake, Hema. "Women and Family in Buddhism." In *Buddhist Perception for Desireable Socieites in the Future,* edited by Sulak Sivaraksa. Bangkok: Inter-Religious Commission for Development, 1992.

Gougeon, Len. "Thoreau and Reform." In *The Cambridge Companion to Henry David Thoreau,* edited by Joel Myerson, 194–210. Cambridge; New York: Cambridge University Press, 1995.

Gowans, Christopher W. *Buddhist Moral Philosophy.* New York; London: Routledge, 2015.

Grabowsky, Volker. "Buddhism, Power and Political Order in Pre-Twentieth Century Laos." In *Buddhism, Power and Political Order,* edited by Ian Harris, 121–42. London; New York: Routledge, 2007.

Gray, John. *Enlightenment's Wake: Politics and Culture at the Close of the Modern Age.* London; New York: Routledge, 1995.

Gray, John. "Two Liberalisms of Fear." *The Hedgehog Review* 2, no. 1 (2000).

Gray, John. "Where Pluralists and Liberals Part Company." *International Journal of Philosophical Studies* 6, no. 1 (1998): 17–36.

Gyallay-Pap, Peter. "Reconstructing the Cambodian Polity: Buddhism, Kingship and the Quest for Legitimacy." In *Buddhism, Power and Political Order,* edited by Ian Harris, 71–103. London; New York: Routledge, 2007.

Gyatso, Tenzin (His Holiness the Fourteenth Dalai Lama). "Buddhism and Democracy." The Office of His Holiness the Dalai Lama, http://www.dalailama.com/messages/buddhism/buddhism-and-democracy.

Gyatso, Tenzin (His Holiness the Fourteenth Dalai Lama). "Buddhism, Asian Values, and Democracy." *Journal of Democracy* 10, no. 1 (1991): 3–7.

Gyatso, Tenzin (His Holiness the Fourteenth Dalai Lama). *My Land and My People.* New York: Potala Corporation, 1977. 1962.

Haar, Michel. "La Critique Nietzscheenne De La Subjectivite." *Nietzsche-Studien* 12 (1983): 80–110.

Hales, Steven D. "Recent Work on Nietzsche." *American Philosophical Quarterly* 37, no. 4 (2000): 313–33.

Hales, Steven D., and Rex Welshon. *Nietzsche's Perspectivism.* International Nietzsche Studies; Variation: International Nietzsche Studies. Urbana: University of Illinois Press, 2000.

Halkias, Georgios T. "The Enlightened Sovereign: Buddhism and Kingship in India and Tibet." In *A Companion to Buddhist Philosophy,* edited by Steven M. Emmanuel, 491–511. New York: John Wiley & Sons, 2013.

Hanson, Jim. "Searching for the Power-I: Nietzsche and Nirvana." *Asian Philosophy* 18, no. 3 (2008): 231–44.

Hare, William L. "Nietzsche's Critique of Buddhism." *The Buddhist Review* 8, no. 1 (1916): 21–35.

Harris, Ian. *Buddhism and Politics in Twentieth-Century Asia*. New York; London: Pinter, 2001.

Harris, Ian, ed. *Buddhism, Power and Political Order*. London; New York: Routledge, 2007.

Harris, Ian. "Something Rotten in the State of Buddhaland: Good Governance in Theravāda Buddhism." In *Destroying Mara Forever: Buddhist Ethics Essays in Honor of Damien Keown*, edited by John Powers and Charles S. Prebish, 221–36. Ithaca, N.Y.: Snow Lion, 2009.

Hartshorne, Charles. "Beyond Enlightened Self-Interest: A Metaphysics of Ethics." *Ethics* 84, no. 3 (1974): 201–16.

Harvey, Peter. *An Introduction to Buddhist Ethics: Foundations, Values and Issues*. Cambridge; New York: Cambridge University Press, 2000.

Hauerwas, Stanley, Chris K. Huebner, Harry J. Huebner, and Mark Thiessen Nation, eds. *The Wisdom of the Cross: Essays in Honor of John Howard Yoder*. Grand Rapids, Mich.: W.B. Eerdmans, 1999.

Heilke, Thomas. "On Being Ethical without Moral Sadism: Two Readings of Augustine and the Beginnings of the Anabaptist Revolution." *Political Theory* 24, no. 3 (1996): 493–517.

Hershock, Peter D. *Buddhism in the Public Sphere: Reorienting Global Interdependence*. Routledge Critical Studies in Buddhism. London: Routledge, 2006.

Hobbes, Thomas. *Leviathan*. Cambridge; New York: Cambridge University Press, 1996. 1651.

Hodder, Alan D. *Thoreau's Ecstatic Witness*. New Haven; London: Yale University Press, 2001.

Houtart, Francois. "Buddhism and Politics in South-East Asia: Part One." *Social Scientist* 5, no. 3 (1976): 3–23.

Houtart, Francois. "Buddhism and Politics in South-East Asia: Part Two." *Social Scientist* 5, no. 4 (1976): 30–45.

Hume, David. *A Treatise of Human Nature*. Oxford: Oxford University Press, 2000. 1739–1740.

Huxley, Andrew. "The Buddha and the Social Contract." *Journal of Indian Philosophy* 24 (1996): 407–20.

Huxley, Andrew. "Buddhism and Law—the View from Mandalay." *Journal of the International Association of Buddhist Studies* 18, no. 1 (Summer 1995 1995): 47–95.

Huxley, Andrew. "Buddhist Law." In *Legal Systems of the World: A Political, Social, and Cultural Encyclopedia*, edited by Herbert M. Kritzer, 205–08. Santa Barbara; Denver; Oxford: ABC CLIO, 2002.

Huxley, Andrew. "How Buddhist Is Theravāda Buddhist Law? A Survey of Legal Literature in Pāli-Land." *The Buddhist Forum* 1 (Seminar Papers 1987–1988) (1990): 41–85.

Huxley, Andrew. "Rajadhamma Confronts Leviathan: Burmese Political Theory in the 1870s." In *Buddhism, Power and Political Order*, edited by Ian Harris, 26–51. London; New York: Routledge, 2007.

Huxley, Andrew. "The Reception of Buddhist Law in S.E. Asia 200 BCE—1860 CE." In *La Réception Des Systèmes Juridiques: Implantation and Destin*, edited by Michel Doucet and Jacques Vanderlinden, 139–237. Bruxelles [Brussels]: Bruylant, 1994.

Huxley, Andrew. *Thai Law, Buddhist Law: Essays on the Legal History of Thailand, Laos, and Burma*. Brussels, Belgium: White Orchid Press, 1996.

Huxley, Andrew. "When Manu Met Mahāsammata." *Journal of Indian Philosophy* 24 (1996): 593–621.

Hyde, Lewis. "Henry Thoreau, John Brown, and the Problem of Prophetic Action." *Raritan* 22, no. 2 (Fall 2002): 125–44.

Invisible Committee, The. *The Coming Insurrection*. Los Angeles: Semiotext(e), 2009.

James, William. *The Principles of Psychology*. Henry Holt, 1918.

Jamspal, Lozang. *The Range of the Bodhisattva, a Mahāyāna Sūtra (Ārya-Bodhisattva-Gocara): The Teachings of the Nirgrantha Satyaka*. New York: American Institute of Buddhist Studies, 2010.

Janaway, Christopher. *Beyond Selflessness: Reading Nietzsche's Genealogy*. New York: Oxford University Press, 2007.

Janaway, Christopher. "Nietzsche, the Self, and Schopenhauer." In *Nietzsche and Modern German Thought*, edited by Keith Ansell-Pearson, 119–42. London; New York: Routledge, 1992.

Janaway, Christopher. *Self and World in Schopenhauer's Philosophy*. Oxford: Oxford University Press, 1989.

Jayasuriya, Laksiri. "Buddhism, Politics, and Statecraft." *International Journal of Buddhist Thought & Culture* 11 (2008): 41–74.

Jayatilleke, Kulatissa Nanda. *Aspects of Buddhist Social Philosophy*. Kandy, Sri Lanka: Buddhist Publication Society, 1969. 1955.

Jayatilleke, Kulatissa Nanda. *Ethics in Buddhist Perspective*. Kandy, Sri Lanka: Buddhist Publication Society, 1972.

Jayatilleke, Kulatissa Nanda. "Principles of International Law in Buddhist Doctrine." *Recueil des Cours* 120 (1967): 441–567.

Jenco, Leigh Kathryn. "Thoreau's Critique of Democracy." In *A Political Companion to Henry David Thoreau*, edited by Jack Turner. Lexington: University Press of Kentucky, 2009.

Joly, Robert. *Le Thème Philosophique Des Genres De Vie Dans L'antiquité Classique*. Bruxelles: Palais des Academies, 1956.

Jones, Ken. *The New Social Face of Buddhism: A Call to Action*. Boston: Wisdom Publications, 2003.

Kalupahana, David J. *Ethics in Early Buddhism*. Honolulu: University of Hawaii Press, 1995.

Kant, Immanuel. *Critique of Pure Reason*. Translated by Norman Kemp Smith. New York: St. Martin's Press, 1929. 1781.

Kateb, George. "Democratic Individuality and the Claims of Politics." *Political Theory* 12, no. 3 (1984): 331–60.

Kateb, George. "Democratic Individuality and the Meaning of Rights." In *Liberalism and the Moral Life*, edited by Nancy L. Rosenblum, 183–206. Cambridge, Mass.; London: Harvard University Press, 1989.

Kateb, George. *The Inner Ocean*. Ithaca, N.Y.; London: Cornell University Press, 1992.

Kateb, George. *Patriotism and Other Mistakes*. New Haven; London: Yale University Press, 2006.

Kawanami, Hiroko. "Japanese Nationalism and the Universal *Dharma*." In *Buddhism and Politics in Twentieth-Century Asia*, edited by Ian Harris, 105–26. New York; London: Pinter, 1999.

Kelly, David, and Anthony Reid. *Asian Freedoms: The Idea of Freedom in East and Southeast Asia*. Cambridge; New York: Cambridge University Press, 1998.

Keown, Damien. "Are There Human Rights in Buddhism?" In *Buddhism and Human Rights*, edited by Damien V. Keown, Charles S. Prebish and Wayne R. Husted. Richmond, Surrey: Curzon, 1998.

Keown, Damien. *Buddhist Ethics: A Very Short Introduction*. Kindle ed. Oxford; New York: Oxford University Press, 2005.

Keown, Damien, ed. *Contemporary Buddhist Ethics*. Richmond, Surrey: Curzon Press, 2000.

Keown, Damien. *The Nature of Buddhist Ethics*. Houndmills; New York: Palgrave, 2001.

Ketcham, Ralph L. "Some Thoughts on Buranelli's Case against Thoreau." *Ethics* 69, no. 3 (1959): 206–08.

Keyes, Charles F. "Buddhist Politics and Their Revolutionary Origins in Thailand." *International Political Science Review/Revue internationale de science politique* 10, no. 2 (April 1989): 121–42.

The King of Glorious Sutras Called the Exhalted Sublime Golden Light. Translated by Losang Dawa. Portland, Ore: Foundation for the Preservation of the Mahayana Tradition, 2006. PDF.

King, Winston L. *In the Hope of Nibbana: An Essay on Theravada Buddhist Ethics*. LaSalle, Ill.: Open Court, 1964.

Kirkland, Paul E. "Nietzsche's Honest Masks: From Truth to Nobility 'Beyond Good and Evil.'" *The Review of Politics* 66, no. 4 (2004): 575–604.

Kotkin, Stephen. *Uncivil Society: 1989 and the Implosion of the Communist Establishment*. New York: Modern Library, 2009.

Kritzberg, Barry. "Thoreau, Slavery, and Resistance to Civil Government." *The Massachusetts Review* 30, no. 4 (1989): 535–65.

Kroeker, Travis P. "Is a Messianic Political Ethic Possible? Recent Work by and about John Howard Yoder." *The Journal of Religious Ethics* 33, no. 1 (2005): 35.

Kyi, Aung San Suu. *Freedom from Fear and Other Writings*. London; New York: Viking, 1991.

Lane, Ruth. "Standing 'Aloof' from the State: Thoreau on Self-Government." *The Review of Politics* 67, no. 2 (2005): 283–310.

Lauter, Paul. "Thoreau's Prophetic Testimony." In *Thoreau in Our Season*, edited by John H. Hicks, 80–90. Amherst: University of Massachusetts Press, 1962.

Ling, Trevor. "Kingship and Nationalism in Pali Buddhism." In *Buddhist Studies: Ancient and Modern*, edited by Philip Denwood and Alexander Piatigorsky. Collected Papers on South Asia, 60–73. London; Dublin: Curzon Press, 1983.

Lipset, Seymour Martin. *Political Philosophy: Theories, Thinkers, Concepts.* Washington, DC: CQ Press, 2001.

Locke, John. *Second Treatise of Government.* Edited by C. B. Macpherson Indianapolis: Hackett, 1980. 1690.

Loy, David. "Beyond Good and Evil? A Buddhist Critique of Nietzsche." *Asian Philosophy* 6, no. 1 (1996): 21.

Macy, Joanna Rogers. "Dependent Co-Arising: The Distinctiveness of Buddhist Ethics." *Journal of Religious Ethics* 7, no. 1 (1979): 38–52.

Mahāvaṃsa. Translated by Wilhelm Geiger. London: Pali Text Society, 1912. c. sixth century CE.

The Mahāvastu. Translated by J. J. Jones. The Sacred Books of the Buddhists. Vol. XVI. London: Luzac, 1949.

March, Andrew F. "What Is Comparative Political Theory?" *The Review of Politics* 71, no. 4 (2009): 531–65.

Mariotti, Shannon L. *Thoreau's Democratic Withdrawal: Alienation, Participation, and Modernity.* Madison; London: University of Wisconsin Press, 2010.

Marshall, Mason. "Freedom through Critique: Thoreau's Service to Others." *Transactions of the Charles S. Peirce Society* 41, no. 2 (Spring 2005): 395–427.

Martin, Raymond, and John Barresi, eds. *Personal Identity.* Malden, Mass; Oxford: Blackwell, 2003.

Marty, Martin E., and F. Scott Appleby. *Fundamentalisms and the State: Remaking Polities, Economies, and Militance.* Chicago: University of Chicago Press, 1993.

Marx, Karl, and Friedrich Engels. *The Marx-Engels Reader.* Edited by Robert C. Tucker. 2nd ed. New York; London: W.W. Norton, 1978.

Marx, Leo. *The Machine in the Garden: Technology and the Pastoral Ideal in America.* Oxford; New York: Oxford University Press, 2000. 1964.

Mathou, Thierry. "How to Reform a Traditional Buddhist Monarchy: The Political Achievements of His Majesty Jigme Singye Wangchuck, the Fourth King of Bhutan (1972–2006)." Thimphu, Bhutan: Centre for Bhutan Studies, 2008.

Mathou, Thierry. "Political Reform in Bhutan: Change in a Buddhist Monarchy." *Asian Survey* 39, no. 4 (1999): 613–32.

Matthews, Bruce. "The Legacy of Tradition and Authority: Buddhism and the Nation in Myanmar." In *Buddhism and Politics in Twentieth-Century Asia*, edited by Ian Harris, 26–53. New York; London: Pinter, 1999.

McCarthy, Stephen. *The Political Theory of Tyranny in Singapore and Burma: Aristotle and the Rhetoric of Benevolent Despotism*. London; New York: Routledge, 2006.

McKenzie, Jonathan. "How to Mind Your Own Business: Thoreau on Political Indifference." *The New England Quarterly* 84, no. 3 (September 2011): 422–43.

McLeod, Melvin. *Mindful Politics: A Buddhist Guide to Making the World a Better Place*. Boston: Wisdom, 2006.

McWilliams, Wilson Carey. *The Idea of Fraternity in America*. Berkeley: University of California Press, 1973.

Meyer, Michael. *Several More Lives to Live: Thoreau's Political Reputation in America*. Westport, Conn.; London: Greenwood Press, 1977.

Miller, J. Hillis. "The Disarticulation of the Self in Nietzsche." *The Monist* 64, no. 2 (1981): 247–61.

Mistry, Freny. *Nietzsche and Buddhism: Prolegomenon to a Comparative Study* [in English]. Monographien Und Texte Zur Nietzsche-Forschung. Berlin: New York, 1981.

Mitchell, Donald W. *Buddhism: Introducing the Buddhist Experience*. New York; Oxford: Oxford University Press, 2008.

Moore, G. E. *Principia Ethica*. Rev. ed. Cambridge: Cambridge University Press, 1993. 1903.

Moore, Matthew J. "Immanence, Pluralism, and Politics." *Theory in Action* 4, no. 3 (July 2011): 25–56.

Moore, Matthew J. "Pluralism, Relativism, and Liberalism." *Political Research Quarterly* 62, no. 2 (2009): 244–56.

Moore, Matthew J. "Political Theory Today: Results of a National Survey." *PS: Political Science and Politics* 43, no. 2 (2010): 265–72.

Moore, Matthew J. "Wittgenstein, Value Pluralism, and Politics." *Philosophy & Social Criticism* 36, no. 9 (2010): 1113–36.

Morrison, Robert G. *Nietzsche and Buddhism: A Study in Nihilism and Ironic Affinities*. Oxford; New York: Oxford University Press, 1997.

Morrison, Robert G. "Response to Graham Parkes' Review." *Philosophy East & West* 50, no. 2 (2000): 267–79.

Myint, Tun. "Buddhist Political Thought." In *The Encyclopedia of Political Thought*, edited by Michael T. Gibbons. New York: John Wiley, 2015.

Nagarjuna. *Nagarjuna's Letter to a Friend*. Translated by Padmakara Translation Group. Ithaca, N.Y.; Boulder, Colo.: Snow Lion, 2008.

Nation, Mark. *John Howard Yoder: Mennonite Patience, Evangelical Witness, Catholic Convictions*. Grand Rapids, Mich.: William B. Eerdmans, 2006.

Nehemas, Alexander. "'How One Becomes What One Is.'" In *Nietzsche*, edited by John Richardson and Brian Leiter, 255–80. Oxford; New York: Oxford University Press, 2001.

Nehemas, Alexander. *Nietzsche: Life as Literature*. Cambridge, Mass.: Harvard University Press, 1985.

Nelson, Truman. "Thoreau and John Brown." In *Thoreau in Our Season*, edited by John H. Hicks, 134–53. Amherst: University of Massachusetts Press, 1962.

Neufeldt, Leonard N. "Henry David Thoreau's Political Economy." *The New England Quarterly* 57, no. 3 (1984): 359–83.

Nichiren. "The Writings of Nichiren Daishonin." Soka Gakkai International, http://www.nichirenlibrary.org/en/wnd-1/Content.

Nichols, Charles H., Jr. "Thoreau on the Citizen and His Government." *Phylon (1940–1956)* 13, no. 1 (1952): 19–24.

Nietzsche, Friedrich. *The Anti-Christ, Ecce Homo, Twilight of the Idols, and Other Writings*. Translated by Judith Norman. Cambridge Texts in the History of Political Thought. Cambridge; New York: Cambridge University Press, 2005.

Nietzsche, Friedrich. *Beyond Good and Evil*. Translated by W. Kaufmann. New York: Viking Press, 1966.

Nietzsche, Friedrich. *Daybreak: Thoughts on the Prejudices of Morality*. Translated by R. J. Hollingdale. Cambridge Texts in the History of Philosophy. Cambridge; New York: Cambridge University Press, 1997. 1881.

Nietzsche, Friedrich. *The Gay Science*. Translated by Walter Kaufmann. New York: Vintage Books, 1974. 1887.

Nietzsche, Friedrich. *Human, All Too Human: A Book for Free Spirits*. Translated by R. J. Hollingdale. Cambridge Texts in the History of Philosophy. Cambridge; New York: Cambridge University Press, 1986. 1878–1880.

Nietzsche, Friedrich. *On the Genealogy of Morality*. Translated by Carol Diethe. Cambridge: Cambridge University Press, 1994. 1887.

Nietzsche, Friedrich. "On Truth and Lies in a Nonmoral Sense." Translated by Daniel Breazeale. In *Philosophy and Truth: Selections from Nietzsche's Notebooks of the Early 1870's*, edited by Daniel Breazeale, 79–97. New Jersey and London: Humanities Press International, 1979.

Nietzsche, Friedrich. *Thus Spoke Zarathustra: A Book for Everyone and No One*. Translated by R. J. Hollingdale. London; New York: Penguin Books, 1961. 1883–1885.

Nietzsche, Friedrich. *The Will to Power*. Translated by Walter Kaufmann and R. J. Hollingdale. New York: Vintage Books, 1968. 1901.

Nietzsche, Friedrich, Giorgio Colli, and Mazzino Montinari. *Sämtliche Werke: Kritische Studienausgabe in 15 Bänden*. 15 vols. München: Deutscher Taschenbuch Verlag: Berlin; New York, 1980. 1967.

Nuccetelli, Susana, and Gary Seay, eds. *Ethical Naturalism: Current Debates*. Cambridge; New York: Cambridge University Press, 2012.

Nugent, John C. *The Politics of Yahweh: John Howard Yoder, the Old Testament, and the People of God*. Theopolitical Visions. Eugene, Ore.: Cascade Books, 2011.

Obeyesekere, Gananath, Frank Reynolds, and Bardwell L. Smith, eds. *The Two Wheels of Dharma: Essays on the Theravada Tradition in India and Ceylon*. Chambersburg, Penn.: American Academy of Religion, 1972.

Ollenburger, Ben C. Koontz Gayle Gerber. *A Mind Patient and Untamed: Assessing John Howard Yoder's Contributions to Theology, Ethics, and Peacemaking*. Scottdale, Penn.: Cascadia, 2004.

Orzech, Charles D. "Puns on the Humane King: Analogy and Application in an East Asian Apocryphon." *Journal of the American Oriental Society* 109, no. 1 (1989): 17–24.

Pardue, Peter A. *Buddhism: A Historical Introduction to Buddhist Values and the Social and Political Forms They Have Assumed in Asia.* New York; London: Macmillan, 1971.

Parfit, Derek. *Reasons and Persons.* Oxford: Oxford University Press, 1986.

Parkes, Graham. *Composing the Soul: Reaches of Nietzsche's Psychology.* Chicago: University of Chicago Press, 1994.

Parkes, Graham, ed. *Nietzsche and Asian Thought.* Chicago: University of Chicago Press, 1991.

Parkes, Graham. "Nietzsche and Early Buddhism." *Philosophy East & West* 50, no. 2 (2000): 254–67.

Parkes, Graham. "Nietzsche and Nishitani on the Self-Overcoming of Nihilism." *International Studies in Philosophy* 25, no. 2 (1993): 51–60.

Parkes, Graham. "Nietzsche and Zen Master Hakuin on the Roles of Emotion and Passion." In *Emotion in Asian Thought: A Dialogue in Comparative Philosophy*, edited by Joel Marks and Roger T. Ames, 213–31. Albany: State University of New York Press, 1995.

Parkes, Graham. "The Overflowing Soul: Images of Transformation in Nietzsche's *Zarathustra*." *Man and World* 16, no. 4 (1983): 335–48.

Parkes, Graham. "Reply to Robert Morrison." *Philosophy East & West* 50, no. 2 (2000): 279–84.

Pasanno, Ajahn, and Ajahn Amaro. *The Island: An Anthology of the Buddha's Teachings on Nibbāna.* Redwood Valley, Calif.: Abhayagiri Monastic Foundation, 2009.

Peek, John M. "Buddhism, Human Rights, and the Japanese State." *Human Rights Quarterly* 17, no. 3 (1995): 527–40.

Pérez Remón, Joaquín. *Self and Non-Self in Early Buddhism.* The Hague; Paris; New York: Mouton, 1980.

Plato. *The Collected Dialogues of Plato.* Edited by Edith Hamilton and Huntington Cairns. Princeton: Princeton University Press, 1961.

Plutarch. "Reply to Colotes in Defence of the Other Philosophers (Adversus Colotem)." Translated by Benedict Einarson and Phillip H. De Lacy. In *Moralia.* Vol. 14. Loeb Classical Library. Cambridge, Mass; London: Harvard University Press, 1967.

Pollis, Adamantia. "Cultural Relativism Revisited: Through a State Prism." *Human Rights Quarterly* 18, no. 2 (1996): 316–44.

Poole, Ross. "Nietzsche: The Subject of Morality." *Radical Philosophy* 54 (1990): 2–9.

Premasiri, P. D. "Moral Evaluation in Early Buddhism." *Sri Lanka Journal of the Humanities* 1, no. 1 (1975): 31–45.

Queen, Christopher S., and Sallie B. King, eds. *Engaged Buddhism: Buddhist Liberation Movements in Asia.* Albany: State University of New York Press, 1996.

Rahula, Walpola. *What the Buddha Taught.* 2nd rev. ed. New York: Grove Press, 1974. 1959.

Ratnapala, Nandasena. *Buddhist Democratic Political Theory and Practice.* Ratmalana, Sri Lanka: Sarvodaya Vishva Lekha, 1997.

Reynolds, Frank E. "Sacral Kingship and National Development: The Case of Thailand." In *Religion and Legitimation of Power in Thailand, Laos, and Burma*, edited by Bardwell L. Smith, 100–10. Chambersburg, Penn.: ANIMA Books, 1978.

Richardson, John. *Nietzsche's System.* Oxford; New York: Oxford University Press, 1996.

Robinson, David M. *Natural Life: Thoreau's Worldly Transcendentalism.* Ithaca, N.Y.; London: Cornell University Press, 2004.

Rosenblum, Nancy. *Another Liberalism: Romanticism and the Reconstruction of Liberal Thought.* Cambridge, Mass.; London: Harvard University Press, 1987.

Rosenblum, Nancy L., ed. *Liberalism and the Moral Life.* Cambridge, Mass.; London: Harvard University Press, 1989.

Rosenblum, Nancy L. "Thoreau's Democratic Individualism." In *A Political Companion to Henry David Thoreau*, edited by Jack Turner, 15–38. Lexington: University Press of Kentucky, 2009.

Rosenblum, Nancy L. "Thoreau's Militant Conscience." *Political Theory* 9, no. 1 (1981): 81–110.

Roskam, Geert. *Live Unnoticed (Λάθε Βιώσας): On the Vicissitudes of an Epicurean Doctrine.* Leiden; Boston: Brill, 2007.

Ruang, King. *Three Worlds According to King Ruang.* Translated by Frank E. Reynolds and Mani B. Reynolds. Berkeley, Calif.: Asian Humanities Press, 1982.

Rudolph, A.W. "Nietzsche's Buddhism." *ITA humanidades* 5 (1969): 33–43.

Saddhatissa, Hammalawa. *Buddhist Ethics.* Rev. ed. Boston: Wisdom Publications, 1997.

Sarkisyanz, Emanuel. "Buddhist Background of Burmese Socialism." In *Religion and Legitimation of Power in Thailand, Laos, and Burma*, edited by Bardwell L. Smith, 87–99. Chambersburg, Penn.: ANIMA Books, 1978.

Sarkisyanz, Emanuel. *Buddhist Backgrounds of the Burmese Revolution.* The Hague: Martinus Nijhoff, 1965.

Schlechta, Karl. *Nietzsches Werke in Drei Bände.* Munich: Carl Hanser Verlag, 1958.

Schmithausen, Lambert L. "Aspects of the Buddhist Attitude Towards War." In *Violence Denied: Violence, Non-Violence and the Rationalization of Violence in South Asian Cultural History*, edited by Jan E.M. Houben and Karel R. Van Kooij, 45–67. Leiden; Boston; Köln: Brill, 1999.

Schmitt, Richard. "Nietzsche's Psychological Theory." *Journal of Existential Psychiatry* 2 (1961): 71–92.

Schofield, Malcolm. "Epicurean and Stoic Political Thought." In *The Cambridge History of Greek and Roman Political Thought*, edited by Christopher Rowe and Malcolm Schofield. Cambridge; New York: Cambridge University Press, 2000.

Schwartz, Ronald D. "Renewal and Resistance: Tibetan Buddhism in the Modern Era." In *Buddhism and Politics in Twentieth-Century Asia*, edited by Ian Harris, 229–53. New York; London: Pinter, 1999.

Scott, David. "Rewalking Thoreau and Asia: 'Light from the East' for 'a Very Yankee Sort of Oriental'." *Philosophy East and West* 57, no. 1 (2007): 14–39.

Scriven, Charles. *The Transformation of Culture: Christian Social Ethics after H. Richard Niebuhr.* Scottdale, Penn.: Herald Press, 1988.

Seery, John. "Moral Perfectionism and Abortion Politics." *Polity* 33, no. 3 (2001): 345–64.

Sextus Empiricus. *Selections from the Major Writings on Scepticism, Man, & God.* Translated by Sanford G. Etheridge. Indianapolis: Hackett, 1985.

Sharma, J. P. *Republics in Ancient India: C. 1500 B.C.–500 B.C.* Leiden: E.J. Brill, 1968.

Shils, Edward. "The Virtue of Civil Society." *Government and Opposition* 26, no. 1 (1991): 3–20.

Shulman, George. "Thoreau, Prophecy, and Politics." In *A Political Companion to Henry David Thoreau,* edited by Jack Turner, 124–50. Lexington: University Press of Kentucky, 2009.

Siderits, Mark. "Buddhist Reductionism and the Structure of Buddhist Ethics." In *Indian Ethics: Classical and Contemporary Challenges,* edited by P. Bilimoria, J. Prabhu and R. Sharma, 283–96. Abingdon, UK: Ashgate, 2005.

Siderits, Mark. *Personal Identity and Buddhist Philosophy: Empty Persons.* Ashgate World Philosophies Series. Aldershot, UK; Burlington, Vt.: Ashgate, 2003.

Silber, Ilana Friedrich. "Dissent through Holiness: The Case of the Radical Renouncer in Theravada Buddhist Countries." *Numen* 28, no. 2 (1981): 164–93.

Simon, Myron. "Thoreau and Anarchism." *Michigan Quarterly Review* 23, no. 3 (1984): 360–84.

Sizemore, Russell F., and Donald K. Swearer, eds. *Ethics, Wealth, and Salvation: A Study in Buddhist Social Ethics.* Columbia: University of South Carolina Press, 1990.

Smith, Bardwell L., ed. *Religion and Legitimation of Power in Sri Lanka.* Chambersburg, Penn.: ANIMA Books, 1978.

Smith, Donald Eugene. *Religion and Political Development.* Boston: Little, Brown, 1970.

Smith, Donald Eugene, ed. *Religion, Politics, and Social Change in the Third World: A Sourcebook.* New York: Free Press, 1971.

Sokoloff, William. "Nietzsche's Radicalization of Kant." *Polity* 38, no. 4 (2006): 18.

Sørensen, Henrik H. "Buddhism and Secular Power in Twentieth-Century Korea." In *Buddhism and Politics in Twentieth-Century Asia,* edited by Ian Harris, 127–52. New York; London: Pinter, 1999.

Spellman, J. W. *Political Theory of Ancient India.* Oxford: Clarendon Press, 1964.

Spinoza, Baruch. *Ethics; Treatise on the Emendation of the Intellect; and Selected Letters.* Translated by Samuel Shirley. Indianapolis: Hackett, 1992.

Spiro, Melford E. *Buddhism and Society: A Great Tradition and Its Burmese Vicissitudes.* 2nd. rev ed. Berkeley; Los Angeles; London: University of California Press, 1982.

Stack, George J. *Lange and Nietzsche.* Berlin; New York: Walter de Gruyter, 1983.

Staten, Henry. *Nietzsche's Voice*. Ithaca, N.Y.: Cornell University Press, 1990.

Steinhart, Eric. *On Nietzsche*. Belmont, Calif.: Wadsworth/Thomson Learning, 2000.

Strong, John S. *The Legend of King Aśoka: A Study and Translation of the Aśokāvadāna*. Princeton: Princeton University Press, 1983.

Strong, Tracy. "Texts and Pretexts: Reflections on Perspectivism in Nietzsche." *Political Theory* 13, no. 2 (1985): 164–82.

Stuart-Fox, Martin. "Laos: From Buddhist Kingdom to Marxist State." In *Buddhism and Politics in Twentieth-Century Asia*, edited by Ian Harris, 153–72. New York; London: Pinter, 1999.

Stuart-Fox, Martin. "Marxism and Theravada Buddhism: The Legitimation of Political Authority in Laos." *Pacific Affairs* 56, no. 3 (1983): 428–54.

Suksamran, Somboon. *Buddhism and Political Legitimacy*. Bangkok: Research Dissemination Project, Chulalongkorn University, 1993.

Suksamran, Somboon. "Buddhism, Political Authority, and Legitimacy in Thailand and Cambodia." In *Buddhist Trends in Southeast Asia*, edited by Trevor Oswald Ling, 101–53. Singapore: Institute of Southeast Asian Studies, 1993.

Suksamran, Somboon, and Trevor Oswald Ling. *Political Buddhism in Southeast Asia: The Role of the Sangha in the Modernization of Thailand*. New York: St. Martin's Press, 1976.

Swearer, Donald K. "Centre and Periphery: Buddhism and Politics in Modern Thailand." In *Buddhism and Politics in Twentieth-Century Asia*, edited by Ian Harris, 194–228. New York; London: Pinter, 1999.

Tachibana, S[hundo]. *The Ethics of Buddhism*. London; New York: Curzon/Barnes & Noble Books, 1975. 1926.

Tambiah, Stanley Jeyaraja. *Buddhism Betrayed? Religion, Politics, and Violence in Sri Lanka*. Chicago and London: University of Chicago Press, 1992.

Tambiah, Stanley Jeyaraja. *The Buddhist Conception of Universal King and Its Manifestations in South and Southeast Asia*. Kuala Lumpur: University of Malaya, 1987.

Tambiah, Stanley Jeyaraja. "King Mahāsammata: The First King in the Buddhist Story of Creation, and His Continuing Relevance." *Journal of the Anthropological Society of Oxford* 20, no. 2 (1989): 101–22.

Tambiah, Stanley Jeyaraja. *World Conqueror and World Renouncer: A Study of Buddhism and Polity in Thailand against a Historical Background*. Cambridge: Cambridge University Press, 1976.

Taylor, Bob Pepperman. *America's Bachelor Uncle: Thoreau and the American Polity*. Lawrence: University Press of Kansas, 1996.

Thera, Ratanapañña. *The Sheaf of the Garlands of the Epochs of the Conqueror: Being a Translation of Jinakālamālīpakaraṇaṁ*. Translated by N. A. Jayawickrama. London: Pali Text Society, 1968. c. fifteenth-sixteenth centuries CE.

Thiele, Leslie. *Friedrich Nietzsche and the Politics of the Soul: A Study of Heroic Individualism*. Princeton: Princeton University Press, 1990.

Thoreau, Henry David. *Political Writings*. Cambridge Texts in the History of Political Thought. Edited by Nancy Rosenblum. Cambridge; New York: Cambridge University Press, 1996.

Thoreau, Henry David. *Walden and Civil Disobedience*. New York: Penguin, 1983. 1849.

Turner, Jack. "Performing Conscience: Thoreau, Political Action, and the Plea for John Brown." *Political Theory* 33, no. 4 (2005): 448–71.

Turner, Jack, ed. *A Political Companion to Henry David Thoreau*. Lexington: University Press of Kentucky, 2009.

van der Braak, André. *Nietzsche and Zen: Self-Overcoming without a Self*. Lanham, Md.: Rowman & Littlefield, 2011.

Villa, Dana. *Socratic Citizenship*. Princeton; Oxford: Princeton University Press, 2001.

Wagner, C. Roland. "Lucky Fox at Walden." In *Thoreau in Our Season*, edited by John H. Hicks, 117–33. Amherst: University of Massachusetts Press, 1962.

Walker, Brian. "Thoreau on Democratic Cultivation." *Political Theory* 29, no. 2 (April 1, 2001): 155–89.

Walshe, Maurice. *The Long Discourses of the Buddha: A Translation of the Dīgha Nikāya*. Boston: Wisdom, 1995.

Wangchuk, Tashi. "The Middle Path to Democracy in the Kingdom of Bhutan." *Asian Survey* 44, no. 6 (2004): 836–55.

Warder, Anthony Kennedy. *Indian Buddhism*. Delhi: Motilal Banarsidass, 1970.

Weaver, Alain Epp. "After Politics: John Howard Yoder, Body Politics, and the Witnessing Church." *The Review of Politics* 61, no. 4 (1999): 637–73.

Weber, Max. *The Religion of India*. Translated by Hans H. Gerth and Don Martindale. New York: Free Press, 1958.

Welbon, Guy Richard. *The Buddhist Nirvana and Its Western Interpreters*. Chicago: University of Chicago Press, 1968.

Welshon, Robert C. "Nietzsche's Peculiar Virtues and the Health of the Soul." *International Studies in Philosophy* 24, no. 2 (1992): 77–89.

Wenman, Mark. "Agonism, Pluralism, and Contemporary Capitalism: An Interview with William E. Connolly." *Contemporary Political Theory* 7 (2008): 200–19.

White, Stephen K. *Sustaining Affirmation: The Strengths of Weak Ontology in Political Theory*. Princeton; Oxford: Princeton University Press, 2000.

Whitecross, Richard W. "Separation of Religion and Law?: Buddhism, Secularism and the Constitution of Bhutan." *Buffalo Law Review* 55 (2007): 707–11.

Whitehill, James. "Buddhism and the Virtues." In *Contemporary Buddhist Ethics*, edited by Damien Keown, 17–36. Richmond, Surrey: Curzon Press, 2000.

Whitehill, James. "Buddhist Ethics in Western Context: The Virtues Approach." *Journal of Buddhist Ethics* 1 (1994): 1–22.

Wilson, Robert A., and Lucia Foglia. "Embodied Cognition." Stanford Encyclopedia of Philosophy. July 25, 2011. http://plato.stanford.edu/archives/fall2011/entries/embodied-cognition/.

Worley, Sam McGuire. *Emerson, Thoreau, and the Role of the Cultural Critic*. Albany: State University of New York Press, 2001.

Wright, Nigel. *Disavowing Constantine: Mission, Church and the Social Order in the Theologies of John Howard Yoder and Jürgen Moltmann*. Paternoster Biblical and Theological Monographs; Variation: Paternoster Biblical and Theological Monographs. Carlisle, Cumbria, UK: Paternoster Press, 2000.

Yoder, John Howard. *The Christian Witness to the State*. Newton, Kan.: Faith and Life Press, 1964.

Yoder, John Howard. *Discipleship as Political Responsibility*. Scottdale, Penn.: Herald Press, 2003.

Yoder, John Howard. *The Politics of Jesus*. Grand Rapids, Mich.: William B. Eerdmans, 1972.

Zimmerman, Earl. *Practicing the Politics of Jesus: The Origin and Significance of John Howard Yoder's Social Ethics*. The C. Henry Smith Series. Scottdale, Penn.: Cascadia, 2007.

Žižek, Slavoj. "From Western Marxism to Western Buddhism." Spring 2001. http://www.cabinetmagazine.org/issues/2/western.php.

Zuckert, Catherine. "Nature, History and Self." *Nietzsche Studien* 5 (1976): 55–82.

INDEX